SEARCHING FOR THE DIVINE IN PLATO AND ARISTOTLE

To scholars of ancient philosophy, *theoria* denotes abstract thinking, with both Plato and Aristotle employing the term to signify philosophical contemplation. Yet it is surprising for some to find an earlier, traditional meaning referring to travel to festivals and shrines. In an attempt to dissolve the problem of equivocal reference, Julie Ward's book seeks to illuminate the nature of traditional *theoria* as ancient festival-attendance as well as the philosophical account developed in Plato and Aristotle. First, she examines the traditional use referring to periodic festivals, including their complex social and political arrangements, then she considers the subsequent use by Plato and Aristotle. Broadly speaking, she discerns a common thread running throughout both uses: namely, the notion of having a visual experience of the sacred or divine. Thus her book aims to illuminate the nature of philosophical *theoria* described by Plato and Aristotle in light of traditional, festival *theoria*.

JULIE K. WARD is Professor Emerita of Philosophy at Loyola University, Chicago. Her publications include *Feminism and Ancient Philosophy* (1996), *Aristotle on Homonymy, Dialectic and Science* (Cambridge University Press, 2008), and many journal articles.

SEARCHING FOR THE DIVINE
IN PLATO AND ARISTOTLE

Philosophical Theoria *and Traditional Practice*

JULIE K. WARD

Loyola University, Chicago

CAMBRIDGE
UNIVERSITY PRESS

CAMBRIDGE
UNIVERSITY PRESS

University Printing House, Cambridge CB2 8BS, United Kingdom

One Liberty Plaza, 20th Floor, New York, NY 10006, USA

477 Williamstown Road, Port Melbourne, VIC 3207, Australia

314–321, 3rd Floor, Plot 3, Splendor Forum, Jasola District Centre, New Delhi – 110025, India

103 Penang Road, #05–06/07, Visioncrest Commercial, Singapore 238467

Cambridge University Press is part of the University of Cambridge.

It furthers the University's mission by disseminating knowledge in the pursuit of education, learning, and research at the highest international levels of excellence.

www.cambridge.org
Information on this title: www.cambridge.org/9781316519417
DOI: 10.1017/9781009023580

First published 2022

A catalogue record for this publication is available from the British Library.

Library of Congress Cataloging-in-Publication Data
NAMES: Ward, Julie K., 1952– author.
TITLE: Searching for the divine in Plato and Aristotle : philosophical theoria and traditional practice / Julie K. Ward.
DESCRIPTION: Cambridge ; New York, NY : Cambridge University Press, 2021. | Includes bibliographical references and index.
IDENTIFIERS: LCCN 2021024936 (print) | LCCN 2021024937 (ebook) | ISBN 9781316519417 (hardback) | ISBN 9781009010450 (paperback) | ISBN 9781009023580 (epub)
SUBJECTS: LCSH: Plato–Criticism, Textual. | Aristotle–Criticism, Textual. | Theōria (The Greek word) | Philosophy, Ancient. | Pilgrims and pilgrimages in literature. | Festivals in literature. | Classical literature–History and criticism. | Object (Philosophy) | Knowledge, Theory of. | Metaphysics. | BISAC: PHILOSOPHY / History & Surveys / Ancient & Classical
CLASSIFICATION: LCC PA430.T48 W37 2021 (print) | LCC PA430.T48 (ebook) | DDC 184–dc23
LC record available at https://lccn.loc.gov/2021024936
LC ebook record available at https://lccn.loc.gov/2021024937

ISBN 978-1-316-51941-7 Hardback

Contents

Acknowledgments

The classical scholar Ian Rutherford notes that the timing of the ancient embassy to Delphi was determined by those set to watch for lightning over Harma on Mt. Parnes, which, in being infrequent, led to the saying "When the lightning flashes on Harma" used in reference to things happening rarely or late. He thus employs the metaphor to describe his research that extended from the 1980s to the 2000s, culminating in the publication of his monumental work on *theoria* in 2013 (Rutherford 2013, xvii). In a more modest context, I would like to redeploy the image to describe the development of the present book that spanned over a decade, with much time spent researching outside my area of ancient philosophy. During this period, I have benefited from scholarly and personal help from various sources including formal readers, conference audiences, students, friends, and family. Beginning with the most immediate group, I thank my family, primarily Ezio Vailati, for frequent critical discussions. As well, I am grateful to my friends and past colleagues, particularly those in Classical Studies at Loyola University, including Drs. Greg Dubrov (now deceased), Laura Galinsky, Pat Graham, Jim Keenan, Brian Lavelle, and Jackie Long, for sharing their knowledge both in writing and informal conversation. In the group of classicists, I also express deep thanks to Dr. Elizabeth Asmis (University of Chicago) who graciously agreed to read an early draft of the book, giving me essential, critical advice. My gratitude is also directed to past graduate students (now postgraduates) who contributed to early discussions about Aristotle and Plato on *theoria* or provided editorial assistance, including Drs. Jean Clifford, Robby Duncan, Marcella Russo Linn, and Carlo Tarantino. Next, I thank Drs. Daryl Tress and Tony Preus, organizers of Society of Ancient Greek Philosophy Conferences, where papers on Plato and Aristotle on philosophical *theoria* were presented. In a related vein, I am grateful to Dr. Owen Goldin and the organizers of the Marquette Summer Seminar on Aristotle and Aristotelianism, and to Dr. Nicoletta Scotti, for opportunities to present papers on Aristotle's treatments of perception and *theoria*. Third, I wish to express deep thanks to the two referees for Cambridge University Press whose comments clarified numerous erroneous or misleading claims made and provided helpful suggestions that have benefited the MS; any errors remaining are, of course, my own responsibility. Finally, thanks go to Hilary Gaskin, Philosophy Editor at Cambridge University Press, for her concerted assistance throughout the process and to her collaborators for their expert help in the book's final stages.

Abbreviations

Aristotle

An. Po.	Posterior Analytics
Ath. Con.	Athenian Constitution
Cat.	Categories
DA	De Anima
De Part. An.	On the Parts of Animals
DM	De Memoria
DS	De Sensu
EE	Eudemian Ethics
EN	Nicomachean Ethics
Meta.	Metaphysics
Meteor.	Meteorology
Phys.	Physics
PN	Parva Naturalia
Pol.	Politics
Protrep.	Protrepticus
Top.	Topics

Cicero

Tusc. Disp.	Tusculan Disputations

Diogenes Laertius (DL)

Lives	Lives of Philosophers

Diels and Kranz (DK)

Diels, H. and Kranz, W.	Die Fragmente der Vorsokratiker.

Euripides

Bacch.   *Bacchae*
Ion   *Ion*

Herodotus

Hist.   *The Histories*

Iamblichus

Vit. Pythag.   *Lives of Philosophers*

Liddell and Scott

LSJ   Liddell, H. G., and Scott, R., Eds. 1968. *A Greek-English Lexicon*

Plato

Apol.   *Apology*
Char.   *Charmides*
Cleit.   *Cleitophon*
Crito   *Crito*
Ep.   *Epinomis*
Hipp.   *Hipparchus*
HM   *Hippias Minor*
Ion   *Ion*
Lach.   *Laches*
Laws   *Laws*
Lys.   *Lysis*
Men.   *Meno*
Phd.   *Phaedo*
Phdr.   *Phaedrus*
Prot.   *Protagoras*
Rep.   *Republic*
Soph.   *Sophist*
Symp.   *Symposium*
Theaet.   *Theaetetus*
Tim.   *Timaeus*

SEG
Supplementum Epigraphicum Graecum.　　Leiden, 1923

Theognis
Eleg.　　*Elegies*

Thucydides
Hist.　　*History of the Peloponnesian War*

Xenophon
Cyr.　　*Cyropaedia*
Mem.　　*Memorabilia*

Introduction

I.I *Theoria* and the Problem of Univocity

To scholars of ancient philosophy, the term *theoria* (θεωρία) signifies a distinctively cognitive activity, one that for Plato and Aristotle belongs to the highest intellectual faculty and marks the possession of scientific knowledge. To classical scholars, *theoria* refers to a long-standing practice of traveling to sites to attend festivals and shrines, a tradition that has little in common with the activity described by philosophers. The contrast is further underscored in that the travel to festivals constitutes the earlier, dominant use of the term, one having its origin in the Archaic period, well before that of Plato and Aristotle. Put more precisely, the dominant use, that which we term "traditional *theoria*," in fact refers to two kinds of religious practice: (i) the travel to periodic festivals (e.g., the Olympic or Nemean) and (ii) travel to religious shrines and healing sanctuaries. The former kind occurs at fixed periods of the calendar year for a specific length of time, and the latter may occur outside fixed periods.[1] The primary point at hand is that both these uses comprise cultural practices that predate the notion of philosophical *theoria* (as contemplation) and persist for centuries.[2] Thus, the ancient practice of *theoria*, namely, the travel to festivals and sanctuaries, comprises the primary referent for the term *theoria*, and predates the philosophical use by at least two centuries.[3] From the standpoint of development and usage then, the reference to contemplation

---

[1] These two uses comprise the "two broad categories" of traditional *theoria* (that which excludes the philosophical use); the use of traveling to healing sanctuaries, oracles, and Mystery sites such as Eleusis also covers cases where the visitor seeks a solution to a particular problem (cf. Dillon 1997, 60).

[2] According to Rutherford, traditional *theoria* spans about 800 years, from 6th c. BCE –2nd –3rd c. CE (Rutherford 2013, Ch. 2, 17).

[3] The generalization holds despite Herodotus' use of *theoria* referring to traveling for discovery or learning; see reference to Solon and Anacharsis (*Hist.* 1. 29, 4. 76).

seems to lie entirely outside the dominant use, that referring to traditional *theoria*.

To philosophers, the recognition that a thing signifies a number of referents invites a consideration about synonymy and homonymy, with synonymy indicating a thing (or term) that possesses a common referent over its applications, and homonymy indicating the lack of a common referent. Put in a more precise sense as Aristotle considers the difference in *Cat.* I, first, homonymy is said to obtain when a general term, like "animal," refers to different things (e.g., a living thing and a picture of one) that lack a common essence and definition (cf. *Cat.* 1a1–3). When we consider the term *theoria*, we appear to be situated in the domain of homonymy. For we seem to have two or three different referents for *theoria* with festival and sanctuary attendance, on one side, and abstract thinking, on the other. The difficulty then lies in suggesting what key common features the referents share – in effect, we wonder whether it is possible to specify a feature definitive both of festival and sanctuary travel, as well as abstract thinking. Compounding this problem is the further issue concerning the unity of reference of philosophical *theoria* across uses by Plato and Aristotle. For example, an initial survey of *theoria* and related terms by Plato reflects homonymy, with wider and narrower uses of meaning. More precisely, the wider *theor/ia/eo* family of terms reveals two general uses with only one referring to *theoria* as abstract thinking. A similar situation concerning a plurality of uses is evident in Aristotle's works, the survey of the *theor/ia/eo* group of terms revealing a basic bifurcation between wider, generic senses and narrower, technical senses. So, for example, Aristotle employs forms of *theoreo* to signify studying or observing something, like the parts and functions of animal kinds (*De Part. An.* I 5) where he employs a wide, generic sense of *theoria*.[4] As well, however, he chooses a narrow, technical sense of *theoria* to signify the kind of scientific thinking he examines in *EN* X 7. Without going into detail on this point, it is fair to say that, fortunately, we find parallels in usage of theoric language between Aristotle and Plato, and this conclusion allows our investigation to proceed. In general, we find a pattern of usage consisting in a wide, general sense and a narrow, technical one with the former referring to studying, or considering, something and the latter having a narrower reference. Having reached this initial finding about

---

[4] See, for example, *De Part. An.* 644b24–645a19; for discussion of the senses, see Ch. 4, fn. 4, and Ch. 5, sec. 5.4.

the overlap in Plato's and Aristotle's uses of *theor/ia/eo* terms, we can consider a further arrangement of meaning.

It seems possible to determine key features common to the wider and narrower uses of theoric terms in Plato and Aristotle. Since both the narrow and wide use are concerned with looking at or observing something, it seems reasonable to propose the activity of observation as the generic feature, and to propose thinking about intelligible objects as the qualification of the generic notion needed to reach the technical definition for the philosophical use of the term. At this point, we have posited two conclusions for the two philosophers' use of the *theor/ia/eo* family, the first concerning the generic notion of the terms, and the second, the technical notion of *theoria*. But, as yet, the previous problem concerning the ambiguity between the traditional sense (festival or sanctuary visitation) and the philosophical sense (intellectual contemplation) remains. However, further study in the history of traditional *theoria* as well as in the lexical range of *theoria, theoreo, theaomai* provides a way out of the problem. To begin with, the etymological connections among the *theor/ia/eo* family is unified in virtue of a root (*theor*) that signifies visual sense-perception, and specifically, looking at a sacred object or one of high significance. The perceptual feature is strongly represented in traditional *theoria*, or festival-attendance, which, while it comprehends several different features, possesses the central notions of observing something divine, and spectatorship as core features. It may be surprising to suppose that a perceptual or observational feature comprises the tether that connects the philosophical and traditional uses of *theoria*, yet, in this regard, we should consider that while philosophical *theoria* for Plato and Aristotle requires apprehending something intelligible, this apprehension is not without its visual, or perceptual, aspect. Coming to this general conclusion, however, was not immediate or obvious, and required reading from a wider range of scholarship about traditional *theoria* than initially planned. However, the synthesis of philosophical and classical concepts allows for a more informed perspective about *theoria* as a historical practice and concept.

In this regard, the work acknowledges a debt to the scholarship on *theoria* from classical studies as well as from that in ancient philosophy, as the former proves pivotal to establishing the possibility that *theoria* is not an ambiguous concept, but one with interrelated senses. Specific mention should be given in this regard to those classicists whose research on traditional *theoria* proved indispensable including Matthew Dillon (1997), Jas Elsner (with Ian Rutherford 2005), Simon Goldhill (1996), James Ker (2000), Andrea Nightingale (2001, 2004, 2005), and Ian

Rutherford (1995, 1998, 2000, 2013) to mention a few central figures. The present study is especially indebted to the work of two scholars, Andrea Nightingale's monograph, *Spectacles of Truth in Classical Greek Philosophy: Theoria in its Cultural Context* (2004), and Ian Rutherford's study, *State Pilgrims and Sacred Observers in Ancient Greece: A Study of Theoria and* Theoroi (2013). Nightingale's monograph on the cultural context of *theoria* added substantially to understanding the relation of traditional *theoria* to philosophical *theoria*, and Rutherford's work supplies the historical scope and scholarly detail necessary to understanding the history and weight of traditional *theoria*. Despite the wealth of resources afforded by these scholars, their work left some space for further research on *theoria* from a philosophical perspective. A strength of Nightingale's work concerns the focus on Plato's and Aristotle's conceptions of *theoria* placed against the historical and cultural background of traditional *theoria*, and in this regard, the present work builds on her study. However, she offers some conclusions about Aristotelian *theoria* that are, to my mind, inadequately supported, and so fail to reflect the complexity of his position, with the fortunate result that it affords scholars the space for more comment. In a similar way, Rutherford's work sets traditional *theoria* in its historical scope, detailing evidence from the eighth century BCE to the second and third centuries CE in Hellenistic and Roman forms of *theoria*, including a wealth of data about its history, geography, and ethnography, but offers only a slim chapter on the intersection of *theoria* and philosophy, which allows some conceptual space for the present study.

As well, a work about philosophical *theoria* owes a debt to scholars in ancient philosophy who have contributed fine work on Aristotelian and Platonic *theoria*. While this group contains too many to list individually, some mention could be made of those whose work aided the research, such as Rachel Barney (2010), Myles Burnyeat (1999), Richard Kraut (1997), Gabriel Richardson Lear (2004, 2014), David Roochnik (2009), Gregory Vlastos (1997), and Matthew Walker (2010, 2018).[5] In the initial stages of research, Roochnik's observation about the narrow scope in the scholarship on Aristotelian *theoria* proved efficient in opening my research into the *theor/ia/eo* family of terms.[6] Gabriel Lear's work linking intellectual

---

[5] Other scholars writing on Aristotle's account of *theoria* influenced my thinking, including Charles (1999, 2014), Cooper (1986), Dahl (2011), Kraut (1995), Nussbaum (1990), Patzig (1979), and Rorty (1980).

[6] Roochnik comments on the lack of attention to *theoria/theoro* in Aristotle's works apart from its consideration in his conception of happiness (Roochnik 2009, 80–81).

theoria with moral virtue alerted me to the link between contemplative and practical faculties, while Walker's monograph turned my attention to the practical effects of philosophical *theoria*. With regard to Plato scholarship, works by Burnyeat (1999) and Barney (2010) on ring composition in Plato aided my postulation of the ring form as a corollary to traditional *theoria* within specific dialogues while those by Kraut (1997) and Vlastos (1997) on the results of Platonic *theoria* on moral character provided a critical lens with which to assess the value attached to the activity.

I.2   The Interdisciplinary Approach, Synopsis of Chapters

Since the problem about the univocity of *theoria* arises from considering evidence from classical studies and ancient philosophy, it is only fitting that the solution to the problem be sought from consulting both disciplines. As a first step to solving this puzzle, we postulated a single, generic element that underlies both the traditional and philosophical notions. This move is supported, first of all, by the etymological connections among the *theor/ia/eo* family of terms, specifically, in noting that the root *theor/* signifies perception or observation, and second, by similarities arising across the *theor/* family of terms from the central literary and philosophical texts. The interdisciplinary approach, combining evidence from both classical studies and philosophy, is motivated primarily by the need to understand the cultural ground from which the accounts of *theoria* by Plato and Aristotle spring which is accomplished by situating the philosophical accounts in context of the earlier practice of *theoria*. As well as placing the philosophical accounts against traditional *theoria*, the present study allows greater sustained critical depth on the accounts of *theoria* by Plato and Aristotle than most current scholarship affords. Working toward the end of enlarging the present philosophical discussion of *theoria*, the initial chapters give an overview of traditional *theoria* and thus provide a comparative basis for the accounts of *theoria* in Plato and Aristotle. By situating their theories in relation to traditional *theoria*, we are able to reach certain novel conclusions about *theoria* at two levels. First, from a broad, comparative level, we see that relating Platonic and Aristotelian *theoria* to traditional *theoria* provides a useful background against which to evaluate the nature, objects, and value of philosophical *theoria*. Second, from a narrower perspective, it becomes evident that Plato's account in particular bears a strong tie to the traditional practice such that specific, perhaps overlooked, features take on pivotal roles in it.[7] Again, at the narrower level, we find that Aristotle's under-standing of *theoria* as an activity of *nous* coincides with that of Plato, while disagreeing with him about the negative value of traditional *theoria*. Lastly, the wider perspective on *theoria* enables the re-conception of the dominant uses of *theoria* as comprising a single entity, albeit one with loosely connected features. We may take some of these loosely related but central features to include visual experience, the object of vision being divine or highly significant, the ideas of circular motion, and of traveling for a religious purpose. As will be developed, these features are characteristic of traditional *theoria*, and also suggestive of philosophical, especially Platonic, *theoria*, for which one may discern close affinities in the notions of visual experience of the divine, undertaking a journey with a spiritual aim, and circularity. The continuity of certain social and political features that belong to traditional *theoria*, such as its utility in expanding shared cultural values, is less obvious with Plato's and Aristotle's accounts at first glance, but in fact may be evident in some dialogues, like *Laws* (cf. Chapter 3).

Having suggested the potential gains to be won by taking a broader perspective in specific chapters, let us turn to a brief synopsis of the chapters. As we have noted, finding the interrelations between philosoph-ical and traditional *theoria* requires a general sketch of the traditional practice which is provided in Chapter 1. In addition to discussing what activities comprise traditional *theoria* – giving precedence to *theoria* as festival-attendance – the chapter introduces the family of terms relating to *theoria*, referenced as the *theor/ia/eo* class of terms, and the notion of *theoria* as philosophical thinking. Chapter 2 provides a more detailed account of the traditional uses in Classical writers, including Herodotus, Thucydides, Aristophanes, and Euripides, and some brief mention of Plato's employment as well. Overall, the two dominant, conjoined features mentioned by writers about the traditional use consist in traveling to a site for the sake of observing something sacred, or highly significant; these interconnected features remain, although in an attenuated sense, through the philosophical development of the notion. Chapter 3 gives a close study of Plato's treatment of both kinds of *theoria*, having the wider framework provided by an overview of traditional *theoria* in hand. To begin, we find that Plato stands at a crossroads between the older, traditional idea of *theoria* and something entirely new, his re-conception of *theoria* as abstract

---

[7] For example, the feature of circularity implicit in traditional *theoria* is employed by Plato as ring form in certain dialogues, as developed in Ch. 3, sec. 3.2, below.

thinking. Yet Plato often pulls both ideas of *theoria* together, as when he makes use of the idea of traditional *theoria* as the dramatic contrast to his notion of *theoria* as abstract thinking. In one example from *Republic* V, Socrates effectively redefines the activity of *theoria* by framing the search as one not concerned with observing spectacular sights and sounds of festivals, but apprehending intelligible objects; he further clarifies that the philosopher, not festival-delegate, is a truth-seeker (cf. *Rep.* 475d–e, 476b–d).[8] Other dialogues (e.g., *Crito, Phaedo, Phaedrus, Symposium, Laws*) reflect an interest in using traditional *theoria* as a contrast to philosophical *theoria*, and some have the further purpose of constructing ring compositions in so doing. These select dialogues, in exhibiting a ring form, point to a further element relating to traditional *theoria*, that of circular motion.

A slight digression for clarification may be useful in relation to the connection of traditional *theoria* to the idea of circular motion. As a way to introduce the feature, we mention the use of an analogy some classicists suggest between traditional *theoria* and pilgrimage: in both, it is claimed, we find the idea of tracing a circular motion.[9] The suggestion may not be obvious; let us set aside for the moment a more evident common feature, namely, traveling for a religious end, and simply consider the motional feature.[10] In the latter regard, we assume that pilgrimage involves moving away from a starting point, one's home city, and returning to one's starting point; in this regard, it reflects a circular motion. The possible objection that the figure traced in such travel is bi-directional – moving from a starting point to a mid-point and moving back along the same path – misconstrues the nature of the return. For, as discussed in Chapter 2, the travel is conceived as passing through a mid-point and following a new path back to the initial starting point. So, in pilgrimage travel, the pilgrim leaves one site, and returns, having had some significant experience that has changed the person; in this sense, the route homeward is, at least figuratively, a new path, not a repetition of the outward path. So, if pilgrimage is accepted as an analogy, the traveling in traditional *theoria* is not properly conceived as a simple, bi-directional motion (e.g., moving from A to B, and from B back to A), but as involving a kind of circular

---

[8] We track Plato's use by way of the employment of the *theor/ia/eo* family of terms, including *theaomai*, a term he prefers both for visual perception and for apprehension of intelligible forms.
[9] Different aspects of the comparison are considered in Dillon (1997), Nightingale (2004), and Rutherford (2013, 12–14), for example.
[10] We note that critical attention of the analogy concerns the extent to which having a religious end is an invariant, or essential, feature of traditional *theoria*, on which see Scullion (2005).

motion. In more detail, it should be noted that Chapter 3 examines Plato's dialogues in relation to this feature: I differentiate it in kinds including spatial, psychological, epistemic, and cosmic, some having reference to philosophical *theoria*. For example, we find the notion of epistemic circular motion in *Rep.* VII, where we find a theoretical ascent and descent proposed in the cave analogy.[11] As well, Plato employs the ideas of rotation and of axial motion with regard to the soul and noetic thinking in various passages, including *Rep.* VII, *Phaedo, Phaedrus*, and *Timaeus* (discussed in Chapter 3).

Chapter 4 is devoted to Aristotle's account of *theoria* which retains Plato's technical understanding of *theoria* considered as philosophical intellection. Broadly speaking, we see the continuity between Plato and Aristotle on the nature of philosophical *theoria*, namely, that the activity consists in the apprehension of the highest objects, namely, forms. For example, in *EN* X 7–8, Aristotle describes *theoria* as the highest activity of the highest faculty, describing it as complete, continuous, pleasant and apprehending the highest objects (cf. *EN* 1177a15–b25), echoing the account from *Symp.* 211a–212a. Yet, while Aristotle retains the essential features of Plato's *theoria*, he departs from him in not once using traditional *theoria* to define his own account.[12] There are other, perhaps more substantial areas of difference between Aristotelian and Platonic *theoria*, such as metaphysical differences about the nature of objects apprehended, and the value accorded to *theoria* that receive extended consideration in individual chapters at the end of this work. As well, Chapters 5 and 6 include the broader perspective as I have adopted from the outset, considering the nature of the objects and the value given to *theoria*, both of the traditional and the philosophical kind.

Stated in more detail, Chapter 5 provides a comparative study of the traditional, Platonic, and Aristotelian conceptions of objects apprehended by *theoria*, reaching a general conclusion that despite some differences, all three accounts hold that *theoria* depends on the apprehension of a perceptible object that stimulates the cognitive faculty.[13] Regarding specifically

---

[11] For discussion of the element of circular motion in Plato, see Ch. 3, sec. 3.2, below.

[12] Two reasons suggest themselves, one concerning compositional differences such as dramatic framing, style, and irony present in Plato, absent in Aristotle, the other, philosophical differences such that Plato proceeds by illustration and analogy whereas Aristotle prefers analytical reasoning; also see below fn. 16, and Ch. 4, sec. 4.2.

[13] Both traditional and philosophical *theoria* depend on visual perception of something significant that leads to higher thought, often by means of memory; the defense of this claim relies on discussion in subsequent chapters, especially Ch. 5.

philosophical *theoria*, we may generalize in concluding that for both Plato and Aristotle the objects of the activity involve forms, with the addition that some discussion is needed concerning the metaphysical distinction between Aristotelian and Platonic objects.[14] Like the previous chapter, Chapter 6 takes a broader perspective by which to examine the three views about the value of *theoria*, including whether the activity is deemed valuable for its own sake, for an instrumental end, or for a combination of these reasons. In general, the chapter finds that within traditional *theoria*, the activity primarily appears to have instrumental value in that: (i) as festival-attendance involving an official delegate, the city seeks certain results through the actions of its representative; (ii) as sanctuary-visitation, typically, the visitor seeks a cure or some kind of help from the priest or the oracle.[15] In contrast, when we turn to Plato's and Aristotle's comments on *theoria*, we find the preponderance of its value residing in the activity itself, in thinking and knowing the forms, and secondary value in its benefits, although we add some qualifications to these findings in our later discussion. So, Aristotle, echoing Plato, praises philosophical *theoria* in *EN* X 7 as the highest activity, but both also seem to suggest that such *theoria* gives rise to practical knowledge. Here we may consider Plato's view that possessing theoretical knowledge about the just and the good is needed for politics (cf. *Rep.* 519c–520e) as suggesting the instrumental value of *theoria*, a view with which Aristotle also seems to concur (cf. *EN* 1177b23–25, 1178a1–8).

In general, Chapters 1 and 2 follow a method similar to Aristotle in *Topics* II 15 where he attempts to discern various meanings associated with the use of a common term, and then, to look for lines of similarity or difference among them; in this case, the focus is on the *theor/eo/ia* family of terms. The initial, discriminating stage comprises one of three levels in the work by analyzing what we consider the primary uses of *theoria* – as festival-attendance, sanctuary-visitation, and abstract thinking – across several thinkers. After discriminating the various uses, we attempt to extract the central elements they share to construct a generic idea of *theoria* that runs through them. Armed with this general notion, we move to the second stage at which we specifically examine Plato's contribution to the concept of *theoria* in representative dialogues, focusing on the structural

---

[14] I use lower-case punctuation generally, i.e., "form" instead of "Form" (also, Grube and Reeve 1992), unless the context requires that a Platonic object, specifically, is signified.

[15] Visitors to healing sanctuaries and oracles alike share the aim of seeking answers to specific problems (Dillon 1997, Ch. 3).

and philosophical implications of his uses. While Plato employs the notion of *theoria* as festival-attendance, he focuses on *theoria* as intellectual activity, redefining the latter kind as philosophical thinking which he identifies with the activity of the philosopher apprehending truth.

Still remaining at the second stage, we find that Aristotle's account retains Plato's technical understanding of *theoria* as the contemplation of essences but offers a refinement of that theory by describing the activity of *theoria* in detail in *EN* X 7–8. Aristotle's account differs from that of Plato in its lack of connection to traditional *theoria*: instead of considering festival-attendance as a foil for his own conception, Aristotle fixes his gaze on the precise notion, detailing the properties of *theoria*, such as being the highest, most complete, continuous, and pleasant of human activities.[16] In a sense, Aristotle continues the direction that Plato initiates with his critical stance toward traditional *theoria*, and his account of *theoria* as a "complete activity" (*energeia teleia*) finalizes some features implicit in Plato's account. The third stage departs from close scrutiny of the philosophers' accounts by returning to central issues arising from the three primary uses, such as, as we have mentioned, the objects each kind of *theoria* apprehends and the value attached to each kind. These questions arise in relation to all kinds, and, by taking a more comprehensive perspective, it is possible to find some similarities among them. For example, if we assume for the moment that any type of *theoria* depends, at least partly, on the activity of looking at something, the activity presupposes specific objects of observation. Yet, it is evident that the objects of *theoria* are not identical in species across kinds, and in this regard, *theoria* has different objects relative to kind. It suffices to say that whereas the objects of traditional *theoria* (namely, as festival-attendance) comprise a subclass of artifacts, including religious statues, those of philosophical *theoria* constitute another kind, namely, intelligible objects. The second question about *theoria* concerns its end, the reason for which traditional and philosophical *theoria* are chosen and pursued, that necessitates taking a broad perspective on the topic so that we may compare how each kind of *theoria* is valued. Consequently, the final two chapters revert to the comparative perspective on *theoria* with which the study begins.

It may be helpful to note, at this point, that the book does not possess an overall linear structure of argument. Considered as a whole, the chapters may be considered as tracing a pattern similar to a "pedimental"

---

[16] Aristotle is not unaware of traditional *theoria*, however, referring to the *architheoros*, or leader of the embassy, in *EN* IV 2 in relation to the virtue of *megaloprepeia* (cf. *EN* 1122a22–25).

construction, named for its relation to the architectural form comprised of stepped bases surrounding a central pillar.[17] By representing different levels of specificity, the chapters represent the various "steps" of the pediment that begin and end at the same level, imitating the pediment configuration. Thus, Chapters 1 and 2 describe the activities comprising traditional *theoria* and suggest ways in which the philosophical tradition accommodates traditional *theoria*. Chapters 3 and 4, devoted to Plato's and Aristotle's accounts, move to more detailed analyses of *theoria*, comprising the core sections of the work. Finally, Chapters 5 and 6, dealing with the objects and value attached to *theoria*, repeat the broader comparative perspective with which the work begins. Across the chapters, a principal, unifying aim of the book concerns the extent to which traditional *theoria* provides the ground in which the philosophical accounts by Plato and Aristotle germinate and come to fruition. In doing so, we come to develop a general account of what *theoria* as such consists in that needs to be kept in mind as we proceed through the analyses of philosophical *theoria*, especially that of Aristotle, as this generic definition stabilizes the exposition. If we are successful, we may achieve the overall objective of situating the accounts of philosophical *theoria* within the context of the larger, existing practice of *theoria*.

---

[17] The term is applied to musical and discursive compositions displaying a stepped internal structure; for definition, see Thesleff (1993, 19, fn. 4), and Douglas (2007) for discussion of ring composition and pediment form.

CHAPTER I

Traditional Theoria

1.1   Traditional *Theoria*: History and Scope

While we have noted that the earliest use of the term *theoria* (θεωρία) refers to the practice of attending religious festivals and sanctuaries, the extension of the practice remains unremarked thus far. Needless to say, a non-specialist student or scholar on first encountering traditional *theoria* would be impressed by its temporal and spatial extension.[1] While not belonging to the essence of *theoria*, they comprise some accidents of its historical manifestation, providing a certain solidity to our understanding of the practice. First, with regard to its temporal duration, traditional *theoria* extends for nearly eight hundred years from the sixth century BCE to the third century CE.[2] The geographical reach of the practice is similarly extensive with festivals drawing populations from all over the Mediterranean area – not only from the Greek and Italian peninsulas but from regions as distant as the Black Sea. In this connection, the Hellenistic historian Dio Chrysostom refers to a festival that attracted visitors from across the Mediterranean, including from areas of present-day France, Italy, Libya, and the Black Sea – for any scholar, a huge land area from which to draw visitors for a festival.[3] In relation to the very large area for place of origin, a third remarkable feature concerns the size of attendance, on which we may find estimates of varying numbers, with the highest end about 700,000 based on Herodotus (*Hist.* II. 60)

---

[1] The phrase "traditional *theoria*" is used to refer to practices encompassing both attendance at various religious festivals and at healing sanctuaries: as is detailed in this chapter, traditional *theoria* includes different activities depending on whether festival-attendance or sanctuary-visitation is being addressed, but in general, "traditional *theoria*" applies to festival-attendance.

[2] Rutherford finds the practice extending for eight hundred years: flourishing in the early 6th through 4th centuries, "reinvigorated" in the Hellenistic period and extending into the 3rd century of the Roman Empire (Rutherford 2013, 3).

[3] His account of an Isthmian festival gives the attendance in "the thousands" (Dio Chrysostom 8.8, 9.5, in Dillon 1997, xiii); festival distances vary depending on land or water route but include figures as high as several hundred to over a thousand miles (one-way).

and the lower end about 20,000, mentioned by Plato referring to a gathering at Epidauros (*Ion* 535d).[4] The considerable difference between Plato's and Herodotus' estimate (Plato's being less than a thirtieth of Herodotus') may be explained by the kind of *theoria* being referenced, with Plato referring to an attendance at a sanctuary dedicated to Asclepius, and Herodotus to an Egyptian festival at which attendance is speculated as much higher.[5] For a modest comparison, if we suggest a figure just twice that of Plato's we have a size about equal to the number of Athenian male citizens in the fourth century, and hence, a very large number of persons routinely engaged in attending festivals and visiting sanctuaries.

A partial explanation for the large number of travelers as well as for the distance they travel is related to the status of certain festivals, in particular, four major festivals, the Olympic, Pythian, Isthmian, and Nemean, that are termed "panhellenic" for the scope of visitors. For example, the Olympic festival held in honor of Zeus, perhaps the largest and best-known, regularly attracts several thousand from across the Greek world. Any of the major festivals typically lasts from several days to a few weeks, taking place during the "sailing period" of the summer when the weather best permits ship travel (the preferred mode for festival-attendance).[6] Both seasonality and periodicity of festivals contribute to the volume of travelers in that we find a relatively large number of major festivals occurring in quick succession from the spring through the late summer months with smaller, regional festivals fitted in between.

Thus, for example during the Classical period, a calendar list would include five to seven major festivals attracting many foreign visitors, and in addition, many smaller festivals for regional visitors. Among the panhellenic festivals, the Olympian Festival is held every four years in Olympia; the Pythian Festival, dedicated to Apollo, every four years in Delphi; the Isthmian Festival, to Poseidon, every two years in Isthmia;[7] the Nemean Festival, to Zeus, every two or three years in Nemea. To this list we may add the Eleusinian Mysteries, dedicated to Demeter, held annually in

---

[4] Plato's figure is repeated by Diodorus Siculus in referring to an Olympic festival in the Hellenistic period (Diodorus Siculus 18.8.5).
[5] Or this is inflated by Herodotus; the Egyptian festival is said to be for the goddess Artemis or Bastet (Dillon 1997, 142).
[6] The four main festivals, every two or four years, occur in the order of Isthmian (April/May), Nemean, Olympian, Pythian (varying years, July/August) allowing the harvest of grapes (Sept.), olives (Nov.–Feb.), and grain (May–July), (Dillon 1997, 30–31, 99–101).
[7] Located on the isthmus between the Peloponnese and northern Greece (Dillon 1997, 100).

Eleusis[8] and two others, the Panatheneia, dedicated to Athena, held every year and the Great Panatheneia, every four years, in Athens. Some smaller but notable festivals may include the Delian Festival dedicated to Apollo, on the island of Delos; the Panionian festival, dedicated to Poseidon, at a sanctuary near Priene; the Great Daedala, dedicated to Hera, in Plataea and the Heraia, to Hera, in Argos and Olympia.[9] While the present list numbers only twelve, one easily reaches a number of more than thirty festivals that are held in a periodic schedule, a quantity implying both frequency of occurrence and cause for the quantity of travelers across Greek territories throughout the year. In this regard, it is worth repeating the observation that festival travelers not only comprise a near constant presence on the landscape, but make up the largest, cohesive mass of people in transit apart from deployed armies.[10] Given the presence and number of these travelers, one must assume that, to writers and philosophers of the fifth and fourth centuries, traditional *theoria*, if not a fixture of everyday life, appears regularly on the cultural horizon. In this regard, let us consider the frequency with which *theoria* takes place. Combining periodic religious festivals as well as trips to sanctuaries for personal health and well-being, it appears that such travel occurs several times a year with each trip lasting from a few days to a few weeks.[11] On this assumption, it does not seem improbable for citizens and non-citizens alike spending from several days to a few full months a year undertaking trips to *theoriai*. In this connection, we mention a suggestion from Plato's discussion about Magnesia's festivals in *Laws* that festival-attendance would comprise about a sixth of the year, or two months, given their twelve-month calendar.[12]

---

[8] The Olympian, Pythian, Isthmian, and Nemean involve "crown" competitions where athletes competed for wreaths, as distinct from those awarding prizes or money, and are considered the most prestigious festivals for *theoroi* (Rutherford 2013, 54–55). The sanctuary at Eleusis drew attendants year-round, but its annual event consisted in initiation into secret rites, differing in content from the festivals concerned with competitions and plays in public spaces.

[9] Among these, Dillon mentions that the Panionian and Great Daedala are largely ethnic festivals while the Delian and Heraia attract a larger scope of visitors (Dillon 1997, 113–14, 126–30, 147–48, 193–96).

[10] Excluding merchants and traders, Dillon concludes that festival travelers comprised a highly conspicuous group on the landscape (Dillon 1997, 294, and xviii).

[11] While there is no reason to think that all members of the state, free and slave, would participate equally in festival attendance, there is evidence that participation by slaves, like those belonging to the wealthy households can be inferred in traveling to festivals; slaves also act as assistants to those traveling to one of the healing sanctuaries like Epidauros and as supervisors of weights at Eleusis, and as traders; evidence suggests itinerant craftsmen like metal-workers, also travel to festivals (cf. Dillon 1997, 58, 80, 215–19).

[12] For discussion, see Morrow (1963, 354); however, as Liz Asmis (in conversation) notes, the number of days Plato gives for festival-attendance in *Laws* need not provide a factual average.

This figure seems a lower estimate than what is calculated based on the extant schedule of festivals occurring in the fifth and fourth centuries, which gives the total from three to four months, up to about one third of the calendar. Needless to say, given the frequency, size of attendance, and breadth of theoric[13] festivals, their effect on Greek culture is considerable: first, inter-city travel among individuals to festival cities and shrines raises the possibility of the positive effects of cosmopolitanism, and second, the frequency and depth of the practice reflects its centrality in Greek culture and thought.[14] So, the prominence of traditional *theoria* as a cultural institution needs to be kept in mind as we come to gauge its significance in the intellectual and practical spheres of classical experience.

In connection with the number of travelers engaged in *theoria*, it is worth repeating that traditional *theoria* signifies two kinds of travel, one aimed at travel to festivals, and another, travel to sacred shrines and sanctuaries.[15] In the case of the latter, we are concerned with more informal travel by individuals (also termed *theoroi*) for the purpose of consulting oracles or seeking medical cures. Again, unlike festival-attendance which involves official delegates, travel to sanctuaries involves private individuals traveling to religious sites, typically outside the periods of the regular festivals. The Eleusinian Mysteries (Greater and Lesser) being devoted to health and curing belong to the second kind, but are held yearly about September for an extended period, like festivals.[16] Other sanctuary travel, such as to one of the best-known sanctuaries, Apollo at Delphi, allows travelers to consult the oracle on political and practical matters, as well as for personal health.[17] By way of brief comparison between sanctuary and festival activities, the differences are evident: festivals offer spectacles, such as athletic competitions, theatrical and musical performances, processions, and sacrifices.[18] In contrast, travel to shrines and sanctuaries presupposes different aims and activities (to be detailed subsequently). Their similarity is less evident, but in my view, the central

---

[13] The adjective "theoric" is used throughout to modify persons, events, and activities that are characteristic of traditional *theoria* as described in this chapter.

[14] Perhaps an analogy can be drawn between traditional *theoria* and the modern practice of summer vacation in industrialized countries, if we keep in mind that *theoria* occurs several times a year and likely is more extended in duration.

[15] The sites of this kind include places devoted to oracles, mystery cults, or a combination of these (Dillon 1997, xiv, 60–73).

[16] For discussion about Eleusinian Mysteries, see Dillon (1997, 60–98).

[17] Two other major healing shrines are Epidauros and Kos, dedicated to Apollo and Asclepius, respectively.

[18] For the temples contain statues of the focal deity; for discussion of the rituals, see Dillon (1997, 99–123, 124–48), Rutherford (2013, 54–62).

feature running through both kinds involves travel for the sake of seeing something (or someone) with religious significance. More specifically, both types of *theoria* essentially depend on the visual experience of something religious. Thus, whether one is seeing an oracle or watching a spectacle, the common element depends on having a heightened perception of something sacred.

1.2 The Observational Element in *Theoria*

The perceptual component proposed is reflected in the LSJ entries for the *theor/ia/eo* family of terms that bear *theor-* as the root.[19] The nouns *theoria* (θεωρία) and *theoros* (θεωρός), adjective *theoretikos* (θεωρητικός), verbs *theorein* (θεωρεῖν) and *theasthai* (θέασθαι) are etymologically related to seeing – more specifically, to watching or observing something. So, while *theoria*, *theoreo*, and *theaomai* reflect a certain range of uses, it seems uncontroversial that they indicate visual perception, and specifically, seeing something highly significant. Thus, it seems fair to infer that a central meaning of *theoria* consists in a heightened level of seeing that differs from garden-variety seeing. The latter can be expressed by conventional perception verbs such as *athrein* (ἄθρειν), *blepein* (βλέπειν), *horan* (ὁρᾶν), or *skopein* (σκόπειν).[20] One might suggest the difference as consisting in that between mere seeing and significant seeing – with the proposal being that the *theor/eo/ia* family of terms implies visual perception in which the perceiver is actively looking at, or watching, something highly significant or sacred.

The notion that observation is central to *theoria* is developed in a particularly striking way by the philologist Karl Kerenyi, for whom it is the essential element in traditional *theoria*: not only are the festival sights seen by humans, but simultaneously, they are seen by the gods.[21] On this interpretation, the observational activity by humans mirrors that of the gods, and this shared component comprises the essence of *theoria*.[22] Thus, Kerenyi's scholarship emphasizes the observational element of *theoria*, making it central at two levels – as an activity of humans and of divine

[19] *Greek-English Lexicon*, ed. H. G. Liddell, R. Scott, H. S. Jones, 9th Edition.
[20] Despite slight differences, all signify kinds of seeing such as regarding, observing, considering, or discerning, and so, may overlap with *theoreo*, *theaomai*; however, these latter two also have a distinctly philosophical meaning in Plato and Aristotle.
[21] See Kerenyi (1942), Tr. Hulme (1962); cf. Rutherford (2013, 143–46).
[22] Rutherford claims that on Kerenyi's view, *theoria* constitutes "a key part of Greek religious experience" (Rutherford 2013, 11).

observers – for the gods, too, are thought to enjoy watching competitions.[23] A relevant text in this context is *Homeric Hymn to Apollo* which
mentions spectacles at the Delian Festival (for Apollo) that are seen by
human visitors are also enjoyed by the god himself (*Homeric Hymn to
Apollo* 46–50). Note that on Kerenyi's interpretation, the activity of
observing that is central to *theoria* brings humans and gods together, or
perhaps, to put it more precisely, in *theoria*, humans as spectators
"approach the condition of the gods" (Rutherford 2013, 144). While
Kerenyi's thesis has received some criticism,[24] his idea that humans and
gods participate in the activity of *theoria* provides a valuable insight for
finding lines of connection among the texts on *theoria* that we survey.[25] In
this regard, we focus on the visual and positional aspects implicit in
traditional *theoria*, specifically, on the notion that humans and gods alike
engage in visual or observational activity. Whether the suggestion holds for
philosophical *theoria* as well remains undetermined for the present; what
we maintain is that an observational element is not accidental to *theoria*,
but essential to it.

1.3   The *Theoros* in Traditional *Theoria*

For most scholars, the presence of a *theoros* (θεωρός), a delegate elected by
the city, constitutes the basic requirement for an event to be considered a
theoria – a central duty of a *theoros* being to attend a specific festival.[26] But
the role requires more than attendance, for an official *theoros* represents the
city as a kind of ambassador who is required to participate in the festival,
and by extension to observe its events.[27] For example, a *theoros* may be
expected to participate in processions, offerings, and rituals, as well as act
as observer of the spectacles, all of which may be part of the report given to

[23] According to Dillon, the gods are thought to delight in athletic competitions over other events
(Dillon 1997, 104).

[24] Rutherford presents two objections against Kerenyi's view, wishing to unseat his view of the *theoros*
as an observer, and so, of observation to *theoria* (Rutherford 2013, 144–45; cf. 12–14); in my view,
these objections are not irresistible.

[25] Leaving aside the theological framework that comprises Kerenyi's larger explanation about the
meaning of ancient festival *theoria* (cf. Rutherford 2013, 143).

[26] An interesting counter-example seems to involve the *amphiktionic* festivals which are administered
by organizations of neighboring cities, like the Delphic Amphiktiony, for these did not require
theoroi announcers as such (or were not so called), and nevertheless are counted festivals, with the
festivals at Delphi, and perhaps, Delos, being so described (cf. Rutherford 2013, 66–67).

[27] So, Rutherford describes what appears to be the standard view among classicists about theoric
festivals: the presence of an official *theoros* is essential (Rutherford 2013, 12–14).

the assembly on return to the city.[28] The mention of an official *theoros* going to a festival site, participating, and returning home recalls a similarity to pilgrimage. In this vein, one scholar has called the *theoros* "the official pilgrim" as being the one who travels to a festival to perform various duties for the city (Dillon 1997, 11). So, for example, the official *theoroi* may participate in formal processions (*pompai*), take part in the religious rituals, and act as observers at events like athletic competitions to make reports back to their respective city-councils. One account of some of these duties is provided by the poet Bacchylides in works describing these festival observers. In one, he depicts the circle of observers watching the discus-throwing event (*Baccl.* 9. 30), and in another, a runner ending his race and sprinkling oil over the visitors (*Baccl.* 10. 20–28). It seems that these observers are the official *theoroi* from neighboring city-states charged with recording the competition results in the official reports they make to their city-councils.[29] In addition to acting as official observers of a festival, the *theoros* may serve as a diviner, or religious interpreter, as seen in a poem by Theognis in the sixth century BCE.[30] From the various functions mentioned, it is not surprising that being elected as an official *theoros* is a high public honor, and restricted to adult male citizens during the Classical period.[31] However, women's participation in festival-attendance is not entirely precluded insofar as some functions related to traditional *theoria*, such as hosting official delegates (*theorodokia*) as well as organizing and participating in smaller, local festivals are open to them.[32] More generally, festival- and sanctuary-attendance are widely available to diverse groups, including women, the poor, children, the aged, and slaves, with the majority even of the major festivals being open to women specifically.[33]

---

[28] Rutherford questions the centrality of an observational role, suggesting it may rather center on his attendance (Rutherford 2013, 143); however, literary and philosophical texts surveyed do reflect a range of functions, including an observational one.

[29] See Rutherford (2013, 208); Thucydides' account of Alcibiades' *theoria* to Olympia has an unofficial attendant reporting to the council on observations at Olympic Games (*Hist.* IV, 16, 2).

[30] The reference is discussed below in Ch. 2, sec. 2.1.

[31] During the Classical period into the 4th century although inscriptions from *c.*200 CE show aristocratic women acting in the role of *theoros* at the Olympic festival (Rutherford 2013, 146).

[32] Both Rutherford (in Elsner and Rutherford 2005, 143, and 2013, 64, 84, 146, 160–61), and Elsner and Rutherford (2005, 19) discuss women acting as *theorodokoi* and *theoroi*; Elsner and Rutherford (2005, 20–21) also consider the young as *theorodokoi* and *theoroi*; while women organize and participate in local festivals for female deities like the Thesmophoria, men retain control of sites and shrines (Dillon 1997, 184, 199).

[33] The exception, the Olympian Festival, bars adult women as spectators, allowing young girls (*parthenoi*) and the priestess of Demeter, but most festivals allow women; the Heraia, games dedicated to Hera, consist in competitions by young women (Dillon 1997, 194–95).

From this basis, the implication drawn is that *theoria* as both festival-attendance and sanctuary-visitation allows a more inclusive demographic class than might be expected from existing legal and political systems like that of Athens. The resulting attendance at sanctuaries and shrines thus mirrors the scope of visitors to the festivals which, as noted, is not restricted to adult, male citizens.[34] For example, like the panhellenic festivals, the Mysteries at Eleusis, Samothrace, and Andania are open to slaves with some festivals allowing their participation and initiation, and in addition, Mystery cults permit the attendance of female slaves.[35] In general, women, both free and slave, may participate in *theoria* as festival-attendance and sanctuary-visitation: in regard to the former, they can organize festivals, and so participate indirectly, and even directly in some festivals.[36] In addition, as household members, they contribute materially to travel to festivals and sanctuaries, undertaking long trips of both kinds, sometimes in the company of male guardians, husbands, or other women and also by themselves.[37] In the context of restrictive laws in Athens and elsewhere concerning women, aliens, slaves, and children, their inclusion within traditional *theoria* is striking. It is possible to consider this aspect of festival- and sanctuary-attendance as comprising a more egalitarian practice by extending participation to non-elite members of the social and political hierarchy.[38] While physical inclusion need not spell political change, this aspect leads to the possibility that over time the practice produces a political, social, or cultural transformation, especially in regard to legal restrictions on personal freedom of movement and agency in the city.[39]

[34] E.g., the panhellenic festivals are generally also open to women and slaves while local festivals often are restricted to group membership, *ethne*, such as Ionians, Dorians, or Boeotians (Dillon 1997, 58, 80, 125–48, 183–203).

[35] For discussion about slaves' participation in the Mysteries, as well as their being barred from attending some other festivals, see Dillon (1997, 61, 150, 151, 168).

[36] E.g., indirectly, by sponsoring chariots at the Olympic Festival, and directly, by *parthenoi* competing directly in the Heraia dedicated to Hera at Olympia (Dillon 1997, 194–95).

[37] Data on women pilgrims attending *theoriai* show they travel hundreds of kilometers (Dillon 1997, 184; cf. the female pilgrim, 183–203).

[38] It may be objected that the practice of traditional *theoria*, rather than extending freedom, merely re-inscribes existing hierarchical roles in society, to which the reply is that even admitting the inequality, the hardships endured in undertaking travel would tend to level differences.

[39] Assuming this aspect of traditional *theoria* holds, it may account for Plato's interest in undertaking a re-conceptualization of traditional *theoria* as intellectual activity from which two alternatives follow: the first is that since intellectual activity is understood as a capacity belonging to male citizens, the social transformational aspect of traditional *theoria* is being rejected by Plato; the second, based on *Rep.* V's proposal for women rulers, that his re-conceptualization of *theoria* as intellection makes good on the promise of *theoria* by extending political emancipation to some women; see also Levin (1996), Vlastos (1989).

1.4   Hosting, Announcing, and Financing *Theoriai*

The complexity of the practice that comprises festival-attendance is evident from related functions supporting the practice, as, for example, those acting as hosts to the official *theoroi* who are called *theorodokoi* (θεωροδόκοι). These are citizens the city appoints to act as hosts for both official delegates and announcers, receiving and looking after them while they are attending the festival (Dillon 1997, 11–12). The announcers, those who announce the sacred truces for the festival (*spondai*) are called *spondophoroi* or *theoroi*, have distinct roles from the official *theoroi* as they declare the truces necessary for the protection of the festival travelers. Further evidence of the depth of civic roles incurred by *theoria* is that the practice of hosting the delegates receives its own term, *theorodokia*, and comprises a hereditary civic honor.[40] The duty of hosting visitors, especially aristocratic ones, provided by the *theorodokos* suggests a connection to the earlier practice of guest-friendship called *xenia* (ξενία) as is seen from the connection to the *proxenos* (πρόξενος), the citizen elected to host city representatives visiting his own city.[41]

There are various means by which *theoroi*, or official representatives to festivals, are financed, including by wealthy private individuals, host cities, or a combination of sources.[42] By whichever source, the incentive to cover the cost of *theoric* officials, which includes that of the delegates and the lead official (*architheoros*), is related to the display of moral virtue: those choosing to cover the cost of the delegations as a public service show their public-spiritedness. Thus, undertaking the expense of a city embassy to a panhellenic festival, with all the public recognition this would receive, is attractive to a public-spirited citizen. In this vein, Aristotle mentions wealthy citizens undertaking the financing of large public affairs in connection with the moral virtue termed "magnificence" (*megaloprepeia*) in *Nicomachean Ethics* IV 2. He discusses this private support of public affairs called "liturgies" (*leitourgia*) in the context of their relative expenses, comparing the cost of equipping a warship (*trireme*) with that of leading the embassy as *architheoros*, where it appears leading the embassy is more costly (*EN* 1122a22–25).[43] The public distinction that is awarded to the

---

[40] For discussion of *theorodokia*, see Dillon (1997, 13; cf. 11–24, 329 fn. 3).

[41] Dillon suggests the tie both in linguistic connection (*proxenos, xenia*) and the practice itself (1997, 14, cf. 154–55).

[42] For discussion, see Dillon (1997, 19–22), Rutherford (2013, 215–17).

[43] Aristotle's point is that supporting the lead official of the embassy, the *architheoros* (ἀρχιθέωρος), is just as proper an exercise of the virtue as outfitting a trireme: the proper amount of the outlay is

elected *theoroi* brings up the fact that traveling to festivals with formal status allowed such persons the possibility of acting as diplomats of sorts in their function as inter-city announcers. In this regard, we find Demosthenes as *architheoros* (ἀρχιθεωρός), or lead official, of the Athenian embassy to Olympia in 324 BCE trying to meet with a Macedonian official at the festival to discuss a political decree of Alexander about exiles.[44] So, the notion of combining the roles of *theoros* and ambassador is not implausible given that the two functions are recognized as requiring very similar political and diplomatic skills. In fact, we find the linkage of the two duties reflected in the titular phrase "ambassador and festival delegate" (πρεσβευτὴς καί θεωρός) that is repeated in inscriptions.[45] From the intricate network of laws and customs comprising the shared practice of *theoria*, one begins to appreciate festival observance as an essential means for inter-city social, political, and cultural communication and, in the long term, for cultural and philosophical continuity.[46]

1.5   The Cosmopolitan Aspect of *Theoria*

The activities involved in festival and sanctuary attendance in conjunction with the experience of undertaking travel often to distant sites and shrines support the notion that the *theoriai* comprise part of a large network of cultural and political exchange and in this regard, they help maintain a level of cultural continuity, and perhaps, cosmopolitanism, that might not be possible otherwise. As one scholar remarks about the role of *theoroi*, "[t]he fundamental activity of the *theoroi* is to represent the city or political community that sends them, and in so doing, communicate to the broader Greek world how the leaders of that community want it to be perceived" (Rutherford 2013, 217). Due to the cultural significance of the institution of *theoriai*, as well as the frequency of their occasion, the practice provides a

---

relative to the circumstance involved (*EN* 1122a25–26); see Dillon (1997, 18) on the relative costs of the two outlays, trireme and embassy. Also note that in *Ath. Pol.* 56, 3, Aristotle mentions that the archon appointed an *architheoros*, a delegation leader, to Delos.

[44] Cited in Dillon (1997, 22), mentioned by Diodorus 18. 8 and Deinarchus, *Against Demosthenes* 199.

[45] See Rutherford (2013, 260–63); one Hellenistic decree shows a *theoros* to Delphi in 226/5 BCE also acting as diplomat for Sardes (cf. Rutherford 2013, 195).

[46] Dillon discusses various laws connected with *theoria* as festival observance including the truce (*ekecheiria*, or *spondai*) and period of truce (*hieromenia*) for participating festival cities, the sanctity (*asylia*) and safety (*asphaleia*) for contestants at festivals of the festival sites, and law concerning safe passage extended to formal festival observers and visitors alike (Dillon 1997, 2–10).

means by which cities may transmit their chosen moral values to other cities. So, from a cultural perspective, we can appreciate how the frequency and distribution of the festivals conjoined with their meaning (whether religious, social, or mercantile) contribute to the longevity of the practice. Conversely, we see that the institution of *theoria* provides significant continuity in social, political, and moral values over a substantial period of Greek history in respect of furthering shared Greek religious and cultural identity.[47] The explanation for the practice of *theoria* having this effect is that in attending festivals, visitors and delegates from many cities engage in a cultural undertaking that is based on common religious values. There are also delegates acting as diplomats, the civic representatives who may carry out meetings with other delegates or political leaders. Should the political aspect of festival *theoria* seem over-described, it is worth recalling that the festivals are a well-established institution of laws and agreements by the fourth century. As Rutherford points out, by the late sixth century traditional *theoria* has a widespread foundation supplied by "a common religious network" over a large area.[48] What the "common network" assumes is a system of shared laws and customs concerning the festivals agreed on by individual cities. For example, cities participating in the festivals have agreements about restricting their powers over the dates of the festivals, including suspending military conflict, protecting festival travelers within the territory and postponing capital punishments.[49] The participating cities find the temporary constraints worthwhile as they are offset by political and cultural gains they attain through the practice of *theoria*. The positive expression of the spirit of the inter-city alliances is reflected in one of their shared values in the fourth century, that of *homonoia*, or concord, which one scholar claims is produced as an effect of the practice of traditional *theoria*.[50] This suggestion, with which I concur, rests on the argument that traditional *theoria* depends on expanding a shared Greek identity and this, in turn, requires *homonoia*, here understood as inter-city concord. In light of the prominence of

---

[47] For discussion on the cultural influence of the panhellenic festivals, see Rutherford (2013, 264–71), Nightingale (2004, 54–63).

[48] Rutherford (2013, 41) states that the structure of common laws and customs undergirding *theoria* is well established by the 5th and 4th centuries.

[49] Typical restrictions include truces between cities that imply the cessation of hostilities, protections for travelers en route between the cities and their territories, inviolability of travelers at the festival or sanctuary site, and postponement of capital punishments for the duration of the festival (Dillon 1997, 1–26).

[50] Rutherford discusses the theoric network of cities from 6th through 4th centuries and *homonoia* (2013, 42–43).

homonoia as a civic value in the fourth century, it is worth observing that its discussion by Plato and Aristotle may signal the influence, albeit indirect, of traditional *theoria* on the subject matter comprising their thinking.[51]

1.6   Common Features in Traditional and Philosophical *Theoria*

It is understood, then, that traditional *theoria* as festival-attendance and sanctuary-visitation is well-established in the fourth century, at the time Plato and Aristotle are developing their accounts of philosophical *theoria* (cf. Rutherford 2013, 297–303). The long background for traditional *theoria* provides the explanation for which central Classical thinkers including Herodotus, Thucydides, Sophocles, Euripides, and Aristophanes refer to *theoria* in relation to festival- or sanctuary-attendance, not as intellectual activity.[52] In several texts that we examine in the next chapter, we find historians and poets mentioning traditional *theoria* or the *theoros* of traditional *theoria* in reference to a range of activities, from presiding as official delegate to being a visitor at a sanctuary to consult an oracle. In general, what marks the activities as belonging to traditional *theoria* is their fundamental connection to having visual experience of something signif-icant, whether this involves acting as observer at a festival or participant at a sanctuary. The starting point for the data supporting this view begins with the lexical evidence about the *theor/ia/eo* family of terms.

According to LSJ, the earliest usage of the term *theoria* is connected to watching a religious performance or ritual, and from this use, other related terms are derived, such as *theorema* (θεώρημα) meaning "that which is seen," a "spectacle" or *theoreion* (θεωρεῖον) meaning "a place for watching performances." The collective group of *theoria, theoreion, theorema,* and other related terms are thus originally connected in referring to activities that comprise or are related to watching public performances, or spectacles. It is not until the fourth century that one finds the term *theorema* being used to signify a theoretical entity, not a spectacle, as, for example, in Aristotle's *DM* 450b25 or at *Meta.* 1083b18. By the third century and

---

[51] For references to *homonoia*, see Plato, *Rep.* 351d5; *Pol.* 311b9, 432e7; *Symp.* 186e2,187c4; see Aristotle, *EN* IX 6 (1167a22–1167b15) in relation to concord in *philia* or among cities.
[52] Aristophanes' use of a mute character *Theoria* in his comedy *Peace* might appear an exception yet she does not represent an intellectual virtue, contemplation, but the civic role of extending peace among cities; we find another comic reference to *theoria* in a fragment of Aeschylus' satyr-play entitled *Theoroi* in which satyrs reflect on truth and imitation in seeing images of themselves on a temple (Goldhill 2000, 162).

following, the term *theorema* refers to a theorem, in the sense of a mathematical theorem as reflected in uses by Archimedes (*Sylph. Cyl.* 1), Pappus (*Math.* 30.6), and Proclus (*In Euclid* 201 F). A final note concerns the connection between *theoria*, *theaomai* (θεάομαι), and *theos* (θεός), *thea* (θεά): while the etymological connections among these terms are not without dispute, some scholars find a close connection, arguing for an overlap among the meanings.[53] According to this view, the family of terms including *theor/ia/eo/theaomai* (θεωρ/ία/εο/θεάομαι) may be understood as indicating something like "observing something divine or sacred," or "seeing the gods."[54] While the etymological issue itself does not appear decisively concluded, their suggestion is not implausible especially given that *theoria* (and *theoreo*, *theaomai*) are specifically related to traveling to religious festivals or shrines for observation. Furthermore, the connection to seeing gods need not be taken literally, as when we find the verb *theaomai* employed by Plato in contexts where an object with divine-like properties, such as a form, is being apprehended. So, seeing something divine may comprise one of the activities that typify *theoria*, and yet it is not necessary to assume that the activity signified must have a deity as its object.

In recapitulating traditional *theoria*, we find a range of activities exhibited in both (i) festival-attendance, which includes citizens traveling from home cities to foreign cities to observe or take part in periodic, religious festivals and (ii) sanctuary-attendance, which involves similar traveling to ritual sites, like Epidauros for the sake of health or Eleusis and other Mystery sites for their religious rituals.[55] From our previous discussion of both kinds of activities, it appears that one defining feature they possess as being traditional *theoria* is their perceptual, observational component. A similar conclusion is drawn from the lexical evidence about the base root of *theoria* and related terms, namely, that it devolves around the observation of an object of special significance. In the case of the notion of *theoros* – namely, one who acts as an announcer or delegate or attends a festival – this role presupposes an essentially observational character, as is evident with the activity of *theoria*. This hypothesis accords with

---

[53] Scholars such as Bill (1901), Buck (1953, 443–44), and Koller (1958, 275), have maintained this basis for finding the connection; others, like Elsner and Rutherford (2005, 12–13) dispute it.

[54] This overlap is reflected in one scholar's reading of *theorein* used in Thucydides' Peace of Nicias (421 BCE): it states that those wanting to travel to "the common shrines . . . to receive oracles" and "to see the gods" (*theorein*) would be safe (Kowalzig 2005, 60).

[55] Again, both kinds are subsumed under the term "traditional" *theoria*; for discussion on sanctuary travel, see Dillon (1997, 60–97).

comprehending the custom of *theoria* as a set of varied activities centered on festival-attendance in which the key feature involves spectatorship, acting as an observer at a significant event or ritual (Goldhill 1996).

1.6.1   Unifying the Two Kinds of Theoria

Having offered a preliminary conclusion about the common features of traditional *theoria*, we need to examine the possibility of shared features between traditional and philosophical *theoria*. As we have noted, the investigation seems initially impeded by a problem of ambiguous reference. From an Aristotelian perspective, we observe what appears to be a lack of synonymy across the various uses of the term *theoria* in that he finds the minimal condition for two or more items being synonymous being a common essence as well as a common name (*Cat.* 1, 1a1–3). Yet this requirement does not seem to hold across the central uses of *theoria* given that the philosophical and traditional uses signify different activities.[56] So, if the two central referents have no common essence, *theoria* is not synonymous but ambiguous. However, our examination aims to show a fundamental connection between the traditional and philosophical uses of *theoria*. For Plato's account of *theoria* continues traditional *theoria* in certain respects, making possible the study of their common features.[57] Having secured the characteristics shared by Platonic and traditional *theoria*, it becomes possible to investigate Aristotle's account for these characteristics, despite Aristotle's account being less securely tethered to traditional *theoria* than Plato's theory. Thus, the task of unifying the traditional and philosophical uses of *theoria* requires a two-step approach. At the end of the constructive process, we take a final critical step backwards, addressing Plato's and Aristotle's philosophical account from the standpoint of traditional *theoria*.

Let us sketch the procedure in more detail, beginning with the areas of reference that appear as common features between the two kinds of traditional *theoria*: these include seeing or observing something, the object of sight being something of high religious significance, and circular motion as traveling away from and back to a starting point. Taking these elements into consideration, two points of intersection between traditional and

---

[56] This formulation about the synonymy of *theoria* skirts the issue of whether Plato and Aristotle themselves use *theoria* in the same way, or with the same sense; the short answer is that their uses overlap, and the full explanation follows below in Chs. 3 and 4.

[57] Discussion of the shared features appears in Ch. 3.

philosophical ideas of *theoria* are evident, with the observational, or perceptual, element being the first common feature. As we noted, the etymological relations among the *theor/ia/eo* family of terms, including the verb *theaomai*, reflect a common signification: the visual activity of "looking at" or "observing" something. The second point of potential overlap involves a feature clearly present in both kinds of traditional *theoria*, namely, seeing something of religious significance. The subsequent step in synthesis concerns determining whether philosophical *theoria* possesses the two features in the same way as traditional *theoria*: it is here that the difficulties arise. For it becomes clear that the two features are not present in both kinds of *theoria* in the same sense. First, while philosophical *theoria* surely requires sense-perception as a prior epistemic state, it does not consist in the activity of perceiving something, as traditional *theoria* does, say, when we are observing religious rituals at festivals or sanctuaries. Again, philosophical *theoria* does not appear to involve perceiving something of high significance – as traditional *theoria* clearly does. However, philosophical *theoria* resembles traditional *theoria* in these features as both kinds of *theoria* have a perceptual or observational element in their respective activities although this perceptual component is not present in the same sense across these activities. Similarly, the religious feature of traditional *theoria* is present in philosophical *theoria* in an extended sense in that we grasp the way that the notion of traditional *theoria* implies this characteristic and apply the relation to philosophical *theoria* by analogy. For example, we may formulate an analogy of the perceptual feature in stating that visual insight is to philosophical *theoria* as observing is to festival *theoria* where the visual aspect of traditional *theoria* provides the *explanans* of that in philosophical *theoria*. The extension of the perceptual feature is supported as well by the linguistic and semantic ties holding among the *theor/ia/eo* family of terms, and so, it is understandable that Plato chooses the *theor/* family for his notion of apprehending forms. In similar fashion, we may construct an analogy of the shared religious feature as follows: studying the eternal and divine is to philosophical *theoria* as observing the gods is to traditional *theoria*. Here it is suggested that the religious aim typical of traditional *theoria* is present in an extended sense in philosophical *theoria* in that the latter consists in studying the eternal and divine as forms. Finally, while the circularity feature is not present in precisely the same sense in philosophical *theoria* as in traditional *theoria*, one can grasp the sense in which it is present by an extension of meaning. Circularity of movement belongs to traditional *theoria* by virtue of starting and returning to one's home city; such motion is also implied in epistemic movements concerning the apprehension of form.[58] In addition to an analytical discussion of the analogy, we may consider the parallel between traditional *theoria* and pilgrimage by way of advancing the matter of shared features.

In the present regard, it is useful to mention a central parallel that some scholars suggest to grasping the nature of traditional *theoria*, namely, pilgrimage.[59] Given that traditional *theoria* includes traveling to sites for religious purposes, the analogy to pilgrimage seems particularly apt, even taken at the level of particular activities, such as taking part in rituals or communicating with a deity.[60] Furthermore, considering traditional *theoria* as akin to pilgrimage provides us with an imaginative motif that enables the extension of pilgrimage to philosophical *theoria*. In so doing, it becomes possible to grasp the way in which the features of observation and seeing something religious, belong to philosophical *theoria*. In essence, the conceptual parallel between traditional and philosophical *theoria* is envisioned by way of a third notion, pilgrimage. By focusing on the two features mentioned, namely, having an observational component and a religious object to view, it becomes more apparent how philosophical *theoria* is analogous to traditional *theoria*, namely, in virtue of both being analogous to pilgrimage. In more detail, the argument works thus: the overlap between traditional *theoria* and philosophical *theoria* depends on certain common features. Stated as a complex component, the two central features of traditional *theoria* can be described as "engaging in visual activity for the sake of observing something sacred or of high significance." This description can be extended without change of sense to pilgrimage, and so traditional *theoria* and pilgrimage are close analogues. The analogy between pilgrimage and philosophical *theoria* works to the extent that we allow for an extension of sense of the observational element in that philosophical *theoria* involves observation of different kinds of objects than traditional *theoria*. In brief, by taking the analogy to pilgrimage seriously, we can grasp the common elements among the kinds of *theoria*, both traditional and philosophical, more easily. We will now examine the textual sources for the kinds of *theoria* in more detail in Chapter 2.

---

[58] For discussion, see Ch. 3, sec. 3.2.
[59] Dillon (1997), Nightingale (2004), and Rutherford (2013) equally discuss pilgrimage, differing about its aptness to theoria.
[60] It seems, furthermore, that since pilgrimage possesses the same features as traditional *theoria*, the parallel is closer than analogical similarity, but not synonymy or core-dependence (see Shields 1999, Ch. 1; Ward 2008, Ch. 1, 3).

CHAPTER 2

Literary and Philosophical Texts on Theoria

Through the brilliance of my *theōria* to Olympia, the Greeks were led
to believe our city greater than she was.
                                          – Alcibiades (Thucydides, *Hist.* VI, 16, 2)

In the previous chapter, we concluded that the primary reference among
the *theor/eo/ia/os* family of terms in the fifth and fourth centuries is one
signifying festival or sanctuary attendance with a secondary one indicating
abstract thinking. In addition, we mention a fifth-century use of *theoria* to
signify traveling for education or generalized sight-seeing. Since this kind,
educational *theoria*, if we may call it such, does not fall neatly under either
traditional *theoria* or philosophical *theoria*, it seems correct to situate it
between the two dominant uses as an intermediate one. Like traditional
theoria, it consists in traveling to religious sites for observation, and like
philosophical *theoria*, it appears directed at gaining knowledge. Let us file it
away for the moment and refer to it later when we study various texts that
mention *theoria*.[1] In conjunction with the task of comparative collection,
it is worth recalling some conclusions about the *theor/ia/eo* family of terms,
namely, that what is typically signified concerns having visual apprehension with objects of high significance as the object. Yet, while the *theor/ia/
eo* family seems to exhibit a unified meaning related to observing, or
watching, something highly significant, differences in the meaning of
the observing activity may arise depending on differences in the objects
seen. Specifically, it is clear that each kind of *theoria*, whether festival-
attendance, intellectual apprehension, or sight-seeing, is directed at a
specific kind of object which affects the nature of the activity. For example,
the objects apprehended in philosophical *theoria* comprise the highest kind
of intelligible objects, and the kind of observation involved differs from
that in festival-attendance which involves seeing spectacles, such as athletic

---

[1] See sec. 2.3, this chapter, for discussion.

games, rituals, or images of deities. It is clear that some objects apprehended in festival- and sanctuary-attendance, like temples, cult statues, sculpted images of deities, and the like, coincide with the kind of objects seen in *theoria* as sight-seeing, and so, the observational activity involved in both the traditional and educational kinds of *theoria* seem similar. But, of course, educational *theoria* does not depend on attending a formal festival nor does it appear to have the kind of public dimension that traditional festival-attendance does.

In fact, the aspect of comprising a public function seems very characteristic of traditional festival-attendance and absent from both educational *theoria* and philosophical *theoria*.[2] For we should note that traditional *theoria* requires public observation: this is fully predictable when we recall that attendance at festivals (and healing shrines) takes place within a shared arena of action. Furthermore, some traditional *theoria* seems to carry with it an element of self-conscious observation or thinking oneself seen, as well as seeing, among its other features.[3] Thucydides' reference to Alcibiades' *theoria* that prefaces this chapter counts in this regard.

2.1 Traditional *Theoria* in Literary Texts

We first turn to some texts reflecting core aspects of traditional *theoria* as both festival- and sanctuary-attendance, here presented by various writers including Theognis, Thucydides, Aristophanes, Euripides, and Plato. The texts reflect differing aspects of traditional *theoria* that, by placing them together, yield a general picture about traveling to sites to watch, observe, or interpret the events connected with the celebration of deities. In the first example, we find an extended description of an official *theoros* attending an oracle at Delphi that reflects an expert capacity and the public aspect of the role central to traditional *theoria*. The text comes from a poem by Theognis in which a young man who is addressed as a *theoros* takes part in the ceremony.[4] So, the speaker addresses the youth and asks him to be more accurate in his predictions "than the carpenter's compass, plumb line

---

[2] While it is possible for philosophical or sight-seeing *theoria* to be engaged in with others, this aspect does not belong to its core features.

[3] While it lies outside the scope of this work, classical scholarship also elucidates a related aspect, a kind of self-conscious observation of art termed *ekphrasis*, on which see Goldhill (1996, 2007), Goldhill and Osborne (1992), and Zeitlin (1992).

[4] The work is attributed to Theognis about a ceremony held by the Delphic Amphiktiony, i.e., the cities in the area administering the Delphic sanctuary (Rutherford 2013, 41, 66).

or set square" (Theognis, *Eleg.* I, 805–806).[5] The scholarly interpretation is that here the *theoros* is acting like a diviner, an interpreter of rituals, called a *theopropos* (Rutherford 2013, 99).[6] Thus, the poem's request for the *theoros* to be "more precise than carpenter's tools" (ll. 805–806) refers to an exercise in divination, and it reveals that, in being asked to provide a level of precision in interpreting what the god wishes to communicate, we see a *theoros* acting as a skilled interpreter of an oracle.[7] Like a delegate acting at a festival, this role carried out at a sanctuary reflects a public aspect in which the proper performance of the task implies being seen to perform it well.

The public aspect of the *theoria* is also reflected in another account of festival *theoria*, this time describing travel to a festival that appears to be informally conducted. Thucydides provides the account, a well-known *theoria* taken by Alcibiades to Olympia in 416 BCE.[8] As Thucydides recounts it, Alcibiades went on an Olympian *theoria* and, on returning home, reported to the Athenian council: "Through the brilliance of my *theoria* to Olympia, other Greeks were led to believe our city greater than she really was" (*Hist.* VI, 16, 2–3).[9] In the rest of his account, he describes his multiple victories in chariot-racing, and his display of magnificence in the ceremonies, actions that would have been considered as reflecting hubris, all of which suggest his acting as a private citizen.[10] In another example from Thucydides, we find an oblique reference to an official delegation abroad, in this case, the Athenians and Ionians attending the Delian Festival. In Thucydides' account, he explains that Peisistratus purified the area around the temple in Delos (in the sixth century), and subsequently, the Athenians purified the whole island, removing old graves, and establishing the Delian festival to be held every five years with games (*Hist.* III, 104, 1–2). Likely better known to readers, Plato provides

---

[5] The Greek lines: τόρνου καὶ στάθμης καὶ γνώμονος ἄνδρα θεωρὸν εὐθύτερον χρὴ <ἔ>μεν, Κύρνε, φυλασσόμενον ... (*Eleg.* I. 805–806).

[6] The term is also used in Herodotus and Homer; Pausanias employs *theoros* in the sense of a delegate who functions as an oracle, on one occasion, describing someone selected as a *theoros* to Delphi because of his expertise in the mantic art (Pausanias, 4.9.3–4).

[7] For discussion, see Rutherford (2013, 93–95).

[8] Alcibiades' being boastful about his appearance rather than carrying out his function bears out his reputation as being lawless and immoderate: see Thucydides, *Hist.* VI, 15, 4; for discussion on his *theoria* as private citizen, see Bill (1901, 200–201).

[9] The Greek: οἱ γὰρ Ἕλληνες καὶ ὑπὲρ δύναμιν μείζω ἡμῶν τὴν πόλιν ἐνόμισαν τῷ ἐμῷ διαπρεπεῖ τῆς Ὀλυμπίαζε θεωρίας (*Hist.* VI, 16, 2).

[10] It is Alcibiades' actions of taking the state emblems and displaying them as his own at the festival that are considered ostentatious and improper; cf. *Against Alcibiades* (25 ff.) attributed to Andocides (Bill 1901, 200).

us with references to the same festival, the Athenian delegation (i.e., a state *theoria*) to Delos in both *Crito* and *Phaedo* that account for the postponement of Socrates' death (cf. *Cr.* 43c9–d1, *Phd.* 58b1–5).

2.1.1 Theoria *in Greek Drama*

Greek drama supplies parallel examples to Thucydides' descriptions of *theoria* as festival-attendance. One brief but dramatic passage about festival *theoria* comes from Aristophanes' play *Peace* (*Eirene*) in which we find a mute character named *Theoria* who is given back to the city assembly, or *boule*, as a gift by the main character named *Peace* (cf. ll. 523 ff.). According to one scholar, this action is to be interpreted as indicating that the character *Peace* is restoring the power of the assembly to appoint festival delegates that had been interrupted by war (Bill 1901, 201–202). If this reading is accepted, the character of *Theoria* may be interpreted as representing the service of state-appointed delegates for attendance at festivals, which is fully consistent with *theoria* as referring to the practice described as festival-attendance. Two other works by Aristophanes employ the idea of festival-going *theoria* as a dramatic backdrop, specifically, two of the lost works entitled *Amphiarius* and *Women Setting Up Tents* (*Skenas Katalambanousai*).[11] In these plays, the mention of *theoria* refers to someone going on a pilgrimage or undertaking travel to a religious shrine. It is worth noting that in the latter play, the plot involves female festival-goers called *theorai* attending a large, non-local festival, a reference that supports the idea of women attending festivals.[12] In Aristophanes' comedy *Wealth* (*Ploutos*) we find a plot in which a man named Chremylus and his slave Carion, on returning from a *theoria* to Delphi meet an old, blind man representing Wealth. Within the course of the play, the three characters devise a plan to travel together – in effect, undertaking another *theoria* – to an Asclepion, a healing shrine dedicated to Asclepius, to find a cure for the old man's blindness.[13]

As well, Greek tragedy provides vivid descriptions of *theoriai* involving travel to shrines and healing sites being carried out by servants as well as free citizens. In Euripides' *Ion*, two main characters, Xuthus and Creusa,

---

[11] Of Aristophanes' more than forty plays, only eleven are extant; we have some fragmentary evidence of the two mentioned, *Amphiarius* and *Women Setting Up Tents* (rough translation).

[12] Noting the evidence is from a literary source; however, other evidence about the festivals supports the view of women's attendance and participation; see Dillon (1997, 183–203), and Rutherford (2013, 146, 160–61) on participation by women and children.

[13] For discussion of these works, see Rutherford (1998).

king and queen, are traveling to Delphi to consult the oracle about conceiving offspring. Unknown to them, the temple-priest at Delphi is Creusa's son, and the plot unfolds.[14] In addition to the main *theoria* by the king and queen, we have a secondary *theoria* made up of Queen Creusa's female attendants who comprise the Chorus whose lines reflect their function as *theorai*, or celebrants on a *theoria*. The servant women describe their observations at the Delphic shrine, comparing it with the sculptures of deities they know from the Acropolis (*Ion*, ll. 184–89, 196–97).[15] The representation of women's participation in non-festival *theoriai* is realized by depicting a Chorus of female servants to the queen who is on a royal *theoria*. Although a fictive account, the play accords with evidence about both women slaves and servants taking part in *theoriai* to major sanctuaries like Delphi where they are free to consult an oracle.[16] This fact is reflected in *Ion* when the temple attendant Ion asks Creusa whether she has come with her husband or alone to the oracle (*Ion*, l. 299).[17] Two other plays by Euripides, *Andromache* (ll. 1086–1163) and *Bacchae*, may be noted in relation to non-festival *theoria* as well. First, *Andromache* concerns a confrontation between Neoptolemus and Orestes that occurs when Neoptolemus is on *theoria* to Delphi – in this case, a sacred mission – to apologize to Apollo for his previous impiety to the god. So, he ends up spending three days in the sanctuary of Apollo "contemplating" the god (ll. 1086–87), at the end of which a crowd of people from Delphi gathers, fearful he will sack the sanctuary again, and he is killed by an unnamed man (ll. 1147–48).[18] An equally grim portrayal of non-festival *theoria* is highlighted in *Bacchae*, where the god Dionysus, describing himself as a *theoros* (l. 1047) and accompanied by the Bacchants, appears in Thebes to inspect his followers. While King Pentheus resists accepting the god, the Theban women follow Dionysus and the Bacchants outside the city to the mountains to celebrate the god. To his great misfortune, Pentheus, driven

---

[14] The plot turns on the background that Creusa was raped by Apollo many years ago, an event she recalls but wishes to forget (ll. 247–54).

[15] See Rutherford (1998, 139, and fn. 21); Zeitlin (1992).

[16] See, for example, discussion of women's activities as attendants in consulting the Delphic oracle and healing sanctuaries like Epidauros, and attending festivals (Dillon 1997, 189–96). In addition, while usually only male citizens act as *theoroi*, some evidence suggests women may be leading extraterritorial *theoriai*, on which see Rutherford (2013, 160–61).

[17] For discussion about participation by women at specific sites including Epidauros, Delphi, Eleusis, and Andania, see Dillon (1997, 60–86); for a general account of the female pilgrim, Dillon (1997, 183–203).

[18] In his discussion of the play, Rutherford emphasizes the visual aspect of the drama, that Neoptolemus "gazes at" the god for three days, and then prays to the god "in full sight" (l. 1117) in a "culmination of the process of sacred contemplation described earlier" (Rutherford 1998, 147).

by his desire to watch them, dresses as a Bacchant and runs off to spy on them. Dionysus savagely punishes the interloper: as Pentheus is watching the Bacchants from his hiding place in the trees (ll. 1058–62), they – including his mother Agave – see him, bring him down, and tear him apart. So, the play turns on events in which someone is seen and not seen or is seen but not recognized: Pentheus, who sees but does not recognize Dionysus, and Agave who sees but does not recognize her son. In this regard, the frequent use of sense-perception verbs signifying watching and looking is highly significant, the terms being pivotal to the central activity of *theoria* the play describes: attending and observing a religious ritual of Dionysus. Moreover, it may be suggested that the play contrasts two different kinds of *theoria*, a legitimate kind consisting of the female followers of Dionysus attending the ritual dance for the god, and an illegitimate kind exercised by Pentheus, who chooses to attend to spy on the female celebrants. In the latter case, Pentheus' activity of looking is not sanctioned; it is improper *theoria* and so, it is a transgression, in part, because he sees what he is not supposed to see (the Bacchants' rite), and as a result, the ritual of *theoria* ends violently.[19]

2.1.2   *Extra-Literary References to* Theoria

Two other references to *theoria* standing outside the literary tradition deserve mention, one related to the participation in the Eleusinian Mysteries, the other, a mundane reference to the Theoric Fund in Athens. In the case of the Eleusinian Mysteries, we find *theoria* used in what we might consider a technical context to describe the kind of vision that belongs to an ordinary follower of the Mysteries. This type of seeing stands in distinction from the kind of activity termed *epopteia* (ἐποπτεία) that is supposed to belong to the fully initiated viewer of the Mysteries.[20] The second case, the so-called "Theoric Fund," is a civic fund that may have been established by Pericles to provide monies for citizens to attend festivals and theater (θέατρον). While its originator and date remain unclear, its purpose is to provide Athenian citizens the means to attend the Dionysia Festival in Athens in the fifth and fourth centuries.[21] While these latter two cases do not coincide with *theoria* as festival-attendance, they may be subsumed under *theoria* in virtue of being related to activities comprising it, as, for example with the viewing implicit in the Mysteries,

---

[19] For discussion, see Rutherford (1998, 150–51).   [20] See Rutherford (2000, 139, and fn. 31).
[21] See Rutherford (2000, 134, fn. 8).

or with being the material means by which festival-attendance is attained, with the Theoric Fund. Consequently, both bear sufficient similarity to the other cases to allow identification with traditional *theoria*.

2.1.3   Collection of Literary References

It is time to take stock of the examples of *theoria* coming from the literary tradition to search for their common characteristics. One method is to review the roles of the *theoros* since his presence confirms that of a *theoria*. From the extension of roles falling under the term, we find a person traveling to a festival or shrine: (i) to observe a festival as an appointed delegate or as a private citizen; (ii) to form part of a delegation to a sanctuary; (iii) to consult an oracle;[22] (iv) to act as a city magistrate, (v) to participate as a non-initiate in the Eleusinian Mysteries.[23] Admitting the obvious differences among these roles, one complex feature they share centers on being an observer of religious ritual or of the divine. Hence, we find viewing, or spectatorship, as a central element in traditional *theoria*, and, in addition, the object of the viewing is something divine, or highly significant. We may mention a third element, suggested by one classicist, concerning the performance of sacred duty as added to the features specified.[24] While this feature may not initially appear to comport well with some kinds of *theoria* such as consulting an oracle or visiting a sanctuary, it is, in fact, perfectly consistent with them insofar as they are performed against a backdrop of belief in the deities' power to aid them. In this light, actions carried out as part of *theoria* assume that the agent is acting under the moral norms imposed by religious belief, and in this sense, the person is acting from duty. It may be less clear that the kind of *theoria* that is mentioned in relation to Solon, namely, educational *theoria*, or traveling for sight-seeing,[25] displays this last feature; so, for the sake of being comprehensive, I propose that the idea of traditional *theoria* has two components, first, the activity of observation, and second, the object observed is divine or of religious significance.[26] With this generic account, the several examples of *theoria* and *theoros* can be subsumed under a

---

[22] As we have seen in Theognis, fr. 88, and Euripides, *Ion*.

[23] We are excluding here festival announcers, variously called *spondophoroi* or *theoroi*, as they have distinct roles from the official *theoroi*.

[24] For discussion, see Bill (1901, 197).

[25] The reference to Solon's trip to Egypt as *theoria* is Herodotus (*Hist.* 1. 29–31).

[26] However, in my view, the third feature comes into play when we come to Plato's depiction of *theoria* in specific dialogues; see Ch. 4.

common account. Taking a comprehensive view of *theoria*, the element of spectatorship, or observation, is central to traditional *theoria* and to sight-seeing *theoria*, the less-mentioned third type. If we consider this element with the other characteristics we commonly find, the list may be expanded to include: (i) purposive looking or observation, (ii) an aim of religious significance, and (iii) circular motion as traveling to and from sites. The last feature has been broached in the Introduction where more attention was promised, which we make good in what follows.

2.2   Traditional *Theoria* and Pilgrimage

The literary and historical references to traditional *theoria* describe it as involving some individual, usually called a *theoros*, who journeys from a home city to a specific site for festival- or sanctuary-attendance and returns. This description, taken in conjunction with the notion of seeing something of religious significance, has suggested the analogy to religious pilgrimage.[27] While scholarly reception of the comparison remains uneven, in my view the analogy offers certain features that are so apt for grasping the ancient practice that it seems overly cautious to reject it.[28] For while we may acknowledge that traditional *theoria*, like pilgrimage, is likely to refer to set of connected experiences rather than one thing with invariant features, we may yet maintain the general suitability of the comparison.[29] After all, another central feature of pilgrimage consists in observing something sacred, which further connects it to traditional *theoria*. Taken together, the common features support the analogy of traditional *theoria* and pilgrimage, despite the reservations of classicists like Scullion (2005).[30] So, with the working hypothesis that the analogy has merit, even if inexact in some respects, let us proceed to examine the idea of pilgrimage further.

For more precision, we may revisit an anthropological account of pilgrimage that, while somewhat dated, bears on the traditional practice of *theoria*. According to the description given by Nightingale, the process

---

[27] See Dillon (1997, Ch. 1), Nightingale (2004, 40–71), Rutherford (2013, 12–14) on the analogy.
[28] See, for example, Elsner and Rutherford (2005, 2–22), Rutherford (1998, 2013, 12–16).
[29] See Elsner (2005, 4–5, and fn. 13); a common criticism is that pilgrimage seems to require feelings of piety and repentance while these appear absent from traditional *theoria*, see Rutherford (1998, 131–32), yet he endorses the comparison, nonetheless.
[30] Scullion (2005) takes a skeptical attitude to its religious aim, claiming that traditional *theoria* is more aptly described as "festival-junketing" than pilgrimage, thus contrasting his view with Dillon (1997), Elsner and Rutherford (2005, 1–38), and Rutherford (2013, 12–14).

consists in three distinct phases, the first leaving the home city, a stage that represents "a fixed point" in one's world in order to reach the second stage, the focus of the travel: this represents the "liminal stage" that lacks "all or most" of the features of one's ordinary existence, and which enables the religious experience of the pilgrim. In the third phase, the pilgrim returns to the stage of ordinary experience, the point of departure, changed.[31] At first glance, traditional *theoria* does not appear to reflect all three stages well: for example, the liminal stage where one's experience lacks most everyday features. For festival- or sanctuary-attendance consists in traveling to well-known sites and shrines that do not seem to reflect this feature. However, on closer consideration, traditional *theoria*, especially travel to sanctuaries, does appear to involve a liminal phase in that such visitors are seeking practical remedies through the mediation of a god, and so, we find parallels to the ideas of being at a threshold and entering a liminal phase in the experiences of the attendee at a sanctuary. As well, the beginning and ending phases of departing and returning home that comprise parts of the pilgrim's journey bear comparison to traditional *theoria*.[32] Consequently, the analogy can be used without expecting all features of monotheistic pilgrimage, like piety, to apply in the same way to all traditional *theoria*. Furthermore, we need not even assume that all pilgrimage requires the feature of piety,[33] as any reader familiar with Chaucer's account of pilgrimage can appreciate.[34] So, the analogy between traditional *theoria* and pilgrimage seems reasonably secure if we are willing to admit a certain plasticity among the items compared. After all, most cases of traditional *theoria* involve traveling to a specific site or shrine to observe or take part in a religious ritual, and in this regard, they appear well-suited for a comparison to pilgrimage.

Overall, my suggestion is to compare traditional *theoria* to pilgrimage in a qualified way for the reason that we may not be able to determine all the specific fixed features of pilgrimage that map onto traditional *theoria*. But we can enumerate a certain number of specific features. For example, we

---

[31] For example, that of Turner and Turner (1978, 2), discussed in Nightingale (2004, 42).

[32] Nightingale (2004, 42–44) discusses *theoria* as traveling for experience in which the structure of leaving and returning home comprises the end points of a journey consisting of detachment, liminal phase, and return.

[33] Namely, the objection cited in Elsner seems to assume that pilgrimage requires pilgrims to have narrowly religious objectives as invariant features, which is not obvious in itself (cf. Elsner and Rutherford 2005, 4, fn. 13).

[34] Consider characters like the Wyfe of Bath with her decidedly secular motives (cf. *Canterbury Tales*, 453–548); even as fictional descriptions, these check our assumption about piety being necessary to pilgrimage.

know that activities within traditional *theoria* include, for example, traveling to attend festivals, seeing spectacles like athletic games, observing religious rituals, consulting or interpreting oracles, seeking cures, and traveling for the sake of health. Taking these into account, it becomes possible to provide a generic description of traditional *theoria* that would allow the comparison to pilgrimage; for this purpose, we propose the following generic definition as sufficient to comprehend the common elements: "traveling for the sake of observing something significant and perhaps sacred." Taking this account of *theoria* as a common starting point has two advantages: first, both cases of *theoria* as festival-attendance and sight-seeing may be subsumed under the generic description, ensuring that the application of the term *theoria* signifies some one thing; second, additional features can be added to the generic account to differentiate the specific kind. It also should be evident that a corresponding generic account of pilgrimage can be provided, and that we will be able to find an overlap with the generic account of *theoria* in ways that may illuminate further features that they share. To begin with, like traditional *theoria*, pilgrimage consists in traveling for the sake of seeing something significant or sacred. Additionally, as we suggested, another typical feature of pilgrimage concerns what me way consider its circular form in having a common starting and ending location.[35] Since the familiar kinds of religious pilgrimage possess end points, they possess a center point which consists in the traveler being at the religious site or shrine to experience a deity or a religious ritual, inasmuch as this experience comprises the focal point of the travel. These three aspects coincide well with the notion of traditional *theoria* that we have discussed in that both festival-attendance and travel to sanctuaries possess the same general structure in virtue of possessing a circular form. These same features prove to be significant with respect to Plato's conception of *theoria* which includes both traditional and philosophical uses.

2.3   *Theoria* as Sight-Seeing and Pilgrimage

As we mentioned, a third use of *theoria* refers to traveling with an aim to see sights, and perhaps, receiving an education; we have placed it between traditional and philosophical *theoria* as it seems to share some features with each kind. It also bears some similarities to the practice of pilgrimage, as may be evident from the generic account of *theoria* mentioned above: traveling

---

[35] This is not to deny that pilgrimage might take place over a long migration to a different location and so compose a linear rather than a circular form.

for the sake of seeing something highly significant or sacred. In terms of the textual examples of *theoria* as sight-seeing, these occur prior to and contemporaneous with Plato and Aristotle, the earliest coming from Herodotus. More specifically, we have two passages in Herodotus, one in Isocrates, one in Thucydides, and one each from Plato and Aristotle. The first text concerns a long trip that Herodotus reports Solon took to Egypt to see foreign sights of interest (*Hist.* I. 29), and the second, a trip (*theoria*) taken by Anacharsis, a non-Greek, who travels to Greece, receiving "much wisdom" (*Hist.* IV. 76). The third text comes from Isocrates in which the speaker, the son of a nobleman, describes himself as being sent to Athens and other places in Greece "for the sake of travel and *theoria*" by his father (Isocrates 17.4). In all of these, we find the notion of going on a *theoria* connected to the idea of gaining wisdom, perhaps in the sense of acquiring cultural education. Let us study these more closely, beginning with Herodotus' account of Solon's extended journey away from Athens.[36] According to Herodotus, after Solon (archon 594/3 BCE) gives Athens its laws, he decides to take a trip to Lydia and Egypt that is described as a *theoria*.[37] According to Herodotus: "Solon, the Athenian, having left Athens to be absent ten years, under the pretext of going on a sight-seeing trip (*kata theories* [κατά θεωρίης], I. 29, 1), but really to avoid being forced to repeal any of the laws which, at the request of the Athenians, he had made for them" (*Hist.* I. 29).[38] In the longer passage from which these lines occur, the term *theoria* is repeated: "On this account, as well as for *theoria*, (*tes theorias* [τῆς θεωρίης], I. 30, 1), Solon went to Egypt to the court of Amasis, and also came on a visit to Croesus at Sardis" (*Hist.* I. 30).[39] As mentioned, Herodotus describes a trip by a non-Greek, Anacharsis, who travels to several cities, Greek and non-Greek, for the sake of sight-seeing: "after surveying [*theoresas*] much land and receiving much wisdom, he brought it to the haunts of the Scythians . . ." (*Hist.* IV. 76; tr. Rutherford 2013, 335). Herodotus employs the *theor/ia* family of terms in a slightly different context in describing an exchange between Solon and Croesus in which Croesus tells Solon that his reputation for

---

[36] This assumes Herodotus' *Histories* was composed about 440 BCE.
[37] It is not known whether the trip described by Herodotus took place; the notion of taking a *theoria* may be used as a *topos* law-giver, see Ker (2000).
[38] The Greek runs: καὶ δὴ καὶ Σόλων ἀνὴρ Ἀθηναῖος, ὃς Ἀθηναίοισι νόμους, ποιήσας ἀπεδήμησε ἔτεα δέκα, κατὰ θεωρίης πρόφασιν ἐκπλώσας, ἵνα δὴ μή τινα τῶν νόμων ἀναγκασθῇ λῦσαι τῶν ἔθετο. αὐτοὶ γὰρ οὐκ οἷοί τε ἦσαν αὐτὸ ποιῆσαι Ἀθηναῖοι· (*Hist.* I. 29).
[39] The Greek runs: Αὐτῶν δὴ ὦν τούτων καὶ τῆς θεωρίης ἐκδημήσας ὁ Σόλων εἵνεκεν ἐς Αἴγυπτον ἀπίκετο παρὰ Ἄμασιν καὶ δὴ καὶ ἐς Σάρδις παρὰ Κροῖσον (*Hist.* I. 30).

wisdom (*philosophia*) and traveling for sight-seeing (*theories*) across many lands precedes him (*Hist.* 1. 30, 2).[40] Aristotle gives a parallel account of Solon's trip to Egypt and also calls it a *theoria*: ". . . as he did not wish to alter these provisions or stay and incur enmity, he went abroad on a journey (*theoria*) to Egypt, for the purpose both of trading and of seeing the country, saying that he would not come back for ten years, as he did not think it fair for him to stay and explain his laws, but for everybody to carry out their provisions for himself" (*Ath. Pol.* II, 1–2, Rackham).[41] Whether Solon took the reported journey or not matters less to us than the fact of Herodotus and Aristotle describing the trip as a *theoria* or for *theoria*.[42] So, in these four texts, we have occurrences of *theoria* referring to travel for the purpose of observing significant sites as educational.

Three other notable passages in which *theoria* is employed in the sense of traveling for exploration, or what one scholar terms "sacred sight-seeing" are drawn from Thucydides, Isocrates, and Plato.[43] Thucydides also mentions *theoria* in this context of generalized sight-seeing in explaining the motivation of Athenian young men undertaking the Sicilian expedition, claiming that they were "yearning for absent sight (*opsis*) and observation (*theorias*), and hopeful that they would be safe" (Thucydides, *Hist.* VI, 24, 3).[44] Other examples of *theoria* as educational travel, or sight-seeing, include a text by Isocrates called *Trapeziticus* about a young man who describes himself sent off by his father to Athens and other Greek cities "for the sake of *theoria*" (*kata theorian*), read either as "for the sake of sight-seeing" or "for cultural education."[45] In Plato, we find the use of *theoria* as sight-seeing mentioned as a civic practice in *Laws* XII (cf. 950d–952d). In a discussion about citizens traveling abroad and foreigners entering the city, the Athenian stranger tells Clinias that while no one under forty years old may be allowed to travel abroad (950d), certain male citizens of

---

[40] Croesus then asks Solon to name the happiest person in the world, thinking he will name him, but Solon names two young men who lived and died honorably (*Hist.* 1. 30, 2–3).

[41] The Greek is: βουλόμενος μήτε ταῦτα κινεῖν μήτ᾽ ἀπεχθάνεσθαι παρών, ἀποδημίαν ἐποιήσατο κατ᾽ ἐμπορίαν ἅμα καὶ θεωρίαν εἰς Αἴγυπτον, εἰπὼν ὡς οὐχ ἥξει δέκα ἐτῶν, οὐ γὰρ οἴεσθαι δίκαιον εἶναι τοὺς νόμους ἐξηγεῖσθαι παρὼν ἀλλ᾽ ἕκαστον τὰ γεγραμμένα ποιῆσαι (*Ath. Pol.* II, 1–2).

[42] Herodotus' phrase *kata theorian* (*Hist.* 1. 29) may be translated as "for [the sake of] *theoria*" or "on the pretense of sight-seeing" depending on whether we suppose Solon's motivation for travel to be absence from Athens or a genuine interest in learning from foreign sites.

[43] For discussion of this sense of sight-seeing, see Rutherford (2000, 135).

[44] Rutherford (2013, 150) compares the sight-seeing example from Thucydides about the young men's desire to see new sights with Neoptolemus looking in Euripides' *Andromache* (cf. ll. 1086–1183), which seems to me to comprise sight-seeing *theoria* in a very different sense.

[45] See Isocrates, *Discourses* 17, 4, *Trapeziticus*; cited in Rutherford 2000, 135; discussed in Rutherford 2013, 149; for analogous cases to the Greek use of *theoria* as sight-seeing in Egyptian and Roman texts, see Rutherford 2013, 149–55.

good character over fifty will be allowed to travel abroad (*theoria*) for the sake of cultural comparison with other states so that when they return, they enable the city to perfect itself and improve its laws (951a–c).[46] Further discussion of this passage can be found in Chapter 3.

Looking over the examples mentioned by Herodotus, Isocrates, Thucydides, Plato, and Aristotle, it seems that the examples of *theoria* described fall into one of two types, one concerned with traveling to specific sights and shrines, and the other with generalized traveling for the sake of learning. While these two mentioned have strong similarities, they differ from the standard kind of *theoria* we have described as festival-attendance. For example, if we compare the *theoriai* taken by Solon, Anacharsis, and Alcibiades, we find some obvious differences: Solon and Anacharsis set out on extended trips for the sake of learning – or, in Solon's case, he also may be wishing to be absent from Athens for a period – whereas Alcibiades' trip has the limited aim of seeing a specific festival and its events. However, in all the cases, we find that those who travel are private citizens undertaking the trips for the sake of seeing something significant and perhaps, for learning something. In contrast to these cases, the description from Thucydides about Athens sending city-appointed delegates to the Delian Festival represents *theoria* as a state-sanctioned event in which the delegates have the function of civic representation and observation, rather than private sight-seeing or learning. Hence, an inductive collection of the kinds of *theoria* we have just mentioned allows us to conclude that: (i) the first two kinds consist in traveling abroad for cultural learning, and possibly for an unspecified length of time, (ii) festival-attendance involves traveling to specific state festivals, like those at Olympia or Delos on set dates for a specific length of time and principally for observing or participating in the events. Having stated the differences in aim and duration of the travel, it is still accurate to claim that both kinds of traditional *theoria* and *theoria* as sight-seeing fundamentally consist in traveling for the sake of observing something significant or sacred.

2.4 *Theoria* as Philosophical Speculation

Another group of texts, one that dramatically diverges from the first two we have discussed, is represented by Heraclides (fr. 88), Plato, and

---

[46] The terminology of *theoria* is clearly invoked here throughout the passage by virtue of the practice of cultural ambassadors sent out to other cities and festivals, and the city delegate is explicitly termed a *theoros* at *Laws* 951c6.

Aristotle, who understand *theoria* as signifying philosophical study or contemplation, not festival travel or sight-seeing. Let us preface the discussion about philosophical *theoria* by mentioning a couple of precursors to *theoria* as abstract thinking. The texts are by Plato and Heraclides but purport to describe the early conception of philosophy found in Thales and Pythagoras. In the first text, Plato connects Thales, albeit indirectly, with the abstract speculation that is associated with philosophical *theoria* in a well-known passage from *Theaetetus*. Plato describes Thales as being someone so captivated in looking upwards to study the stars (*astronomounta*) that he falls into a pit, earning him the mockery of a Thracian servant girl who claims he is "so eager to know things in the sky he could not see what was under his feet" (*Theaetetus* 174a). In a similar vein, Heraclides of Pontus mentions a parable attributed to Pythagoras connecting *theoria* with contemplation. Briefly put, the story represents Pythagoras as praising the life of contemplation (*theoria*) in contrast with the lives that aim at wealth or glory (Heraclides fr. 88).[47] A common feature in both accounts concerns the connection of philosophical contemplation (*theoria*) with "useless" wisdom, a link that remains constant from the sixth through the fourth centuries. Yet, while the uselessness of *theoria* may have been a common conceit, both Plato and Aristotle overturn the criticism with the argument that *theoria* is unique in that its value does not depend on its effects, but on the activity itself. From this perspective, one may describe *theoria* as useless, but the charge loses its force insofar as philosophical contemplation does not aim at utility, but at theoretical knowledge. For the philosophers, it is the intrinsic value of *theoria* that renders the activity supreme, unlike the kinds of activities associated with becoming wealthy or famous. While we are brushing aside the complex differences among these views at present, when we engage Plato and Aristotle as well as the traditional practice about the value of *theoria*, we find a more nuanced account emerges (cf. Chapter 6).

2.4.1   Plato's Uses of Theoria

With the wealth of references to traditional *theoria* in the literary tradition, Plato's use of *theoria* in this context will not be surprising. For example, Plato draws upon the traditional practice in referring to the reason for

---

[47] Another version of the parable is by Cicero, which, according to Rutherford, may have been invented in the fourth century, likely by Heraclides (Cicero, *Tusc.* V 8–9/fr. 88 Werli.); it is corroborated in Diogenes Laertius VIII 8, and Iamblichus, *Vit. Pythag.* 58 (Rutherford 2013, 325).

Athens' postponing Socrates' death sentence in the *Crito* and *Phaedo*. In *Crito*, the reason for the postponement is given as the departure of the Athenian delegation for the Delian Festival (*Crito* 43c9–d1) with the explanation being the Greek law prohibiting death sentences being carried out spanning the theoric delegation's departure and return to the city.[48] In addition, Plato employs the notion of *theoria* as festival-attendance in the compositional frames for certain dialogues, including *Crito*, *Phaedo* (58b1–5), and *Republic* (556c10). It is fair to say, however, that in Plato's hands the notion of *theoria* as festival-attendance is neither the sole nor the dominant use; rather, he develops his own philosophical use. Thus, the majority of the *theor/eo/ia/os* and *theaomai* group of terms in Plato's dialogues can be divided in two main categories: (i) that concerned with traditional *theoria*, principally, with festival-attendance; (ii) that concerned with intellectual activity directed at abstract objects. Plato has some reference to the third use, the hybrid of the previous two, that involves traveling for the sake of learning, not for festival-attendance. Thus, the last use of *theoria* does not coincide with either festival-attendance or with philosophical *theoria*, yet it shares features with both. For, like traditional *theoria*, it involves traveling to a religious site to view a significant spectacle, and like philosophical *theoria*, it involves intellectual thinking. Plato includes a reference to what I consider the third kind of *theoria* in *Laws* XII, where we find the reference to citizens of Magnesia traveling for the sake of learning about foreign laws and constitutions. The explanation for such travel in *Laws* XII is that foreign *theoria* is useful for citizens understanding the laws and constitutions of other cities with an eye to improving their own. Specifically, in *Laws* XII (950d–952d), Plato describes virtuous citizens who are chosen by the assembly to travel to other cities to view the laws and constitutions with the aim of learning about them for political reasons. It should be evident that the value of the hybrid kind of *theoria* is not the same as that of Platonic philosophical *theoria* in that the former has primarily instrumental value, while the latter kind, directed at intelligible objects, forms, has primarily intrinsic value for epistemic reasons.[49]

---

[48] Among the various names for the festival period requiring specific truces or suspension of laws are *hieromania* (sacred month), *spondai*, and *ekecheiria* (the latter also referring to political truces); these differ in length, running from one to four months for panhellenic festivals, and fifty-five days for the Greater and Lesser Eleusinian Mysteries (Dillon 1997, 2–5).

[49] As evident from the various passages in dialogues concerned with knowledge such as *Rep.* V through VII as well the ascent passage from *Symp.* 210a–212b; I am using "intrinsic value" to signify something good in itself; for discussion on terms, see Ch. 6, sec. 6.1.

One specific observation about Plato's usage concerns the fact that looking across the *theor/eo/ia* family of terms, Plato shows a preference for using forms of the verb *theaomai* over *theoreo* as is evident by the former outnumbering the latter by a third.[50] Since *theaomai* is closely related in etymology and meaning to *theoreo* (both referring to looking at or observing something significant), his use of *theaomai* and related terms forms part of the evidential basis for developing an interpretation about how Plato employs the *theor/eo/ia* family of terms. Taking these two groups together, the references are divided along the lines we noted between the traditional and the philosophical uses. Thus, Plato employs the *theor/eo/ia/ theaomai* group of terms both for: (i) observing at festivals and sanctuaries, and (ii) philosophical "observing," or contemplation. As to textual examples of the first kind, we may mention *Rep.* I where Plato describes Socrates and company viewing spectacles at the festival for Bendis (*Rep.* 328a–b) or look to *Crito* (43c9–d1) where Plato refers to the Athenian delegation to the Delian Festival: here Plato's use overlaps with references to festival-going that are dominant in the literary authors we surveyed. For textual examples of the philosophical kind – of which there are far more examples in Plato's works – we can do no better than refer to his use of the family of terms across various dialogues such as *Phaedo, Republic, Phaedrus, Symposium,* and *Laws.* As we find in passages from *Symp.* (212a–b), *Rep.* VII (516a–b, 517b–c), *Phd.* (99d–e), Plato employs the *theor/eo/ia* family of terms to refer to the apprehension of form, not festival sights and sounds. When Plato employs the *theor/* family of terms in passages such as those just cited, he uses them to convey a more technical sense: they consistently signify the apprehension of form. So, we may generalize Plato's usage of the verbs *theaomai, theoreo,* and the substantive *theoria* as reflecting two distinct meanings: the traditional use for the activities of festival-attendance (e.g., *Rep.* I and *Crito*), and the technical use for apprehension of abstract form.

While the distinction of two central uses in Plato's terminology might suggest that they are conceptually separable, our previous analysis of the similarities among the main features between traditional and philosophical *theoria* holds true for Plato's usage as well. In addition, subsequent discussion (Chapter 3) shows that the two uses reflect a structure of overlapping use and meaning for Plato. In this chapter, we find that Plato's unique contribution on the topic consists in developing the notion of *theoria* in a new direction, namely, philosophical contemplation as the highest human

---

[50] In his lexicon, Des Places cites thirty occurrences of *theaomai* as compared to twenty of *theoreo* in Plato (Des Places 1970 vol. 1).

activity. In so doing, he extends the idea of *theoria* as festival-attendance to develop a second notion of *theoria* as intellectual activity, one according to which abstract thinking may be considered akin to a kind of traveling, and the apprehension of intelligible objects as a journey.[51]

2.4.2   *Aristotle's Uses of* Theoria

Aristotle takes Plato's lead in choosing the *theor/eo/ia* family of terms to refer to abstract thinking; indeed, Aristotle defends this activity as comprising the highest of human achievements at length in *EN* X 7. In addition to the technical sense, investigation across various works shows that Aristotle follows Plato in employing the *theor/ia/os/eo* family of terms in referring to learning or investigation.[52] Yet, Aristotle's use of *theoria* and related terms differs from that of Plato on two counts. First, unlike Plato, Aristotle does not typically employ terminology related to *theoria* to refer to festival-attendance – in fact, he uses *theoria* in the sense of festival-attendance only once in his works at *EN* IV 2 (1122a24–25)[53] which I consider a break with Platonic usage, likely due to the difference in their forms of composition. Second, the frequency with which Aristotle uses *theoria* or related terms to refer to the highest kind of thinking is relatively rare compared with that of Plato. A possible explanation for the difference may lie with Plato's strong preference for using verbs related to visual sense-perception for referring to modes of knowing something. In summary, despite the break with Plato on *theoria* as festival-attendance, Aristotle's work reflects continuity with two elements of the Platonic account, first, that the activity of *theoria* consists in observing something highly significant or sacred, and second, that such activity consists in intellectual, not perceptual, apprehension.

Aristotle's unique contribution to the conception of *theoria* consists in the careful delineation of its features which is given particular focus in *EN* X 7–8, where he classifies it as an activity of *nous*, the highest faculty. In *EN* X 7 in particular, Aristotle gives arguments that extend Plato's account

---

[51] While Nightingale (2004, 2005) and Rutherford (2013, 324–28) have advanced interpretations of Plato along these lines, my analysis (Ch. 2) offers a new dimension concerning the nature of *theoria* and its role as a compositional element in Plato's dialogues.

[52] The canvassing of Aristotle's use of *theoria* and *theoreo* shows that they have two referents, one meaning "to study," or "to investigate" something, and another signifying "contemplation," in the sense of thinking of the highest objects; the dual usage follows Plato.

[53] The reference is to the *architheoros*, or the head of an embassy to a festival (*theoria*); the context occurs in reference to the virtue of magnificence, using one's wealth for a public expenditure.

of *theoria* by delineating both the nature of the activity and its objects. Among the additional features that *theoria* possesses are that it is the most complete, most continuous, most self-sufficient, and most pleasant of activities, allowing this activity to occupy a pre-eminent place in the activity termed *eudaimonia* (*EN* 1177a17, b24–25). Since we analyze Aristotle's specific arguments for these features at length in Chapter 4, at present we provide only a sketch of what he describes as *theoria* from various texts. First, he is consistent across texts in naming *theoria* an *energeia* (ἐνέργεια), or activity. In addition to *EN* X 7, we find mention of this description in *DA* II 1, II 5, and *Meta.* IX 6, XIII 10. Thus, in *DA* II 1, Aristotle distinguishes two kinds of actuality (*entelecheia*) with one kind referring to a state of having knowledge, and the other referring to an exercise of knowledge: for clarity, he mentions *theoria*, using the verbal substantive form *to theorein* (τὸ θεωρεῖν) at *DA* 412a10–11 and *DA* 412b22–23.[54] He returns to the familiar distinction between the state and its exercise in *DA* II 5, specifying that one may have but not use a capacity, like knowing grammar, or one may be using one's capacity for it (*DA* 417a21–24). The significant point for us concerns his analogy: namely, that someone using one's knowledge is similar to one who is "contemplating," *theoroun* (θεωροῦν, *DA* 417a29). Further, he asserts that this state of activity signifies someone who knows "in the most precise sense" (*kurios*, *DA* 417a29).[55] *Meta.* XIII 10 confirms the present account from *DA* II 5 about someone with grammatical knowledge being like one who "contemplates" (*theorei*) "the particular A" (*Meta.* 1087a20–21). Taken together, the passages make two points abundantly clear: first, *theoria* consists in the full actuality of what one knows, and second, the underlying cognitive state of *theoria* is *episteme*. So, *theoria* consists in the full exercise of the state of knowing, and specifically, one arising from the state of scientific knowledge, or *episteme*.[56]

The nature of *theoria* as an activity also figures centrally in an early work attributed to Aristotle, *Protrepticus*, which, although lost, is extant in a version from the Neo-Platonist Iamblichus.[57] According to the

---

[54] The precise term for active exercise of a capacity is *energeia* while *entelecheia* covers having and not exercising, as well as actively exercising a capacity, see *Meta.* IX 3 1047a30–35; cf. IX 6 1048a27–35.

[55] On my reading, the sentence is: "The one who is presently contemplating (*theoroun*) is in actuality (*entelecheia*), and in the proper sense (*kurios*) knowing the specific A" (*DA* II 5, 417a28–29).

[56] This accords with the technical definition of *theoria* as the *energeia* of *episteme* (Burnet 1900, 461).

[57] The history of the authentication of Iamblichus' account is long and vexed: see Chroust (1965) on the nineteenth- to twentieth-century history of scholarship, and more recently, Nightingale (2004, 18, 230–31), Hutchinson and Johnson (2005), Walker (2010).

reconstruction based on Iamblichus' account, Aristotle compares *theoria* to the activity of spectators at the Olympic Games or the Dionysiac Festival. In this reconstruction, Aristotle seems to argue for one conclusion, namely, that *theoria* is worthy in itself, having non-utilitarian value. The conclusion is based loosely on the argument that since *theoria* is not chosen for being useful (*chresimos*) or profitable (*ophelimos*), its value resides wholly in itself, not in an end outside the activity. According to the reconstructed passage, the purpose of *theoria* is compared to that of spectators going to attend festivals which they attend "for the sake of the spectacle itself" (*autes heneka tes theas*), not for anything useful resulting from the activity (cf. *Protrepticus* 53.1526/B44).[58] Leaving aside the details of the argument for the moment, we may note a comparison to Heraclides' parable of the three lives. Like the *Protrepticus* passage, Heraclides draws an analogy between the three kinds of lives one might follow and the three classes of spectators at the Olympic Games (Heraclides, fr. 88). According to the parable, the activity of *theoria* is compared to that of the spectators at the Games in that the spectators – unlike athletes and traders – attend the Games solely for the sake of observation not for fame or money.

Aristotle gives what may be a brief analogy to the parable of the three lives in *EN* I 5, where he is developing a conception about the highest good, viz., happiness, from the kinds of lives that people lead, mentioning the lives of enjoyment, politics, and contemplation (*theoretikos bios*, *EN* 1095b16–17). Leaving aside the discussion of the contemplative life for the time being, he points out that the lives directed at pleasure or honor have incomplete or partial goods as ends, which being such do not deserve consideration for being the highest (cf. *EN* 1096a5). However, one common idea emerging from the three texts (*Protrep.*, Heraclides, *EN* I 5) involves the impracticality of *theoria*: the notion of *theoria* as an activity that is done for its own sake, not for the sake of producing something useful. However, from this claim it does not follow that philosophical *theoria* is "useless" in the sense of not being good for something; in addition, it is wise to distinguish between something being "good for" another thing in an instrumental and in a constitutive sense. For example, it is apt to claim that, for Aristotle, philosophical *theoria* produces good results in that its nature is such as to bring about certain positive benefits.

---

[58] The argument line in *Protrep.* strikes this author as being logically loose, atypical of Aristotle: for he (much less Plato) does not argue for *theoria* being good in itself by arguing against it being useful; in addition, the argument here uses the terms "useful" (*chresimos*) and "profitable" (*ophelimos*) that do not appear in any other discussions by Aristotle about *theoria*.

Hence, claims about the disutility or impracticality of philosophical *theoria* are acknowledged, but need further clarification. This aspect of Plato's and Aristotle's conception of *theoria* will be addressed in Chapter 6.

Reflecting on the ways in which previous thinkers have employed *theoria* leads us to consider, if only briefly at this point, the extent to which Aristotle's conception overlaps with theirs. To begin, it is evident both from the range of terms used and from the nature of the activity described that Plato is Aristotle's closest colleague in thought. For example, Aristotle follows Plato in employing the verb *theoreo* to refer to studying or investigating something as well as using *theoria* to refer to the highest kind of intellectual activity. However, there are two less evident aspects of Aristotle's view about *theoria* that may be seen to recall that of previous thinkers: one aspect concerns the aim of *theoria* as learning, in which case the pivotal phrase used is *kata theorian* meaning "for the sake of *theoria*" (understanding, study). The second feature concerns the scope of *theoria* in the sense of what kinds of objects it has, where the phrase used is *theoria tou pantou* or "contemplation of the whole [universe]." The first feature, that *theoria* involves acquiring wisdom, perhaps scientific knowledge, arises from surveying Aristotle's use of *theor/ia/eo* terms, and especially his use of the verb *theoreo*, across his works. What we find is that the majority of references fall outside the ethical works (namely, *Nicomachean* and *Eudemian Ethics*) belonging to the domain of the biological, psychological, and metaphysical treatises, in which the verbal forms using *theoro* relate to the study, or investigation, of the subject's properties, namely, whether they belong to biological kinds or types of souls, such as we find in *De Part. An.* I 5. This use may be seen as comparable in kind, if not degree, to Herodotus' account of trips taken by Solon and Anacharsis that are said to be done *kata theorian*, "for the sake of sight-seeing," or "for learning."[59] Another text mentioned that describes *theoria* as concerned with learning is Plato's *Laws* Book XII (950d–952d) where the provision is made for mature, virtuous, male citizens to travel to other cities for the sake of learning the political arrangements to benefit their home city (*Laws* 951a–c). Thus, what seems to be continuous across this use concerns the idea of *theoria* as observation for the sake of learning and education. The second feature of *theoria* linking Aristotle's usage to earlier views concerns the use of the phrase *ten theoria tou pantos*, "the contemplation of the whole [universe]," that appears in the *Protrepticus* and resembles a line

---

[59] A different view is given by Rutherford who suggests that Herodotus' account of Solon's trip supports the connection of *theoria* to philosophy (2013, 324).

from Anaxagoras stating that *theoria* "of the sun, moon, and heavens" is the purpose of human life (DK59A1, DL 2.10).[60] Aristotle records very nearly the same statement in *Eudemian Ethics* I, 5 where he links Anaxagoras to the view that "contemplating (*theoresai*) the heavens and the whole order of the universe" is the reason for human life (*EE* 1216a10–11). So, again, we find a possible line of connection between Aristotle's view of the scope of *theoria* and a pre-Socratic view, like that of Anaxagoras, about *theoria* as the study of the heavens as its subject matter.[61]

2.4.3   Intersecting Uses of Theoria in Plato and Aristotle

We have observed and will develop further in subsequent chapters that what is distinctive about the Platonic use of the *theor/ia/eo* family of terms concerns the duality of application. More precisely, Plato preserves the traditional use of *theoria* as festival- and sanctuary-attendance, and at the same time, develops a new conception of *theoria*. While the Platonic view may have received inspiration from the earlier notion of *theoria* that we see at work in, say, Herodotus' account of Solon's trip to Egypt, it is clearly sui generis. As we will show in Chapter 3, Plato's conception of *theoria* employs the notion of traveling abstractly, to refer to an epistemological journey that involves intellectual apprehension. This does not mean that Plato discards the notion of traditional *theoria* entirely for philosophical *theoria*, but rather that he intertwines the two uses. Thus, in specific dialogues, we find that *theoria* as festival-attendance appears side by side with *theoria* as intellectual vision, typically, with the latter emerging as the successor to the former. This double application, or pairing, of the traditional with the philosophical uses is quite characteristic of Plato's work. In contrast to Plato's tendency to join or combine two main uses, Aristotle's employment of *theoria* is almost entirely restricted to describing the highest form of intellectual activity. Such an account we find well-described at some length in the canonical text, *EN* X 7–8. In effect, Aristotle's account

---

[60] *Protrep.* reads: "the contemplation of the universe is to be honored more than all useful things" (*Protrep.* 53.1526/B44); DL reports a query to Anaxagoras about the reason for his birth, and he replies "for *theoria* [of the heavens]" (ἐρωτηθεὶς ποτε εἰς τί γεγέννηται, "εἰς θεωρίαν," ἔφη, DL 2.10).

[61] We have two central pieces of evidence linking Anaxagoras to the study of the heavens, first, his observation of the solar eclipse in 478 BCE, which he may have used for calculating the relative sizes of the sun and moon, and second, his prediction of a meteor at Aegospotami in 467/6 BCE (see Aristotle, *Meteor.* 344b31–34; DL 2.10; Pliny, *Nat. Hist.* 2.149; for discussion, see Graham 2013, 149–55).

narrows and refines the Platonic conception of *theoria*, focusing our attention on several features of the activity prominent in his teacher's conception, such as being an activity of the highest faculty, *nous*, and being able to apprehend the most elevated objects, forms. But whereas in Plato the references to the *theor/ia/ eo* family of terms occur throughout the length and breadth of the corpus, from *Crito* through *Phaedo, Republic, Symposium*, and into *Laws* and *Timaeus*, in Aristotle, the frequency and range of use is more restricted. More specifically, Aristotle employs the *theor/ia/eo* family of terms to refer almost exclusively to intellectual activity considered as either observational study or activity of the intellect (*nous*) specifically. It is possible to suggest, then, that Plato's lexicon is wider than that of Aristotle in that Plato employs terms from the *theor/ia/eo* family as well as using his preferred verb *theaomai* throughout his works to indicate a range of experience from seeing, or beholding, something to apprehending form, or the eternal.

CHAPTER 3

Plato's Contribution to Theoria

... turning toward the great ocean of beauty, and gazing (*theorōn*)
upon it, one brings forth many beautiful accounts and magnificent
thoughts in a fruitful philosophy ...

(*Symposium* 210d4–5)

3.1 Bridging Two Kinds of Vision

Given the dominant presence of traditional *theoria* throughout the fifth
and fourth centuries, its influence on Athenian intellectual culture is
unsurprising: Plato's dialogues comprise a clear case in point. As we
mentioned, a characteristic feature of Plato's references to *theoria* is its
dual directionality, some recalling *theoria* as festival- and sanctuary-attendance, others looking ahead to *theoria* as philosophical thinking. The
evidence from Plato's usage of the *theor/ia/eo/os* family of terms reflects
its reference to two principal activities: travel to festivals and shrines, and
intellectual vision of form. These two uses are not accidentally combined
but often linked so as to contrast the latter with the former; as we shall see,
Plato weaves the mention of traditional with philosophical *theoria* across
two planes in the dialogues, one being structural, the other being metaphysical and epistemological. Prior to the discussion, however, we might
reflect on the history of some key perception terms that Plato employs,
paying particular attention to *theoreo* and *theaomai*.

3.1.1 Plato's Language of Looking

A survey of usage shows that Plato employs various terms to indicate
looking, observing, and visual thinking. In addition to *theoreo* (θεωρέω),
Plato employs perception verbs to refer to visually oriented cognitive
activities. In this regard, we note that Plato possesses a generous lexicon
for visual perception: he employs verbs like *blepein* (βλέπειν), *apoblepein*

(ἀποβλέπειν) that generally meaning "look" or "look at," *athrein* (ἄθρειν) meaning "consider," *horan* (ὁρᾶν) meaning "see," and *skopein* (σκοπεῖν), for "to examine," or "to reflect on." While these primarily signify seeing, looking, or observing in the perceptual realm, the five terms may signify mental perception as well, and in this regard, they function more like *theaomai* in having uses that bridge physical and intellectual perception. In a comparison between just the verbs *theoreo* and *theaomai*, we find Plato showing a preference for *theaomai* (θεάομαι) over *theoreo*, with *theaomai* appearing a third more frequently than *theoreo*.[1] Yet the two terms display a high degree of synonymy with both signifying visual perception, broadly speaking, and specifically, a complex state of visual awareness (LSJ). As a brief aside, in Homer, *theaomai* signifies gazing at something in awe (cf. *Iliad* 7. 444, *Odyssey* 2. 13), as, for example, in *Odyssey* when it is used in reference to Calypso's cave which presents a visually arresting scene of dark woods, trailing vines, colorful birds, and rushing springs: "Why even a deathless god who came upon that place would gaze in wonder, heart entranced in pleasure" (*Od.* 5. 59–84).[2] Taking the implied meanings a step farther, one scholar asserts that in Homeric poetry, verbs like *theaomai* and *theoreo* imply "a felt experience of cognition in the presence . . . of viewing and apprehending beauty."[3]

The Homeric description of visual experience that culminates in both wonder and knowledge seems to anticipate the Platonic usage of *theoreo* and *theaomai* where these terms are employed for apprehending forms as well as gazing at spectacular sights. There is some reason, then, to comprehend the history of the *theor/ia/eo* family of terms as signifying, in general, a positive cognitive state occasioned by a powerful visual experience of something linked to feelings of wonder, or awe. Plato's subsequent usage of the *theor/ia/eo* family thus reflects a connection between seeing and knowing even as it highlights a difference between physical perception and visual cognition. While the larger issue is developed in our analysis below, a brief example from a well-known passage in *Republic* V may suffice to exhibit Plato's differentiation between two modes of visual apprehension, one marking a contrast between sight as an apprehension of physical objects and sight as a faculty that combines visual and

---

[1] Des Places counts thirty passages containing *theaomai* compared to twenty for *theoreo* (Des Places 1970, vol. 1, 246, 252).

[2] Tr. Fagles (1996), and in the longer passage here, *theaomai* is employed twice, with one scholar observing that a specific use of *theaomai* in poetry is for beholding spatial settings (Worman 2015, 292–94).

[3] Thus, Scarry (1999, 3–4), cited by Worman (2015, 292).

intellectual awareness. In a particularly vivid passage that sets out the powers and the percipients (*Rep.* 475b6–476d3), Socrates distinguishes someone who seeks beautiful sights and sounds, the festival-goer, from someone who seeks truth and wisdom, the philosopher – the former pursuing beautiful appearances and the latter, beauty itself. The present point at issue concerns the way in which Plato contrasts what we might consider a physical visual experience with a cognitive visual experience where the latter kind is that which calls for the use of verbs *theoreo* and *theaomai*. Yet throughout the *Republic*, Plato continues to observe a connection among forms of seeing even as he emphasizes the noetic aspect of philosophical perception that is Platonic *theoria*. But, as we seem to be anticipating the main course overly, we should make mention first of Plato's other highly innovative use of *theoria*, his employment of *theoria* as a structural device in ring composition, one that conveys philosophical meaning. In distinguishing these aspects, we arrive at what I term the structural and philosophical planes of Platonic *theoria*.

3.2   The Four Components of Platonic *Theoria*

There are four components of Platonic *theoria* and they are subsumed under two planes, one structural and one philosophical. The two main features of the structural plane include theoric reference and ring form while those of the philosophical plane include visual cognition and circular, or elliptical, motion. Thus, Plato's conception of *theoria* rests on four components that, while divided along two planes, somewhat bleed into one another in certain respects. For example, the feature of ring form that I have placed on the structural plane has a corollary in that of elliptical motion on the philosophical plane. Hence, the two planes are sub-divided such that the structural and philosophical planes each contain two components. According to this division, the structural plane contains the components of theoric reference and ring form, and the philosophical plane contains the elements of visual experience and circular movement. Finally, the four features must be understood as intersecting with what we have called traditional and philosophical *theoria* in the sense that the feature of theoric reference or ring form may be observed operating within either kind.

Prior to examining dialogues reflecting theoric ring form in Plato, it is worth reiterating two prominent features. The first is that which we have described as comprising the basic requirement for theoric ring construction; the second recalls a characteristic of *theoria* as festival-attendance. To

reiterate our earlier conception of strong theoric construction: this characteristic obtains when the dialogue contains references to events or activities
relating to *theoria* at both the starting and end points of the work
constituting the overall ring form. Smaller internal rings may also comprise
subordinate sections of the work containing matching beginning and
ending phrases, or images. The second feature arises from the consideration, previously mentioned, that insofar as traditional *theoria* consists in
departing from one's city and returning to it, the practice of *theoria* reflects
circular motion. Thus, the specific dialogues comprising ring composition
that are strong theoric works also reflect an element of circular motion, or
circular direction, that serves to reinforce the ring form. Furthermore, the
connections among these components, namely, the reference to theoric
events, ring composition, and circular motion, provide means for emphasizing certain aspects of the work. Specifically, their interconnection conveys meaning at both a compositional and a philosophical level. First, on a
compositional level, ring composition carries significance for the connection of traditional *theoria* with circular motion, and second, on a philosophical level, the link between *theoria* and circular motion bears import
for Plato's epistemic theory in that specific dialogues, like *Republic*, reflect
a movement from perceptual experience to intellectual apprehension of
form and a return – this last detailing how theoretical apprehension is
applied, or finds practical use. On an additional level, I suggest that since
the ring composition exhibited in some dialogues is intended to imitate the
motion of traveling to festivals or sanctuaries, it is possible these works are
to be read as if the reader herself is taking a *theoria*. As a corollary, a further
suggestion concerns taking subordinate rings within such works as reflecting other individual *theoriai*, namely, epistemic journeys of specific characters in the dialogue.[4] In these various ways, Plato implements and infuses
elements of traditional *theoria* in his works to create a wholly innovative
result in the ring composition within the dialogue.

3.2.1   Structural Plane: Theoric Reference and Ring Form

Taking the structural plane first, let us begin by discussing the element of
theoric reference, which simply denotes any mention of various events
or activities such as traveling to a festival, attending a religious ritual,
watching a performance, visiting a shrine, or the like. Thus, when we

---

[4] While I do not develop this aspect here, my suggestion includes looking at *theoriai* of characters like
Thrasymachus in *Rep.*, or Phaedrus and Meno in the eponymous dialogues.

encounter references to traveling to a festival or sanctuary in the introductory section of a dialogue, it signals Plato's use of traditional *theoria* as a narrative frame for the subsequent philosophical discussion. For example, Plato's mention of Socrates and friends attending a *theoria*, the festival for Bendis, in the opening lines of *Rep*. I (327a2–b1) bears on the work's philosophical significance; similarly, the reference to the Athenian *theoria* to Delos in *Cr.* 43d1 and *Phd.* 58a occurring at the time of Socrates' imprisonment. In addition, specific works may also contain a reference to a theoric event at the closing. Plato provides us with a variety of theoric references across his works, such as, for example: an Athenian embassy to Delos, noted by Socrates (*Cr.* 43d1); the same Athenian embassy reiterated by Phaedo (*Phd.* 58a); a festival of the goddess Bendis⁵ attended by Socrates and friends (*Rep.* 327a1–4); mention of *Hermea*, rituals for Hermes, attended by Socrates and friends (*Lysis* 206d1); seeing an altar to Boreas on the Ilissus, where Socrates and Phaedrus are situated (*Phdr.* 229b–c, 227a); reference to a festival for Asclepius at Epidauros, described to Socrates and attended by Ion (*Ion* 530a1–2); a festival at Olympia described by and attended by Hippias (*Hippias Minor* 363c7–d1); a temple and shrine of Zeus in Crete to which the Athenian stranger, Clinias, and Megillus are walking (*Laws* 621b1–5). While this list is not exhaustive, it provides some sense of the range of references to religious festivals or sites that Plato uses. While some locations, like the altar to Boreas, appear insignificant in comparison to a panhellenic festival, the import of the reference may gain significance in concert with the presence of a companion theoric reference.

Continuing on the structural plane, we arrive at the second element of the structural plane, ring composition. The name refers to a formal element present in a composition (written or musical) that contains a matching theme, phrase, or image in the opening and closing sections of the work such that it comprises a ring. In a Platonic dialogue, the ring form can be manifested by means of paired references to theoric events or activities. Put more specifically, if we find a reference to a *theoria* (or similar event) in the opening and the closing of the dialogue, we have the formal requirement for a ring composition: the opening and closing of the work have mirror references, comprising a ring form. In addition, I am terming a dialogue that has a reference to a theoric activity (e.g., attending

---

⁵ Although the first reference is "the god" (*Rep.* 327a2) which may imply Athena, the later reference to "the festival of Bendis" (*Rep.* 354a7), a Thracian deity introduced to Athens, confirms this name; see Adam (1965, vol. 1, fn. 2) for discussion of foreign cults in the Piraeus; see also Holm (1894–1902, vol. 3, 189).

a festival or religious ritual) in the beginning section and another mirror reference in the end section a work that has a "strong theoric" structure, a feature that specific dialogues exhibit. Hence, in following the requirements for ring form, the minimal formal features for a strong theoric structure are: (i) a beginning section that includes the reference to *theoria* or theoric activity; (ii) an ending section that includes a *theoria* or theoric element (the two references need not mention identical events). The presence of the ring form also implies the presence of a third feature, a mid-point, that will have special significance for the philosophical meaning of the dialogue, as will be discussed.

We might mention basic features of ring form including names, schematic formulas, and textual examples.[6] In terminology, the ring form is known by several terms, including chiasmus, chiasm, *inclusio*, bookending, pediment, and pedimentality, but among them certain common features appear, namely, well-defined beginning and end point that mark a mid-section.[7] Having said this, some differences persist: a pediment form has steps leading to a center point where the construction turns and descends in a step formation "like the wide-angled pediments on doorways" (Douglas 2007, xiii); a chiastic construction uses inverted word order to organize the whole; an *inclusio* construction contains the same element repeated to form a kind of envelope, sometimes with a smaller ring within a larger one. So, although the exact structures of the various ring forms are not identical, each exhibits this feature of "bookending" producing a mid-section, or turning, that has special significance in that, first, it structures the second half of the work, and second, it contains meaning essential to the overall work. In definition, the form is simple with "the minimum criterion for ring composition [being] for the end to join up with the beginning" comprising a kind of "envelope" within which individual rings may also be found.[8] Put a bit more precisely, ring composition depends on the repetition of structural elements of meaning, or in poetry of rhyming, that occurs in a predictable sequence such that the later elements invert the earlier ones. This fine-grained pattern allows both simple and complex constructions with significant variations. For example, a simple ring

---

[6] The ring form has a long history and wide span appearing in lyric, epic, historic, and dramatic genres across ancient Greek, Roman, Hebrew, Indian, and Chinese traditions; for discussion, see Douglas (2007, 1–16).

[7] In parallelism, the opposed elements are set side by side whereas in ring form the elements are placed in opposition to each other in order following the mid-point; see Douglas (2007, 1–8).

[8] Accordingly, "the linking up of the starting point and end creates an envelope that contains everything between the opening phrases and the conclusion" (Douglas 2007, 1).

composition in one of the most basic forms consists in the pattern A B B^I A^I, while a more complex kind can comprise the pattern A B C D E D^I C^I B^I A^I. In addition, complex ring structure admits the main elements of the ring (e.g., A B C D) themselves consisting of smaller, individual rings.[9] As well, note that in the complex pattern mentioned, the initial elements A B C D are mirrored in reverse order in the second sequence D^I C^I B^I A^I following the mid-point E, which marks the point where the subordinate elements reverse the initial sequence (D C B A) and holds some critical meaning.[10] Thus, the mid-section, or turning, structures the second half of the work, and a fine-grained analysis will reveal not only the presence of the corresponding smaller rings within the larger overall ring, but the significance of the mid-section.

To mention two familiar examples of ring composition, first, the story of Abraham's binding Isaac (*Gen.* 22:1–18): this account consists of rings within an overall ring with a middle section that clarifies the meaning given in the outer rings. To be more precise, the mid-section of the ring provides the resolution to the question about the justice of Abraham binding Isaac: the statements each one makes in the mid-section display the trust between God and Abraham, not the lack of trust. Hence, the ring analysis reveals that Abraham never doubts that God would require him to sacrifice Isaac and this explains why he chooses to follow God's command.[11] Without the meaning provided by the mid-section, the reason for Abraham's acquiescence to God's command remains obscure, and his intended action, unethical.[12] The *Iliad* presents a second example, much more extended, of ring composition, with the outer ring formed by the opening scene with Chryses coming to the Greek camp asking for his daughter, Briseis, and a mirroring ending scene comprising Priam going to Achilles' camp to ask for the body of his son, Hector. Briefly described, the simplified schema of the *Iliad* ring construction consists in A B C B A, with the eight-day war in the mid-section.[13] With these elements of ring form in mind, in looking ahead to theoric ring form in Plato we find that our analysis reveals the feature of bookending using theoric references, and

---

[9] For example, the hunt of Autolycus in the larger ring story about Odysseus in *Il.* X: see Douglas (2007, 18), and Van Otterlo (1948) for analysis of Homeric ring form.

[10] As one scholar states, "the prime test of a well-turned ring is the loading of meaning on the center, and the connections made between the center and the beginning" (Douglas 2007, 31–32).

[11] Interpreting the passage as a ring form reveals that Abraham trusts that God will provide a substitute for the sacrifice, and so never considers his son in peril (cf. Douglas 2007, 19–26).

[12] At least, it has always seemed so to this writer.

[13] For discussion, see Douglas (2007, 104–14); the ring form interpretation provided here relies on matching number of days and sums, not matching words or themes (Douglas 2007, 108).

more importantly, emphases on the mid-section of the dialogue. As we shall see, the mid-section of a Platonic dialogue having ring form typically is marked by two features: first, being the philosophical core of the work, and second, having a distinct style or change in tone. Thus, often the mid-point in a Platonic ring composition is indicated by the presence of stylistic differences in the text that differentiate it from its neighboring parts, one familiar example being the sun-line-cave mid-section of the *Republic*. However, dialogues exhibiting ring form may not qualify as theoric ring compositions in that they do not contain mirroring theoric activities, while three counting as theoric ring form are *Republic*, *Phaedo*, and *Phaedrus*; hence, these three receive our attention in due course.[14]

The Platonic dialogues have long been judged amenable to ring compositional analysis, but no one to my knowledge has tried to connect ring composition with the *theoric* elements they exhibit. Instead, various scholars in classics and ancient philosophy, such as Barney (2010), Burnyeat (1999), Dorter (2006), Gibson (2011), Sparshott (1982), and Thesleff (1993), have shown that specific dialogues reflect some ring compositional structure. It comes as no small surprise that among the dialogues the *Republic* stands out as receiving the most scholarly attention (Barney, Burnyeat, Dorter), with a secondary level of concern directed at *Sophist* and *Hipparchus* (Gibson). In addition, *Charmides, Laches, Meno, Phaedo,* and *Theaetetus* are also mentioned by Barney as displaying what she terms "book-ending," the equivalent of ring form with a repetition of dramatic elements in the opening and closing sections.[15] Let us consider views of the *Republic* as this work has received attention by Barney and Burnyeat. According to Barney (2010), *Republic* is composed of five rings, each of which is composed of two corresponding parts (standard in ring form) such that ring A corresponds with ring A[I], ring B with ring B[I], and so on. More precisely, the correlating rings are structured as follows: ring A represents the opening scene with Socrates returning from a festival at Piraeus (*Rep.* 327a) which corresponds to the closing ring A[I] with the myth of Er (*Rep.* 614b–617d), and the cave analogy in *Rep.* VII comprises the mid-section, or turning (cf. *Rep.* 514a1–518d1). It is worth pointing out in advance that the mid-point need not correspond to the literal mid-point of a work; it may be determined by its dialectical mid-point. For the

---

[14] I concur that *Symp.* exhibits ring form, with Diotima's speech, stylistically distinct, comprising the mid-section (Slings 2004, 33–34), but while I agree with Slings on its ring form, the work does not qualify as a theoric ring composition.

[15] Barney notes that it may also employ a "transposed resolution," as *Laches* (Barney 2010, 36).

sake of clarity, the literal mid-point of the *Republic* would be the halfway point which occurs after the third wave, *Rep.* V (*Rep.* 474a); the dialectical mid-point is usually taken as the cave analogy, *Rep.* VII (cf. *Rep.* 514a).[16] Clearly, the two mid-points do not coincide, yet since the cave (and the related analogies) provide the central philosophical insight for the work, there is good reason to prefer it as the mid-section of the ring as further analyses of Barney and Burnyeat show.[17]

Let us begin with the plan developed by Barney (2010). On her view, the structure of the *Republic* exhibits a sequence of individual rings (A, B, C, D, E) that move toward the mid-point, which is followed by a sequence of corresponding individual rings (A¹, B¹, C¹, D¹, E¹) that return us to the beginning of the work. Thus, in structure, the *Republic* has an overall ring form that is itself composed of five subordinate rings, with A is linked to A¹, B to B¹, C to C¹ and so on, in the manner we have described. Described in more detail, Barney finds the outer ring has two parts consisting of element A and element A¹, where element A represents the descent, or *katabasis* (κατάβασις), of Socrates going down to a festival at Piraeus at the opening (*Rep.* 327a1), and element A¹ represents the return described by the myth of Er in the closing section (*Rep.* 614b–e).[18] While not being mentioned by Barney, I would argue that the closing section concerning the myth of Er itself comprises a ring that begins with Er's descent to Hades (*Rep.* 614b–e) and ends with Er's return to earth (*Rep.* 617d, 621b). It may be noted, in passing, that while I concur with Barney that *Republic* has a genuine ring structure, other scholars describe the work's overall composition somewhat differently, suggesting that the construction more closely resembles the parallel, or stepped, structure described as "pedimental."[19] Mention of the pediment form of construction seems timely in that, while Burnyeat claims that the *Republic* displays a ring form, he sketches it in such a way as to suggest a series of stepped

---

[16] The literal mid-point is, using Stephanus numbering, 147 pages into the text at *Rep.* 474a, and the dialectical mid-point (Barney, Burnyeat) 37 pages later is at *Rep.* 514a; no matter what page numbering method used, the two center points do not coincide.

[17] Thus, I concur with Barney (2010, 39) in making the dialectical middle the ring center.

[18] Socrates' *katabasis* in *Rep.* I (going down to Piraeus) may not seem to mirror Er's *katabasis-anabasis* in *Rep.* X, yet, Socrates and friends are returning to Athens when Polemarchus and his servant intercede so that they return (*Rep.* 327b); for my purposes, however, the festival *theoria* in Piraeus pairs with the content of Er's account, satisfying the conditions for theoric ring form.

[19] The term is used by Thesleff (1993) to describe a structure in the Platonic dialogues having a layered, or stepped, composition reflecting the architectural principles of the pediment: "by 'pedimentality' I mean an arrangement of things as to put the most important or intrinsically interesting ones in the centre, as the figures are arranged in the triangular pediment (*tympanum*) of the Greek temple" (Thesleff 1993, 19, fn. 4).

structures within a larger circle reminiscent of the pediment. So, he describes the structure of the *Republic* as consisting of "poetry-city; Soul-Forms-city; soul-poetry" (Burnyeat 1999, 288).[20] We can immediately see that if we were to diagram the structure he describes using letters marking the elements, we would have three segments: (i) A-B, (ii) C-D-B, and (iii) C-A, which do not comprise what is described as a well-formed ring for obvious reasons. However, if we leave aside the slight anomaly in the outer ring composed of C-A, and divide the work in two halves, we have the following result: (i) a first half comprising A-B-C, and (ii) a second half comprising B-C-A, leaving D as the mid-point of the work. Recalling that the mid-point of the ring carries the weight of the ring composition's significance, the fact that D represents the sections concerned with apprehension of the forms is pivotal for the interpretation. In effect, we conceive the form here consisting of the sequence: poetry-city-soul – forms – city-soul-poetry. While they differ in other respects, the analyses of Barney and Burnyeat coincide in what they consider the mid-point of the dialogue, even though the revised version of Burnyeat's ring section which is represented by A-B-C- (D) -B-C-A does not yet reflect the reverse symmetrical ordering in the second half of C-B-A, and so, the symmetry of the form is not quite attained. In any case, their analyses concur in that the mid-section of the work comprises the sun-line-cave sections, those concerning apprehension of forms that Burnyeat identifies.

3.2.2 *Philosophical Plane: Visual Cognition and Elliptical Motion*

The idea that the mid-point exhibits the focal point of the dialogue brings us to the philosophical plane, which intersects with the structural plane to bear the substantive meaning of the dialogue. Two features characterize this level, one, the strongly visual aspect typical of *theoria* and the other, its directionality, specifically, the elliptical, or circular, motion that is implied in Plato's notion of various kinds of thinking.[21] Let me expand upon these two elements briefly, and then analyze each in more detail. The first element, the visual component, consists in the fact that in specific dialogues characterized by *theoria*, one of the central characters, typically one of Socrates' interlocutors, undergoes a change in his thinking that is often

---

[20] In this analysis, it appears that Burnyeat marks the mid-point as the section on Forms, *Rep.* VI–VII, which excludes Bk. I from the ring (Burnyeat 1999, 288, fn. 8).

[21] The terms are used synonymously since in geometry the circle is a species of ellipsis, and as motion, it is irrelevant whether the path is that of a circle or an ellipsis.

indicated by his having a visual experience toward the mid-point of the dialogue. While verbs of seeing and sense-perception have been used up to the mid-point of the dialogue, what we find in the center section of such dialogues is an increasing reference to seeing, or visual perception. For example, in *Republic*, Plato's increased emphasis on visual experience is indicated by frequent verbs of sight or kinds of seeing occurring in the middle of the work, the section that holds special significance in ring composition. Broadly speaking, finding an emphasis on visual experience in the mid-point of the dialogue is significant in that an essential feature of *theoria* consists in its relation to visual activity, specifically, to intentional looking at something, which involves something more than seeing an object. Plato's emphasis upon kinds of seeing, and specifically, the emphasis on the terminology of *theoria*-related terms is pivotal to such dialogues. The passage that best exemplifies the range of visual experience, including intellectual insight, open to Plato is the cave analogy in the dialectical mid-section of *Rep.* VII (*Rep.* 514a–517b).

The cave analogy in *Rep.* VII comprises just over two pages of Greek text and contains over twenty references to visual perception. To begin with, the chained prisoners are compelled "to see only in front of them" (τὸ πρόσθεν μόνον ὁρᾶν, 514b1) being unable to "see" themselves or one another, but only shadows cast on the cave wall (cf. 515a5–8). Suddenly, when one of them is released and forced to turn around "to look toward the light" (καὶ πρὸς τὸ φῶς ἀναβλέπειν, 515c6), he is "pained, dazzled, and unable to see things he had seen before as shadows" (515c c6–d1).[22] The subsequent experience of being dragged upwards, out of the cave, into the sunlight results in a temporary state of blindness, the prisoner being "unable to see a single one of the things now said to be true" (516a2–3).[23] Eventually, the blindness wearing off, the prisoner is able to look at things in the outside world, at first, shadows, then images, sensible objects, and the heavens (cf. 516a5–b1).[24] At the final stage of vision, the prisoner can "see the sun itself" and not merely its images in water (cf. 516b5).[25] This moment of the prisoner's new visual capacity marks the dramatic, but more significantly, epistemic high-point, as the individual "is able to see

---

[22] The Greek runs: πάντα δὲ ταῦτα ποιῶν ἀλγοῖ τε καὶ διὰ τὰς μαρμαρυγὰς ἀδυνατοῖ καθορᾶν ἐκεῖνα ὧν τότε τὰς σκιὰς ἑώρα (515c6–7); Greek line references to *Rep.* follow Adam's text.
[23] The Greek runs: ὁρᾶν οὐδ' ἂν ἓν δύνασθαι τῶν νῦν λεγομένων ἀληθῶν (516a2–3).
[24] The Greek runs: καὶ πρῶτον μὲν τὰς σκιὰς ἂν ῥᾷστα καθορῷ, καὶ μετὰ τοῦτο ἐν τοῖς ὕδασι τά τε τῶν ἀνθρώπων καὶ τὰ τῶν ἄλλων εἴδωλα, ὕστερον δὲ αὐτά (516a4–6).
[25] The Greek runs: τελευταῖον δὴ οἶμαι τὸν ἥλιον, οὐκ ἐν ὕδασιν οὐδ' ἐν ἀλλοτρίᾳ ἕδρᾳ φαντάσματα αὐτοῦ (516b2–4).

the sun itself in its own place, and study it" (*theasasthai*) (516b5–6),[26] coming to the conclusion that it rules everything in the visible realm, being "the cause of all things seen" (516b7–c1).[27] With this epistemic clarity of vision, the liberated prisoner returns to the cave; in so doing, we find reference to the second element proper to the philosophical plane, the completion of a motion formed by following an ascending and then a descending path described in the cave passage.[28]

The second feature of the philosophical plane consists in elliptical, or circular, motion that arises, first, from the notion of traditional *theoria* insofar as the practice involves leaving and returning to one's home city, as has been suggested.[29] Plato references this aspect of traditional *theoria* in mentioning the Athenian delegation traveling to and from Delos for a festival in two dialogues (*Phd.* 58a–b, *Cr.* 43c9–d1). Thus, traditional *theoria* reflects – or implies – the idea of elliptical motion in regard to its tracing an elliptical spatial pathway. However, Plato goes further in developing other aspects of elliptical motion, such as rotational motion, or the motion of a body turning on its axis that are used in regard to motion and cognition of humans and gods in *Phaedrus, Phaedo, Republic*, and *Timaeus*. For example, in *Phaedrus*, the human soul is likened to a charioteer driving a chariot that "runs around the whole heaven" (*panta de ouranon peripolei*, *Phdr.* 246b), and similarly, the gods are described as being carried by "a revolution of the heavens" (*periphora . . . tou ouranou*) to see things beyond the heavens (*Phdr.* 247c1–2). In *Timaeus*, Plato mentions circular motion as an analogy for thinking as he describes it as involving "revolutions of the soul" (*psyches periodous*, *Tim.* 43a5) or "inner revolution of the soul" (*ten gegonuian . . . psyches periodon*, *Tim.* 47d5), and finally, to assert that the motions of our souls resemble "the intellections and revolutions of the universe" (*hai tou pantos dianoeseis kai periphorai*) (*Tim.* 90c8–d1). But, in the latter cases, the circular motion used as an image for thinking is rotational motion, a kind of motion that differs from elliptical linear motion that we spoke of in regard to traditional *theoria*. In *Tim.* 34a1–4, Plato describes one of the seven motions, one that is "proper to

---

[26] The Greek runs: ἀλλ' αὐτὸν καθ' αὑτὸν ἐν τῇ αὐτοῦ χώρᾳ δύναιτ' ἂν κατιδεῖν καὶ θεάσασθαι οἷός ἐστιν (516b4–5).

[27] The Greek runs: καὶ ἐκείνων ὧν σφεῖς ἑώρων τρόπον τινὰ πάντων αἴτιος (516b7–c1).

[28] The two motions implied in the cave analogy comprise a ring within the larger ring of the dialogue; more discussion is provided in sec. 3.2.4.

[29] Nightingale suggests circularity as an aspect of traditional *theoria* (Nightingale 2004, 42–44) but does not connect it to ring composition nor links circular motion with noetic thinking, as we find reflected in Plato.

thought (*nous*) and intelligence (*phronesis*)," which consists, roughly, in
something "turning on itself (*periagagon*), in the same spot . . . in a circle."
Plato's subsequent description of rotational motion as connected to
thought at *Tim.* 40a7–b1 is briefer, but consistent on the connection.[30]
In any case, as Lee points out, the analogy between circularity and noetic
thinking in *Timaeus* passages (e.g., *Tim.* 34a1–4, 40a7–b1) does not imply
the motion of a body moving in a circle like "a train moving around a
circular track," but signifies axial rotation, which, in its continuous regularity, turns around one point, in one direction (Lee 1976, 74–76).
A passage in *Laws* X (898a8–b3) concerning the kind of motion involved
in *nous* specifies the properties precisely, including regularity, uniformity,
and unidirectionality. So, Lee claims, for Plato the idea of regular, axial
rotation provides the image for *nous* in that it implies certain "qualities of
thought . . . in virtue of which [thinking] qualifies as *noetic*," more specifically, by its lack of perspectivity and timelessness (Lee 1976, 80–81).[31]
Finally, I would add in passing that the character of Plato's *nous* conceived
as a rotating whole, as distinguished from a body moving in a circle,[32]
suggests Aristotle's distinction between complete and incomplete activities
in that the former include activities that are "complete" (*teleia*) at each
moment, such as seeing or being happy (cf. *EN* 1174b4–6), while the
latter include motions like walking or building that are temporally
extended and consist of heterogeneous parts.[33]

A distinct, extended use of circular motion that is connected to reasoning but standing apart from the noetic activity described by the image of
axial rotation in *Timaeus*, appears in the theoric ring dialogues, *Phaedo*,
Republic, and *Phaedrus*, in passages involving ascent and descent. While
this topic is discussed in more detail below (Section 3.2.4), in brief, the
present notion of reasoning linked to circular motion has two components,
the notion of an epistemic route to and from first principles, and an image
of a racecourse – both borrowed from *EN* I 4. Specifically, toward the end

---

[30] Also note that *Tim.* 90dc–d7 suggests that by following the proper motion of our *nous*, one that is
disturbed at birth, we would make "the part that thinks like the object of thought" which is best for
humans: as Menn states, "[w]e can then be completely restored to rationality by a process of
education" through the ears and eyes perceiving harmonies "akin to the motions of the soul within
us" (*Tim.* 42d2–6) (Menn 1995, 53).

[31] Lee suggests the non-perspectivity of *nous* by analogy to Steinberg's description of a Picasso painting
of woman's head conveying front and rear perspectives simultaneously (Lee 1976, 81).

[32] The distinction in motions being between the motion of something rotating on its axis, which is
complete and uniform, and that of a body (or point) moving in an orbit around another body in
circular spatial motion.

[33] For discussion of complete and incomplete activities, see *EN* X 4, and Ch. 5, sec. 5.4.

of *EN* I 4, Aristotle mentions Plato's distinction between reasoning up to and down from first principles, comparing it to two phases of running a race where one can distinguish the first half as running to the mid-point and the second as running back to the finish line (cf. *EN* 1095a33–1095bb1).[34] What we have, then, is Aristotle comparing two kinds of scientific reasoning with running a racecourse where one segment represents the upward route to discover first principles (we assume) and the other, the downward route that employs first principles.[35] Aristotle's image of the racecourse, or of a body tracing a semi-circular or elliptical shape, finds support in various passages in Plato's work as well. For example, the cave analogy presents a familiar passage in *Rep.* VII, according to which a prisoner following a track moves up out of the cave and then returns to exercise political science (cf. *Rep.* 515c–517e, 519c–d). Again, briefly, other passages reflect a kind of circular motion that may best be described as rotational motion in regard to the psychic *peritrope* mentioned several times, say, in *Rep.* VII where the term signifies a "turning round" of the soul that is effected by education (cf. *Rep.* 519b2–3, 532b5, 533d3).[36] Taken together, these passages suggest three distinct kinds of circular motion generally: (i) axial rotation describing noetic activity in *Tim.* and *Laws*, (ii) linear elliptical motion describing the standard path of discovery and return, (iii) *peritrope*, or "turning around" of the soul in *Rep.* VII relating to change in alignment of desires. Although the motion of *peritrope* seems similar to that of axial rotation, I suggest it is distinct in respect to the qualities of motion characterizing noetic activity, such as regularity, continuity, and timelessness. For, the motion of the *peritrope* mentioned above seems to comprise a one-time realignment of the parts of the soul, not a continuous, rotational motion. Thus, three kinds of motions are connected to distinct kinds of reasoning, and while the motion associated with noetic activity clearly requires special consideration, that describing epistemic ascent and descent is worth observing as well.

---

[34] Ostwald asserts a U-shaped course where runners move down one arm to a mid-point and back along the other arm (Ostwald 2000, 7, fn. 12), in effect, following an elliptical shape.

[35] The subsequent lines in *EN* I 4 mentioning the familiar difference being known "to us" and "in itself" (*EN* 1095b2–3) refer to *An. Po.* 72a1–5, *Top.* 141b5–7; for Burnett, the larger passage (*EN* 1095a33–b3) distinguishes *a priori* and *a posteriori* reasoning (Burnet 1900, 17).

[36] The rotational motion here is distinct from that in *Rep.* passages suggesting unidirectional motion such as implied by upward reasoning in the divided line (*Rep.* VI, 510b7–9) or in regard to dialectic where Plato describes its power to draw the intellect upward to first principles (*Rep.* VII, 533c–d) as it is the only "inquiry that travels this road" (*Rep.* 533c7–d1) so that if the soul becomes distracted, "dialectic gently pulls it out and leads it upwards" (ἠρέμα ἕλκει καὶ ἀνάγει ἄνω, *Rep.* 533d2).

3.2.3   Structural and Philosophical Planes Combined

Having distinguished the elements of the structural and philosophical planes, let us now see how joining them advances the interpretive task of addressing specific philosophical problems arising from the texts in advance of detailing a close analysis of two theoric ring texts. One of the most studied philosophical difficulties concerns an issue in *Rep.* VII about philosophers being compelled to return to the cave, and more broadly, how justice of the individual fares against civic justice and what maximizes social coherence.[37] So Glaucon questions why the framers of *kallipolis* would do philosophers an injustice "by making them live a worse life when they could live a better one" (*Rep.* 519d9).[38] Socrates' reply that since the philosophers have been raised and educated precisely to become rulers, it does them no injustice to return to the city to carry out their function (*Rep.* 520c), predictably, has not been received with satisfaction by scholars or readers in general. For, the objection concerns the nature of Platonic justice, specifically, how Plato can conceive the forced return of philosopher-rulers to the city as just – a criticism that is underscored by Plato's consistent use of compulsion language to describe the philosophers' return (cf. *Rep.* 519d–520e). Clearly, if the bar of justice is set at the level of maximizing everyone's happiness (read liberty), any measure that conflicts with this aim is unjust, but the antecedent is obviously false. As Socrates points out, the city has raised and educated one group "to bind the city together" (*Rep.* 520a4); the laws compel them to rule (*Rep.* 519e1–4) but this need not be onerous if it does not conflict with their desires, and in my view, it does not. In this regard, the picture suggested follows that of Kraut (1997) and Vlastos (1997) who offer what Brown terms an "imitationist" thesis about how the moral character of philosophers is changed by their education such that ruling does not conflict with their best interests (Brown 2000, 4–5). While much more may be said about the philosophical aspect of the issue, let me interject a reminder about the significance of the ring form, namely, that the mid-section provides an interpretive key. The *Republic*'s mid-section consisting in three analogies places special focus on the cave, which contains the problem of compulsion and its resolution suggesting why the trained philosopher does

---

[37] See, for example, Annas (1985), Cooper (1997), Kraut (1997), Vlastos (1997), all of whom are discussed in Ch. 5, sec. 5.2.2.

[38] The Greek runs: ἀδικήσομεν αὐτούς, καὶ ποιήσομεν χεῖρον ζῆν, δυνατὸν αὐτοῖς ὂν ἄμεινον (*Rep.* 519d6–7).

not yearn for the purely academic life. First, the philosopher's soul has undergone *peritrope*, or reversal, effected by character education, cemented by right practice, and finally, charged by the vision of the forms. More specifically, the full effect of education implies having one's soul "turned around" (variously, *periagoge, metastrophe, peritrope*) by character training (cf. *Rep.* 519b2–3, 532b5, 533d3), and subsequently, by studying forms, especially the form of the good (cf. *Rep.* 518c6–d1). In fact, the psychic "turning around" is mentioned at various points throughout *Rep.* VII, including one where Plato affirms that dialectic is that which effects the soul "turning around" (*sumperiagein, Rep.* 533d3). In this regard, we find that theoretical study of the forms is an activity providing a lasting effect on virtuous character,[39] an effect that, in reorienting the philosophers' vision, ensures that what they desire, their individual good, coincides with a larger, social good rather than with a purely egoistic good as Glaucon's objection presupposes.[40] The view the philosopher-rulers have about justice is, then, rightly circumscribed by the fact of their upbringing prescribed by law, so that they agree, in principle, that what the laws require of them is just.

Thus, the philosophers may acknowledge an obligation to return to the city, but this duty is not onerous, rather, it is chosen by them. So, the language of compulsion that Plato employs describing the philosophers' return to the city in *Rep.* VII does not contradict the view that it is chosen. First, as Shields argues, compulsion in Plato takes many forms, not all of them incompatible with deliberation and choice.[41] Second, if we permit ourselves to adopt the position of traditional *theoria* and the traditional *theoros*, the state-appointed festival attendant, we may discern another, distinct view about Plato's dilemma. For, the goal of the just city is not to maximize the happiness of one individual or class, but that of the whole city, an end that requires training the most intellectually able citizens and ensuring their return to the city "to bind the city together" (*Rep.* 1–520a4). Taking the standpoint of traditional *theoria* suggests a way in which we may conceive the city's side of the issue in the *kallipolis* such that the

---

[39] As the philosopher seeks to become like the forms, on which see Kraut (1997), Vlastos (1997), and discussion in Ch. 5.
[40] It is duly noted that Socrates states the framers of *kallipolis* "compel" philosophers to guard and care for the city (*Rep.* 520a8, cf. 520e2), but, as he assures Glaucon, their words and actions are just (*dikaion*) (*Rep.* 520a7–8).
[41] For example, what Shields terms "nomic" compulsion, the kind arising from seeing logical entailment, is not incompatible with deliberation, see Shields (2007); on my view, the compulsory aspect of the law is similar to Kantian hypothetical necessity, see Brown (2000, 6).

philosophers' return to the political sphere is not incompatible with civic justice. For, in the case of a state-appointed delegate to a festival, the *theoros*, whose presence is sanctioned by the city, is obligated to return as reporting to the city counts as one of his official duties. To consider whether an official *theoros* who deliberately fails to carry out his duties to the city to maximize his own happiness is acting justly is to misapply the standard: he acts unjustly given his agreement with the city; an appeal to individual justice is irrelevant.[42] So, Glaucon's objection that the philosophers' forced return to the city is inconsistent with individual justice is not conceived correctly: there is no injustice in returning if the question is presented from the standpoint of those who were raised and nurtured in the *kallipolis*, as Socrates suggests, but there is from the standpoint of those who raised themselves, for "what grows of its own accord and owes no debt for its upbringing has justice on its side when it isn't keen to pay anyone for that upbringing" (*Rep.* 520b2–4). However, he reminds them, in *kallipolis* the philosopher rulers are "better and more completely educated than others," and so are "better able to share in both kinds of life" (*Rep.* 520b5–c1).

3.3   Theoric Ring Analyses: *Phaedo* and *Republic*

In the present section, we turn to consider two central theoric dialogues, *Phaedo* and *Republic*, using elements of the structural and philosophical planes to highlight the focus on *theoria*. Our examination reflects some confluence with the scholarship by Barney, Burnyeat, and Nightingale,[43] but diverges from their work on three grounds. First, we develop the reasons for Plato's contrast between traditional *theoria* (and the *theoros*) and philosophical *theoria*; second, we formulate a link between circular motion and Platonic *theoria* at two levels, structural and philosophical; third, we argue for a conceptual continuity between traditional and Platonic, or philosophical, *theoria* using the notion of observational experience of the divine as the common element. Both works reflect the

---

[42] An analogy from national responses to COVID-19: citizens in specific countries (e.g., South Korea, Japan) act for the public good by wearing masks and distancing while those in others (e.g., UK, USA) argue that their individual rights not to wear masks or socially distance outweigh the public good: the appeal to individual rights is misguided here since: (i) society has contributed to their upbringing and education and (ii) public health requires these measures; in *Rep.* VII, the city raised philosophers with their tacit consent to "bring the citizens in harmony with one another" (*Rep.* 519e3–4), so they are bound by a contractual agreement to do what the law requires since it is just; cf. Brown (2000, 9).

[43] The principal works of Nightingale (2004), Barney (2010), and Burnyeat (1999).

contrast between the idea of *theoria* as festival-attendance and that of an intellectual journey culminating in cognitive apprehension of reality. Despite the contrast, certain features of traditional *theoria* can be seen as carried over to the philosophical concept in some form, such as: a *theoros* who undertakes a journey to a different, perhaps foreign, site; the *theoros* having a visual experience of the divine; the *theoros* returning, perhaps with greater understanding. These features are, of course, not present in pre-cisely the same sense, or univocally, across traditional and philosophical *theoria* but analogically. So, for example, the second element concerning a visual experience of the divine implies direct visual observation and par-ticipation in religious rituals in festival and sanctuary *theoria* but implies a visually intellectual apprehension of the divine in philosophical *theoria.*[44] We might suggest that the features are present across both in the relation of an analogical proportion, for example, that visual apprehension of the divine is to traditional *theoria* as intellectual insight of form is to philo-sophical *theoria.*[45]

3.3.1 The Phaedo

The external ring of the *Phaedo* contains references to elements of tradi-tional *theoria* with the opening referring to the Athenian delegation to Delos (*Phd.* 58a3–5), and the closing, a sacrifice to the god Asclepius (*Phd.* 118a7–8). So, the opening of *Phaedo* presents one half of the ring frame with Echecrates, who was absent the day Socrates died, asking Phaedo about Socrates' conversation and the reason for the delay in his death following the court's decision (cf. *Phd.* 58a3–5). Phaedo, having been present at the discussion, provides detailed accounts to both questions: the reason for the delay in punishment involves the departure of an Athenian delegation on their annual *theoria* to the shrine of Apollo on Delos. As Phaedo explains, the Athenian dedication of a ship for the journey to Delos commemorates the story of Theseus saving the fourteen Athenian young men and women from being sacrificed in Crete (cf. *Phd.* 58a10–58c5). As we recall, during the period of the ship's absence to a festival (*hieromenia*), Athenian law prohibits public executions to ensure purity of the city (*Phd.* 58b5–6). Since the ship was crowned the day

---

[44] Again, philosophical *theoria* is visual: the use of *theor/ia/eo* terminology with its implicitly visual aspect binds philosophical *theoria* in Plato and Aristotle to its traditional meaning.

[45] The analogy holds for Aristotle's use of philosophical *theoria*, although he does not employ traditional *theoria* as a conceptual foil as Plato does.

before the trial began, Socrates must remain in prison for the time extending between the trial and the return of the Athenian *theoria* (cf. *Phd.* 58a10–c5).[46] Other internal elements structuring Phaedo's account include the four arguments for the immortality of the soul, the cosmological myth (*Phd.* 107a–114d) and the final account of Socrates' death (*Phd.* 114e–118a). Thus, *Phaedo* contains frequent allusions to departures, returns, traveling, and cyclical motion: Socrates describes his upcoming death as a "journey from home" (*apodemein*, 61e1), comparing the route of the true philosopher to a kind of passage (61c, 61e, 65a, 67b, 70c5–7), and recommending the poet Evenus follow him as "quickly as possible" (ὡς τάχιστα, 61b4). In this vein, we find Socrates' subsequent reference to "an ancient doctrine" (παλαιὸς μὲν οὖν ἔστι τις λόγος, *Phd.* 70c3–4) about the soul returning from Hades to earthly life, the first argument for the soul's immortality, suggesting a circular, or elliptical, motion in the notion of continual dying and being reborn.[47] Thus, Socrates' repeated reference to dying as "going there from here" (61e1) or a "change of abode" (*apodemia*, 67c1) presupposes a background of the soul in continual cyclical rotation. Among the four strict arguments, that from recollection (*Phd.* 73c–77a) reflects central features relating to *theoria* including visual elements (perception, recollection), elliptical motion, and apprehension of forms, that require examination. From there, we proceed to the cosmological myth for providing perhaps the most significant image pertaining to philosophical *theoria* and its goal. Finally, viewing the work as a whole suggests tracing an elliptical figure beginning with Socrates' references to dying as the soul traveling to Hades and ending with an account of Tartarus that includes judges evaluating souls in Hades, some of which mount upwards to reach the surface of the earth and some even higher (cf. *Phd.* 113d1–114c8).

Each of the arguments for the soul's immortality falls short in some way, yet taken together, they comprise an abstractive sequence in the following respect. The cyclical argument (*Phd.* 69e–72e), universally accepted as weak, depends on premises drawn from sense-perception and applying to humans, animals, and plants – all that is generated – to establish that

---

[46] According to Xenophon, the length of time was thirty days (*Mem.* IV, viii, 2).

[47] Related references to "an ancient doctrine" (70c3–4) include "according to the old accounts" (63c6), "an account of long ago" (67c5–6) in connection with *katharsis* (67c5), and those who established "the initiations" (69c3), this last referring to Mystery rituals (Burnet 1989, 44); yet, even if all of these refer to Orphism or its followers (cf. Bluck 1955, 52, fn. 1, and 195–96), Plato's mention is likely ironical (Burnet 1989, 44–45) which supports my view that Plato mentions cases of traditional *theoria* (i.e., attendance at Mysteries) to contrast with philosophical *theoria*.

everything having an opposite is borne from its opposite (cf. *Phd.* 70d8–e2). Socrates' examples, predictably, are drawn from perception, as in relation to growth: we see the smaller thing becoming larger, the weaker thing, stronger, and the slower, faster; we also perceive the young becoming old, and the living, die. Similarly, the generalization that opposite states arise from their opposites also relies on sense-perception.[48] While the recollection argument (*Phd.* 73c4–77a5) contains premises dependent on sense-perception, its pivotal distinction consists in the referential character of a power that compels the perceiver to the cognition of a thing not presently perceived. In effect, recollection moves someone from perception toward the cognition of form, the object of Platonic *theoria*. In this regard, the recollection argument possesses a special epistemic role, situated as it is between the opening and closing references to traditional *theoria* and after an introductory section replete with references to vision, sights, and the journey of the soul in death. Overall, the argument stands out as significant in relation to *theoria* for two reasons. First, the argument depends on the special nature of recollection, a hybrid faculty that depends on perceptual and rational components, which, in activity, has the power to catapult the mind toward the intelligible. Second, the recollection argument, unlike the cyclical argument, provides a road map showing how, beginning with perceptual elements, we use reason to grasp the non-empirical bases of complex perceptual judgments. Socrates begins the reasoning by reminding us that recollection consists in the perception of one thing and the calling to mind of another thing which is absent, or not presently perceived (cf. *Phd.* 73c5–d1). Insofar as the recollection argument presupposes the existence of forms (e.g., the form of equality), the proof serves as a preparation for third and fourth proofs with their explicit premises about certain properties of forms. The premises in the affinity argument and final proof are in turns less reliant on empirical premises than the recollection argument, where, for example, Socrates states that "through the senses, we learn that all sensible things strive for the equal itself but fall short" (*Phd.* 75b1–2). For, the affinity argument begins with the postulation of two general ontological kinds, the composite and the incomposite, assigning being itself, equality itself, beauty itself, and such forms, to the kind whose nature is to remain unchanging (cf. *Phd.* 78d1–4) whereas sensible things that are homonymously equal or beautiful are constantly changing

---

[48] While it is possible to generate the argument from *a priori* premises based on the meaning of contrary terms (e.g., "larger" and "smaller"), Socrates seems to be appealing to the sense-experience of his interlocutors for their initial plausibility.

(cf. *Phd.* 78e1–2). Little surprise, then, that the argument leads to a section disparaging the soul's mode of inquiry using the senses for their confused reports, extolling the soul's mode of inquiry by itself (cf. *Phd.* 79c2–d5) for its accuracy about what is and concluding that the soul is more like what is divine, deathless, intelligible, uniform, indissoluble, and simple (cf. *Phd.* 80b1–3). But the likelihood of these properties being linked and being connected to the soul does not yield demonstrative certainty, that which the final proof tries to provide (or partly establish).[49] As is familiar, the final proof aims to show that since the immortal is indestructible, nothing immortal can perish, and since the soul is immortal, it, too, is imperishable (cf. *Phd.* 106d2–107a1), a conclusion that does not rely in any way on sense-perception; hence, the last proof reaches its goal without appeal to empirical premises. The upward progression of the mind toward what is eternal and imperishable, away from what is generated and perishable, begins with the recollection argument.

Turning back to examine the argument from recollection, we find that it begins with recollection defined as coming about when a sense-perception triggers the awareness of something absent (cf. *Phd.* 73c–e), and it moves to the intermediate conclusion that sense-perceptions of specific properties, like the equal, lead to the recollection of intelligible forms, like perfect equality. Armed with the further premise that sense-perception is inadequate to generate the notion of perfect equality by itself (cf. *Phd.* 74d–e), Socrates drives to the conclusion that there must be a subject or substance in us adequate to produce such an idea, an immortal soul (cf. *Phd.* 76d–e). Leaving aside the details of the reasoning, I suggest the following pared-down line of argument:

(1)   We have a present perception of equal particulars (74b7–8).
(2)   We also possess an idea of perfect equality (74a11–12).
(3)   Since perception of equal particulars is inadequate to generate the idea of perfect equality, the idea of perfect equality is not derived from perception. [1, 2]
(4)   Recollection involves the perception of one thing that gives rise to the awareness of another thing that is absent (73c6–9).
(5)   In recollection, the thing recollected may be like or unlike the thing perceived (74a2–3).[50]

---

[49] Socrates' comment to Simmias (who expresses some doubt) that the "first hypotheses" of the argument need to be re-examined suggests that the proof is not yet fully formulated (cf. *Phd.* 107b2–7).
[50] Socrates' examples are in seeing a picture of Simmias, I may recollect Simmias, or equally, in seeing Simmias' lyre, I may recollect Simmias (cf. *Phd.* 73e5–10).

(6)   Since we may recollect something unlike the thing perceived, we may recollect the idea of perfect equality from the perception of imperfectly equal particulars. [3–5]

(6') The idea of perfect equality is distinct from the perception of equal particulars (74c4–5).

(7)   Our idea of perfect equality is non-empirical. [5, 6, 6']

(8)   A subject pre-existing sense-experience provides our idea of perfect equality. [6, 6', 7]

(9)   The pre-existing subject is an immortal soul having intelligence (76c12–13).

Accepting the above argument as roughly accurate, we see recollection plays a pivotal role, both logically and philosophically: what is particularly noteworthy is that in recollecting, a present sense-perception triggers the idea of something not presently perceived, but an idea called up by a present perception. Socrates argues that when we perceive what appear to be equal particulars, in effect, the present perception stirs up an idea of perfect equality, an idea that cannot be derived from perception or from sensible abstraction. Since the idea must be non-empirical, it requires positing a suitable subject, a soul, to which it belongs. We may also note that that argument depends on the implicit activity of philosophical *theoria*, the highest cognitive state in the epistemic process, for the discovery that the equal particulars are imperfectly equal. For unless we possessed the idea of perfect equality, we could not know that the sensible particulars were imperfectly equal. Let me suggest that in this step, logically, we have completed a kind of elliptical motion in that we moved from the present perception of the sticks' length upwards to the notion of perfect equality, then downwards to conceive a judgment, say, that the sticks are imperfectly, or relatively, equal.

Taking a broader perspective for the moment, consider a comparison between Platonic and traditional *theoria* using the account of perceptive recollection in the argument and recalling aspects of a visitor's experience at a shrine or sanctuary in traditional *theoria*. Two features of Plato's recollection account stand out in regard to the observational activity in traditional *theoria*: first, the person recollecting sees particular sensible objects that bring to mind something similar but absent, and second, the absent object recollected differs in ontological kind from the object perceived. In both Platonic and traditional *theoria*, the absent recollected object is something eternal and divine, although for Plato, the highest object recollected is a non-empirical form, not a deity.[51] Broadly considered, we might suggest that the logical progression of searching for and finding premises in argumentation is similar to the activity of a *theoros* visiting a temple in traditional *theoria*. Another feature shared by Platonic and traditional *theoria* is elliptical motion: in the recollection argument, we are concerned not with spatial motion but with its logical shape. More specifically, the reasoning moves from the perception of (equal) particulars to the apprehension of the form by means of the activity of recollection, and back to the particulars. The apprehension of the form of equality is not the last step in the discursive argument but a penultimate rung by means of which the interlocutors grasp that the equal particulars are not perfectly equal. Of course, the apprehension of the form of equality is necessary to the judgment that the particulars are not perfectly equal: the interlocutors return to an initial starting point with the premise suitably revised. In this regard, the process of discovery that the argument follows suggests a route not unlike that exhibited in situ by those participating in traditional *theoria*. For, as we have noted, the practice of sanctuary-visitation, for example, depends on the visitor, or *hikates*, walking in an elliptical direction around the site where individual icons of the divinity are exhibited.[52] The movement followed at these sites is explained by the fact that they offer numerous images, including statues as well as temple images of the resident deity (or deities) spread out over the area of the temple or sanctuary. Whether the site is purposed primarily as a healing sanctuary or festival temple, the activity of the visitor consists in walking around the divine representations, looking at them, recollecting, and reflecting on the gods and the characteristics being represented by the sculptures and icons.[53]

The cosmological myth and its frame (*Phd.* 108d4–114d7) comprises a ring section distinct from the arguments, with Socrates' claims that he is stating, not proving, what he believes the earth to be like (*Phd.* 108d4–6) and that the myth is "likely to be true" (ἢ ταῦτ᾽ ἐστὶν ἢ τοιαῦτ᾽ ἄττα, *Phd.* 114d2–3) forming the opening and closing of the section. The myth

---

[51] Assuming that in traditional *theoria*, an observer infers the presence of a deity conceived along the lines of the conventional Greek pantheon; Ch. 4 provides a parallel between the objects of Platonic and traditional *theoria*.

[52] On the overlap between the *theoros* (the one who sees) and the *hikates* (the one who arrives), see Naiden (2005).

[53] It is not unreasonable to compare the activity of the traditional *theoros* to a pilgrim following Via Crucis, a route consisting of images relating to significant points in the life of Jesus displayed in some Western Christian churches: the stations typically follow a circular or semi-circular route (in or outside the church) similar to that of a frieze atop temple walls, like the Parthenon frieze.

contains references to epistemically advantaged seeing and observing using two verbs, *horan* (see) and the critically important verb *theoreo* (to contemplate) as primary terms. In the first part of the myth, Socrates describes the earth as being perfectly balanced in the middle of the heavens (*Phd.* 108e4–109a6) with humans living in the hollows of its surface but unaware of the fact (*Phd.* 109c1–4). He presents an analogy with striking visual imagery: suppose humans believed they were living on the upper surface of the earth but were like those living deep in the ocean who look up at the sun and stars through the water, thinking that the sea is the sky (*Phd.* 109c4–7). Due to sluggishness or weakness, Socrates explains, they have not breached the surface of the water and remain unaware of the heavens above (cf. *Phd.* 109c8–d5). As Socrates develops the comparison, such a person "has never reached the surface of the sea nor risen with his head above the water or come out of the sea to our region here nor seen (*heorakos*) how much purer and more beautiful it is than his own region nor has he heard it (*akekoos*) from anyone who has seen it (*heorakotos*)" (*Phd.* 109d1–5). This situation mirrors our own: we believe we are living on the surface of the earth, not in its hollows, yet due to our weakness or slowness, "we are not able to make it to the upper limit of the air, since if anyone were to come to this upper limit, if anyone were to reach it on wings and his head rose above it, then just as fish on rising from the sea see things in our region, he would see (*katidein*) things there, and if his nature could endure to contemplate (*theorousa*) them, he would know that there is the true heaven, the true light, and the true earth" (*Phd.* 109e2–110a1).[54] In fact, Socrates makes a double analogy, one between those living deep in the ocean and those who are unaware of the true heavens, another between those able to breach the surface of the water and those who know what is real, what Socrates terms "the true heaven, the true light, and the true earth" (*Phd.* 110a1). Plato's repeated use of verbs of visual perception is evident throughout the passage with the verbal form *theorousa* receiving subsequent attention in relation to an appearance (*Phd.* 109c4–110a1).

Rowe offers two points in reference to Plato's striking image comparing someone searching for truth to a fish leaping out of the water (*Phd.* 109e2–110a1), both of which, we should note, relate to the central visual aspect of *theoria.* The first comment concerns the line rendered as ". . . if his nature could endure to contemplate them" (*Phd.* 109e6) which he

---

[54] The Greek lines (109e6–110a1) run: καὶ εἰ ἡ φύσις ἱκανὴ εἴη ἀνασχέσθαι θεωροῦσα, γνῶναι ἂν ὅτι ἐκεῖνός ἐστιν ὁ ἀληθῶς οὐρανὸς καὶ τὸ ἀληθινὸν φῶς καὶ ἡ ὡς ἀληθῶς γῆ.

interprets more suggestively as ". . . if his nature were capable of holding up under the sight," explaining that "in the first place, he would be out of his element, like a fish out of water, but there is also the suggestion that the sight itself would be overwhelming" (Rowe 1993, 274). Here Rowe's translation makes better sense of *theorousa* (109e6) in the context insofar as it implies seeing something awe-inspiring, apprehending something divine, that gives an intimation of the dramatic, visual element in Platonic *theoria*. Rowe's second point concerns the reference to someone rising above the limit of the air to see or getting wings and flying up (*Phd.* 109e2–4), to which he gives two parallel texts, one in *Phaedrus* (248a ff.), the other in *Republic* (514a–517a). The *Phaedrus* passage is that of the charioteer, where the soul "of the most god-like of the non-divine souls manages to stick his head through the outermost rim of the universe, so glimpsing the true reality beyond" (*Phdr.* 249c3–4), and the *Republic* passage concerns the prisoner in the cave "finding himself freed and dragged up into the true light of the sun" (cf. *Rep.* 515c6–d1).[55] The significance of the three passages concerns not only the level of difficulty of the upward process, but that "what Socrates is urging is a complete change of perspective" (Rowe, 1993, 274). The terminology he chooses is significant in relation to Platonic *theoria* in that the texts describe an ascent with an achievement, an epistemic change so great that one both knows and sees things fully differently when the end is realized. These points are pivotal to grasping the nature of the path to Platonic *theoria* and its goal, viz., that the process leading to up the vision is arduous and prolonged, but when successful, it affords "a complete change in perspective" (Rowe, 1993, 274), the end of which is the reversal of vision that culminates and preserves philosophical *theoria*, similar to the effect of what Plato terms *peritrope* in *Rep.* VII.[56] For, while *Phd.* 109e2–6 does not employ the term *peritrope*, the image of the leaping fish broaching the water's surface to see above conveys much the same meaning as the soul "turning around" in *Rep.* VII passages. Considering the double image in *Phaedo* more closely, we see that both parts reach a similar goal: the fish, in breaking the surface of its medium, sees unseen things above the water

---

[55] Thus, Rowe (1993, 274), as to which we may note the line in *Rep.* 515c6–7 runs: ". . . when one of them was freed and suddenly compelled to stand up, turn his head around (*periagein*), walk, and look up toward the light (*pros to phos anablepein*) . . . he would be unable to see (*adunatoi kathoran*) things whose shadows he had seen before."

[56] Discussed earlier in this chapter, passages mentioning *peritrope* include *Rep.* VII, 519b2–3, 532b5, 533d3; while the leaping fish does not revolve on itself, the effect of the ascent is the same as in turning around.

just as the individual whose nature can "bear the sight" of the upper region, by climbing to the top realizes that this reveals the real sky, real light, and real earth (*Phd.* 109e6–8).

It is evident, of course, that the sky, light, and earth being mentioned in the above analogy (*Phd.* 109e7–8) are not apprehended by the faculty of sight and sense-perception at all, but by another faculty that involves cognition. The intellectual nature of the apprehension described in regard to seeing ethereal objects such as heavens, light, and earth (*Phd.* 109e7–8) has led scholars to suggest the identity with celestial bodies that Plato elsewhere describes as central to the apprehension of the forms.[57] In this regard, the activity of the *theoros* in the closing myth, that of someone seeing the spectacle of the real sky, sun, and earth (*Phd.* 109e6–110a1), fulfills the earlier account of the philosopher that Socrates describes, according to which one pivots from the care of the body to that of the mind, moving upward to the intelligible realm (cf. *Phd.* 64a–66e). The closing myth, then, may be interpreted as completing the upward direction afforded by the four single arguments for the soul's immortality by providing a sense of the experience of philosophical *theoria*. The upwards path in *Phaedo* that culminates in the vision of intelligible form is described in various stages in the section comprising the cosmological myth. Interpreting the levels of the cosmos that Socrates describes in the myth, we find the ocean, the hollows of the earth, the ethereal earth, and finally, the stars – together representing an ordered ontological series. We may conceive, then, a philosophical *theoros*, or observer, moving along an upwards path, using objects in the various levels, including celestial bodies, as stepping-stones in reaching the apprehension of forms.

Broadly speaking, the cosmological myth is replete with features relating to traditional and Platonic *theoria* such as visual sense-perception, sudden intellectual vision, spatial motions including departing and returning, moving up and down, reverse motion, and rotational motion. These elements, in conjunction with the fact that the mythic section stands apart by Socrates' claim that his account is not a proof (cf. *Phd.* 108d5–6), contribute to seeing the cosmological myth (*Phd.* 108e2–114c8) as an individual ring, one of the final rings in the work. Succeeding it we have the closing scene with its reference to the sacrifice of a rooster to Asclepius that Socrates requests of Crito (*Phd.* 118a7–8); the formal, compositional significance of the sacrifice to Asclepius, quite apart from any symbolic meaning, is that it provides a "closing," or "latch," to correspond to the

---

[57] See, for example, Bluck (1955, 131, fn. 2), Nightingale (2004, 145, 153).

opening reference to traditional *theoria*, the Athenian delegation sent to Delos (*Phd.* 58a10 ff.).[58] So construed, the two references comprise the overall ring of the dialogue. There are substantive results relating to the embassy to Delos that Plato includes, such as that the extended period of the Delian *theoria* is what leads to Socrates' extended prison stay, making possible the philosophical discussion about the nature of the soul that provides an occasion for Platonic *theoria* on the part of the interlocutors.

3.3.2 The Republic

One of the most distinct features of the *Republic* consists in its marked concern to elaborate the similarities and contrasts between traditional and philosophical *theoria*. While visual experience of the divine and kinds of elliptical motion appear as common characteristics of *theoria* in this dialogue as in *Phaedo*, Plato here develops the epistemic differences between traditional and philosophical *theoria* in detail, giving attention to the practitioner and the activity alike. As well, he shows that the differences between specific faculties and objects involved in, say, festival observance versus those of apprehending the forms are considerable, as the images of sun, line, and cave in *Rep.* VI–VII reflect. But first, let us give an overview of the theoric highpoints of the work: we have the opening frame containing a reference to traditional *theoria*, a festival in Piraeus from which Socrates and his companions are returning home, but are detained (cf. *Rep.* 327a1–b5). This reference comprises the first half of the external ring structuring the dialogue. Second, the ring's center consisting of the central analogies of *Rep.* VI–VII reflects Plato's primary attention to philosophical *theoria*, including the activity as a kind of vision, its objects, its connection to politics, as well as its distinction from traditional *theoria*. Thus, the first half of the dialogue shows Plato moving the reader away from traditional *theoria* toward philosophical *theoria* such that the proof of the third wave in *Rep.* V (473c11–480a13) turns on the central epistemic difference between traditional and philosophical *theoria*: that the former depends on pursuing only appearances, not being, whereas the latter is practiced by philosophers "who study the things themselves" (*Rep.* 479e).[59] The contrast between the two kinds of *theoria* is then developed fully in the central analogies in *Rep.* VI–VII, and in the closing section, the

---

[58] Douglas claims a double closure, or latch, in ring compositions represents both the completion of the form and the "thematic correspondence" of the start and ending (Douglas 2007, 37–38).

[59] The Greek is: τοὺς αὐτὰ ἕκαστα θεωμένους καὶ ἀεὶ κατὰ ταὐτὰ ὡσαύτως ὄντα (*Rep.* 479e4–5).

myth of Er (*Rep.* 614b–621b), that describes a journey to the underworld
and a return comprises the second half of the external ring.[60] Overall, the
dialogue presents three different contexts of *theoria* for which we find
structural and conceptual aspects: (i) that of traditional *theoria*: the festival
of the goddess in *Rep.* I (structural), the lover of spectacles in *Rep.*
V (conceptual); (ii) philosophical *theoria*: apprehension of intelligible
forms in *Rep.* V, VI, VII (conceptual); (iii) the myth of Er detailing the
journey of souls in Hades in *Rep.* X (structural, conceptual). Let us now
examine these specific elements and passages in more detail.

Plato's reference to traditional *theoria* begins, as was noted, with the first
lines of *Rep.* I where Plato, using Socrates as narrator, describes himself
with friends returning to Athens from Piraeus having attended the festival
"to offer prayer to the goddess" (327a2), but after being detained by
Polemarchus, they stay over to see some "sights," namely, certain night-
time festival events (cf. *Rep.* 327a1–328b1).[61] Plato employs the verbs
theaomai and *theoreo* several times throughout the passage referring to
them watching spectacles: they had seen the festival parade that day and
anticipate seeing the torchlight race on horseback and other events the
following night (cf. *Rep.* 328a1–7).[62] The opening description of festival-
attendance thus reflects the use of *theor/eo/ia* language both retrospectively,
referring to having seen the festival procession, and prospectively, in
anticipation of the upcoming horseback race at night and other spectacles
(cf. *Rep.* 328a1–7). In the mid-section of the work, specifically, the ending
of Bk. V, and the analogies in Bks. VI–VII (*Rep.* 507a–517b), we find a
turn from *theor/eo/ia* language referring to traditional *theoria* to philosophical *theoria* as the apprehension of forms. More precisely, when Plato
employs *theoreo* and *theaomai* in *Rep.* V and following, the gazing in
question is directed at intelligible objects, viz., forms, not the sights and
sounds of a festival. From an epistemological perspective, the two types of
theoria could not appear more distinct, as one kind consists in standard

---

[60] If we assume that the myth of Er comprises an individual ring, its middle, *Rep.* 618b6–619b1,
consists in Socrates' recommendation about the long-term desirability of choosing the virtuous life.

[61] Adam queries "which goddess, Bendis or Athena?" but he notes that a later reference to the feast of
Bendis (*Rep.* 354a10–11) seems to decide the issue (Adam 1965, vol. 1, 1); also, the festival of
Bendis, a newly introduced Thracian goddess (Grube and Reeve 1992, 2) is a local, not a major
festival, and this reference is, to my knowledge, the only occasion where Plato credits Socrates as
attending a *theoria*; whether this gives evidence for Socrates' adherence to conventional religion (or
its lack) is unclear to me; see McPherran (1996, 2013), Lannstrom (2011).

[62] In the opening section (*Rep.* I, 327a–328b1), Plato employs *theaomai* three times and *theoreo* one
time, showing Plato's preference for the former, although Des Places claims the two are
synonymous (Des Places 1970, 246, 252).

visual perception, the other, intellectual apprehension. Let us describe Plato's shift in focus from *theoria* as an activity concerned with sensible objects to that concerned with intelligible objects, beginning in *Rep.* V where he contrasts the lover of spectacles with the lover of wisdom.

Plato develops the contrasting activities, truth-seeking and spectacle-watching, by sketching the two practitioners, the philosopher and the lover of sights and sounds, in *Rep.* V (475d1–476d5). First, the philosopher, or lover of wisdom (φιλόσοφος) and the lover of spectacles (φιλοθεάμονες) differ in virtue of what each wants to attain (cf. *Rep.* 475b6–7, 475d1, 476a6–476b5). Specifically, the philosopher alone pursues truth as a goal (*Rep.* 475b5, 475c3, 474c7, 475d3, 475e1, 476b1) whereas the lover of sights and sounds pursues pleasant things to see (*Rep.* 475d1, 475e4, 476b3) or to hear (*Rep.* 476b4). As the discussion develops, a second difference between the lovers of spectacles and lovers of truth arises concerning the way in which they pursue their activity: the lovers of spectacles are those who "never willingly attend serious discussion … but run around to all the Dionysiac festivals omitting none" (*Rep.* 475d5–6).[63] In their haphazard fashion, "the lovers of sights and sounds delight in beautiful sounds, colors, and shapes, and everything fashioned from such things, but their thought is unable to see and embrace the nature of the beautiful itself" (*Rep.* 476b4–8).[64] The failure of the lover of spectacles is serious indeed: he is not, and perhaps, cannot become, the true philosopher, for his aim is mistaken, and his focus, diffuse. The reason arises from two related causes, one epistemological, the other moral. First, as the passage implies, what prevents the lover of spectacles from becoming a philosopher concerns his inability to perceive correctly: he confuses beautiful shapes, colors, and sounds with the beautiful itself, and so cannot see true beauty (cf. *Rep.* 476b4–8). Second, the epistemic confusion arises from a deeper, moral defect: having the wrong desires, the lover of spectacles loves and pursues perceptual goods, pleasant sights and sounds, instead of what is truly good.[65] As he does not desire correctly, so he cannot see properly. Since the lover of spectacles cannot see and does not

---

[63] The full Greek line is: πάντων χορῶν περιθέουσι τοῖς Διονυσίοις οὔτε τῶν κατὰ πόλεις οὔτε τῶν κατὰ κώμας ἀπολειπόμενοι (*Rep.* 475d5–6); we use Grube and Reeve (1992).

[64] The Greek line is: οἱ μέν που, ἦν δ᾽ ἐγώ, φιλήκοοι καὶ φιλοθεάμονες τάς τε καλὰς φωνὰς ἀσπάζονται καὶ χρόας καὶ σχήματα καὶ πάντα τὰ ἐκ τῶν τοιούτων δημιουργούμενα αὐτοῦ δὲ τοῦ καλοῦ ἀδύνατος αὐτῶν ἡ διάνοια τὴν φύσιν ἰδεῖν τε καὶ ἀσπάσασθαι (*Rep.* 476b4–8).

[65] A moral, or character, failure would account for why the lover of spectacles is not drawn up to the form of beauty by the beautiful appearances, as the charioteer passage in *Phdr.* 254b1–4, the recollection argument in *Phd.* 74c–e, and the ascent in *Symp.* 210a–e require.

pursue genuinely beautiful objects, the activity of *theoria* is limited to pursuing appearances, viz., festival sights and sounds, not forms. Mired in epistemic confusion, the lovers of spectacles are bound to look, fruit-lessly, for the beautiful itself in more and more appearances of beauty. Unfortunately, the misunderstanding is not uncommon with Plato adding that few are able "to reach ... and see (*horan*) the beautiful by itself" (*Rep.* 476b10–11).

Plato continues an epistemological focus on *theoria* in *Rep.* VI–VII, extending the contrast between the lover of spectacles and lovers of wisdom to describe two distinct kinds of apprehension based on different kinds of objects in the divided line, *Rep.* VI (507b–509c, 510d–511e). As in *Rep.* V where he differentiates the practitioner by the objects of the discipline, he finds that philosophers are those "who study (*theomenous*) the things themselves that remain the same and unchanged" (*Rep.* 479e6–7), so in *Rep.* VI, they are those "who study (*theomenoi*) the highest truth" (*Rep.* 484c8), and engage in "the study (*theoria*) of all time and all existence" (*Rep.* 486a8).[66] Plato's subsequent sketch in *Rep.* VII of the prisoner's ascent from inside to outside the cave is paralleled by the change from crepuscular seeing in flickering, reflected light to precise, noetic apprehension of the forms in clear sunlight (*Rep.* 514a–518b). It is worth noting that in the last section of the cave analogy, Plato uses the term *theaomai* to signify the philosopher's "sight" of the sun itself (*Rep.* 516b4–5), thus contrasting noetic apprehension of the form of the good with a less clear, imagistic seeing that apprehends, first, reflections of things in water, and then, sensible things (*Rep.* 516a5–7).[67] So, it seems fair to assert that the employment of *theaomai* and *theoreo* in reference to the apprehension of intelligible objects, especially forms, in the middle books of the *Republic* comprises what we may consider Plato's narrow, technical usage of the terms, one that contrasts with the broader, generic sense of seeing that he uses with regard to the lovers of spectacles in *Rep.* V with that of the central analogies in *Rep.* VI–VII.

Setting aside differences in theoric activity and their objects, both the perceptual and intellectual kind of *theoria* are linked by a basic, common feature mentioned earlier, the visual apprehension of something signifi-cant, perhaps divine. The generic feature holds despite the epistemic

---

[66] The latter two Greek lines are: καὶ θεώμενοι ὡς οἷόν τε ἀκριβέστατα (*Rep.* 484c8), and θεωρία παντὸς μὲν χρόνου, πάσης δὲ οὐσίας (486a8).

[67] It should be noted that the use of verbs in this section (*Rep.* 516a1–7) includes standard perception verbs like *apoblepein, horan.*

difference Plato sketches between belief and knowledge in *Rep.* V (476c9–d6) and the kinds of observers he contrasts. As we saw in *Rep.* V, the lover of ordinary sights enjoys the sight of beautiful things and ignores the beautiful itself, whereas the philosopher loves and pursues what is genuinely beautiful (*Rep.* 475e3–4). Moreover, having knowledge of the beautiful, the philosopher in seeing beautiful things does not confuse them for the beautiful itself (*Rep.* 476c2–7). Rather, as the cave passage makes clear, the philosopher, liberated from the level of the shadow-watchers, becomes one who "studies" (*theaomai*) the sun outside the cave, concluding it is the cause of all sensible things (cf. *Rep.* 516c1).[68] Looking over Plato's use of the verbs *theoreo* and *theaomai* across these sections of *Rep.* V–VII, specifically, *Rep.* V at 475d–476d, and sun, line, cave sections at *Rep.* 508a–516c, we see that while the verbs refer to the apprehension of forms, they may also refer to apprehending physical objects or their reflections in conjunction with more standard verbs of perception (e.g., *horao*, *blepo*).

3.3.3   *Plato and the Language of* Theoria

Plato frequently employs the verbs *theoreo* and *theaomai* belonging to the *theor/ia/os* family in referring specifically to the apprehension of forms in the *Republic*, and they are also so used in the ascent passage in *Symposium* (210a–e).[69] For, while the latter is not counted as a strong theoric dialogue, it is worthwhile considering its use of the terms in the present context.[70] We also find Plato making use of these verbs in reference to physical sights, or spectacles, as we have seen, in the opening of *Rep.* I (*Rep.* 327a1–328b1) where the terms are used with reference to the activity of spectators at the spectacles, like processions and races (cf. *Rep.* 328a1–7).[71] We find another example of these terms used for sight-seeing in *Rep.* V (475d–476d) where the term for "lover of sights," or *philotheamones*, embeds the noun *thea* (related to *theaomai*) within it but its referent is a festival spectacle, not an intelligible form. In a further example, Plato employs the term *thea*, "sight," in Er's myth (*Rep.* X, 614b–e) where the souls of the dead are described as marching happily onto a meadow "like a

---

[68] The reference to the sun is taken together with the analogy to the sun as the good and the cause of being in *Rep.* VI, 509b (Adam 1965, vol. 2, 93).

[69] See Des Places (1970, 246).

[70] This is despite theoric language in the ascent passage (*Symp.* 210a–e); see sec. 3.2.1, and fn. 13.

[71] A number of related passages include references to seeing sights as at festivals, e.g., in *Laws* 12 (947a, 950e–951a, 951e, 953c), and, as well, we find references to perceptual apprehension in watching the sun at *Phd.* 99d6, and perhaps, in the cosmological myth, at *Phd.* 109e6.

crowd attending a festival" (*panegorizo*, 614e3) and using phrases like "a sight worth seeing" (619e6) and "the extraordinary, beautiful sights" (615a4) seen by souls from heaven.[72] But, as I have suggested, the uniquely Platonic use of these terms is in their conjunction with the apprehension of forms. So, we find their use in *Rep.* VI, where true philosophers are "those who contemplate the highest truth" (καὶ θεώμενοι ὡς οἷόν τε ἀκριβέστατα, *Rep.* VI, 484c8), whose minds tend toward high thoughts, "the study (*theoria*) of all time and all existence" (θεωρία παντὸς μὲν χρόνου, πάσης δὲ οὐσίας, *Rep.* VI, 486a8), which echoes the description of philosophers in *Rep.* V as those who "study the things themselves that remain the same and unchanged" (*Rep.* V, 479e6–7). Again, he employs *theaomai* and *theoreo* in describing the activity of the prisoner who has ascended from the cave: the nascent philosopher is described as becoming accustomed to seeing ever more abstract objects, from reflections in water, and then as one "able to contemplate (*theasaito*) the things in heaven and heaven itself more easily by night" (*Rep.* VII, 516a8).[73] Finally, the philosopher has an ability to look at the sun itself (αὐτὸν καθ᾽ αὑτόν), not its reflection, and be able "to study" (*theasasthai*) the sun itself (*Rep.* VII, 516b6). Considered together, the use of the verbs in our *Republic* passages indicate a change both in objects apprehended and vision involved, from sensible sights and sounds to intelligible natures – and from perceptual awareness to intellectual vision.

The other dialogue that reflects a concerted use of the *theor/ia/eo* family in relation to the apprehension of forms is *Symposium* (210a–212b). Let us mention some of the linguistic connections Plato draws between the family of terms including *theaomai* and intelligible objects in the well-known ascent passage, *Symp.* 210a–212b. Leaving aside the constituent stages of the ascent, we find the person at an advanced stage "compelled to contemplate (*theasasthai*) the beautiful in practices and laws" (*Symp.* 210c3),[74] and, rising to a higher intellectual level, he "turns toward the great ocean of beauty, contemplating (*theoroun*) it ..." (*Symp.* 210d3–4).[75] Ultimately, the student "who is contemplating (*theomenos*) the beautiful in the right

---

[72] Adam (1965, vol. 2, 437 fn.) notes that *Rep.* 615a4 recalls the beatific visions of *Phdr.* 247a ff.

[73] The Greek line (*Rep.* VII, 516a8) runs: ἐκ δὲ τούτων τὰ ἐν τῷ οὐρανῷ καὶ αὐτὸν τὸν οὐρανὸν νύκτωρ ἂν ῥᾷον θεάσαιτο.

[74] The Greek runs: ἵνα ἀναγκασθῇ αὖ θεάσασθαι τὸ ἐν τοῖς ἐπιτηδεύμασι καὶ τοῖς νόμοις καλὸν (*Symp.* 210c3).

[75] The Greek phrase is: ἐπὶ τὸ πολὺ πέλαγος τετραμμένος τοῦ καλοῦ καὶ θεωρῶν πολλοὺς καὶ καλοὺς λόγους ... (*Symp.* 210d3–4).

order" (210a3)[76] has "a wondrous thing, beautiful in nature ... suddenly revealed" (*Symp.* 210e3),[77] and so comes to know the beautiful itself, and in this state, he finds the best life in contemplating beauty itself (θεωμένῳ αὐτὸ τὸ καλόν, *Symp.* 211d2). Two comments about seeing in the ascent passage (210b1–211e3) are worth making: first, visual perception verbs abound in the passage, with over ten occurrences of verbs relating to sight, namely, *idein* (ἰδεῖν), *blepein* (βλέπειν), *horan* (ὁρᾶν), and *kathhoran* (καθορᾶν), but there are half again as many occurrences of *theoreo* and *theaomai* in the same passage. Second, the occurrences of *theoreo* and *theaomai* are employed with respect to seeing – in the sense of apprehending – the beautiful in abstraction, either the beautiful in laws and sciences or the beautiful itself. Hence, it seems fair to conclude that Plato's use of *theoreo* and *theaomai* in the ascent passage in *Symposium* is continuous with using the *theor/eo/ia* family of terms meaning intellectual apprehension in the way we have seen from *Rep.* V–VII where it signals an activity of the intellect. Similar to *Rep.* V–VII, Plato repeatedly chooses *theaomai* and *theoreo* as the preferred terms to signify the highest stage of intellectual apprehension.[78]

In summary, from our discussion, we may formulate three general conclusions about Plato's use of *theoric* language. First, while Plato treats *theoreo* and *theaomai* as synonymous terms, he employs *theaomai* much more frequently than *theoreo*, retaining a special use of *theaomai* for application to apprehending intelligible forms. Second, Plato also employs *theoreo* and *theaomai* in more mundane contexts for apprehending physical sights, or spectacles, in contexts that reflect some coincidence of meaning with verbs of sense-perception, such as *blepein*, *apoblepein*, *athrein*, *horan*, and *skopein*, which signify kinds of seeing that involve the physical senses.[79] Third, in the *Republic*, Plato's use of *theoreo* and *theaomai* specifically reflects a shift in focus from the apprehension of spectacles and sights to that involving the intellectual apprehension of form in the mid-section of the dialogue.

---

[76] The Greek phrase is: θεώμενος ἐφεξῆς τε καὶ ὀρθῶς τὰ καλά (*Symp.* 210a3).
[77] The Greek phrase is: ἐξαίφνης κατόψεταί τι θαυμαστὸν τὴν φύσιν καλόν (*Symp.* 210e3).
[78] As in *Rep.* V–VII, he uses *theaomai* about three times as frequently as *theoreo*.
[79] Two verbs, *apoblepein* and *skopein*, seem to play unique roles in bridging physical and intellectual seeing, connecting seeing with cognition as seeing a thing's nature, e.g., with painters who, "looking toward (*apoblepontes*) what is most true study (*theomenoi*) it as precisely as possible" (*Rep.*VI, 484c8–d1), or "he who studies (*skopoumenon*) what is by means of definitions" (*Phd.* 100a1–2); cf. Des Places (1970, vol. 2, 64, 457).

3.4 Structural Connections: Platonic *Theoria* and Ring Composition

The analysis of Platonic *theoria* in conjunction with the ring form leads us to formulate some implications about its significance to the dialogues. One conclusion is that, by using the ring form, Plato highlights the mid-section, giving emphasis to this part, and allowing its significance to color that of the surrounding sections. The larger strategy conforms with Plato's aim of contrasting philosophical *theoria* with traditional *theoria* for the sake of enlarging our understanding of the former kind in particular. In the *Republic*, he uses references to traditional *theoria* and traditional *theoros* to provide touchstones for readers (as he does for Glaucon) to grasp the nature of philosophical *theoria* and of the *theoros*, the true philosopher.[80] In generalizing about the ring form, we find two aspects relating to its construction, one philosophical, and another structural. With regard to the structural aspect, a strong theoric ring form is present when we find references to *theoria* or a related activity in the opening and closing sections of the work, creating a ring shape. In this regard, we find Plato referring to various events typical of traditional *theoria* such as embassies going to festivals, individuals attending festivals, traveling to shrines, or performing religious rituals like sacrifices. When the beginning and ending are related thematically by containing references to *theoria*, the composition provides two distinct advantages: first, the form gives special emphasis to the meaning residing at the mid-point of the structure, and second, the form enables special connections between the mid-point and the beginning.[81] So, we should look to this part to find the focal point of Plato's philosophical ideas and provide conceptual connections between the opening and the mid-point. The expectation concerning the significance of meaning focusing on the middle section is borne out with evidence in the *Republic* – whether we consider the mid-point its literal middle (third wave, Bk. V, 474a ff.) or the dramatic mid-point of the work (cave analogy, Bk. VII, 514a).[82] In either case, the mid-point represents the most philosophically dense passage of the work, consisting in the central

[80] In *Phaedo*, the *theoros* figure is played by Socrates; possibly, he does also in *Republic*.
[81] As argued in sec. 3.2.1, the ring form allows for complex layers of meaning, on which also see Douglas (2007).
[82] As mentioned, Barney (2010, 39) and Burnyeat (1999, 288) share the view that the cave analogy begins the mid-section of the ring in *Republic*; the literal mid-point (474a ff) has some claim to the mid-point on account of contrasting philosophers with lovers of spectacles which is central to the contrast between traditional and Platonic *theoria*.

metaphysical and epistemological theories, as illustrated by the contrast between the lover of sights and sounds and the true philosopher, as well as the triple analogies of sun, line, and cave. In addition, the connections between the initial movement of going down to Piraeus is matched by the mid-point motion of ascending the cave. Morever, both the individual rings and the large, external ring reinforce the ring form by reflecting the elliptical motion exhibited in traditional *theoria* in the form of moving away from and back to a home site so that the elliptical travel of *theoria* mirrors the ring structure considered at an abstract level.

A structural feature of the ring form contributes to its philosophical meaning as well. For example, the element of elliptical motion arises in relation to traditional *theoria* in that the traditional *theoros* travels away from and back to the home site; this feature may be present by analogy or by metaphor at the philosophical level. We have concluded that Plato considers various senses in which a feature of elliptical motion may be imitated, including linear elliptical motion, axial rotation, and revolution around a fixed body.[83] Plato considers all three kinds of bodily motion, and, significantly, he also considers them with regard to the mind, or soul, in reasoning. Thus, as we have seen, Plato compares the noetic thinking of philosophical *theoria* to axial rotation (cf. *Tim.* 40a7–b1); he also uses a rotational analogy in describing "the revolutions of the soul" (*psyches periodous*, *Tim.* 43a5) or "the inner revolution of the soul" (*ten gegonuian … psyches periodon*, *Tim.* 47d5), that are naturally akin to "the thoughts and revolutions of the universe" (*hai tou pantos dainoeseis kai periphorai*, *Tim.* 90c8–d1). In addition, we have a different kind of motion, linear and non-regular, traced by the ascent and descent of the philosopher in *Rep.* VII in the cave analogy, as well as that of the turning around (*peritrope, peristrephein*) said of the soul in *Rep.* VII (cf. *Rep.* 519b3–4, 532b5, 533d3). The latter, the "turning around" of the soul, refers to its liberation from "the leaden weights" of bodily pleasures that "pull the sight of the soul downwards" (*Rep.* 519b2–4). While the concept of elliptical, or circular, motion is, of course, being applied to the mind or soul analogically, as there is no material object traveling in uniform motion, Plato's choice of the comparison underscores certain features, like regularity, uniformity, or continuity – in the case of axial motion – that aid grasping, say, the nature of the mind's noetic activity (cf. Lee 1976, 73–77). While the reader may, of course, be led to grasp these features of the soul or mind independently, having an awareness of a ring structure

---

[83] For discussion on the species of circular motion, see sec. 3.2.2.

reinforces the philosophical meaning of the work by giving emphasis to a structural element, like elliptical motion or visual apprehension.

In brief, specific dialogues that have a kind of ring composition that I term "strong theoric" ring form exhibit certain features such as having end points of the ring mentioning a theoric event and the mid-section containing the philosophically significant section of the work. For example, the mid-section may include discussion of Platonic *theoria* as the highest intellectual activity, even as other sections include references to traditional *theoria* as traveling to the sanctuary or festival, as we find in *Republic*. We also discover that Plato employs notions of traditional *theoria* and the *theoros* partly to familiarize the reader with philosophical *theoria*, and partly to separate philosophical *theoria* – and the true philosopher – from them. In this regard, one of Plato's more compelling, critical character portraits must include the "lover of spectacles" (*philotheamones*) described in *Rep.* V (cf. 475d1–476d5), he who "runs around to all the festivals omitting none" (*Rep.* 475d5–6) so as to "delight in beautiful sounds, colors, and shapes," but, lacking philosophical potential is unable "to see . . . the nature of the beautiful" (*Rep.* 476b4–8). Plato's contribution to the history of *theoria*, then, is both highly original and far-reaching. For, while we find the notions of *theoria* as cultural travel, or sight-seeing, in Herodotus (*Hist.* 1. 30, 2. 31), and that of *theoria* as intellectual study in Heraclides (fr. 88), nothing approaches Plato's account of philosophical *theoria* both as the highest theoretical activity and as one having a practical dimension. In Plato's hands, philosophical *theoria* represents the culmination of a hard-won epistemic process that requires the acquisition of genuine moral character on the part of the nascent philosopher.[84]

---

[84] See Ch. 5: Platonic *theoria* both causes and preserves moral qualities in the thinker, a view favored by Burnyeat (2000), Kraut (1997), and Vlastos (1997); *Laws* X may be read as a suggestion about the way in which thinking cures bodily maladies; see Menn (1995), esp. 53–59, and fn. 30.

CHAPTER 4

Aristotle's Refinement of Theoria

He who at the moment is exercising his knowledge (*theorōn*) is in actuality and is wise in the most precise sense.

(*DA* 417a26–27)

4.1 Relating Aristotelian *Theoria* to Platonic *Theoria*

Plato's conception of *theoria* as an intellectual activity directed at intelligible forms distinguishes itself from traditional *theoria* even as it stands on its shoulders. Aristotle's conception does not bear such ties to traditional *theoria*, in part due to the limitations of the compositional form in which his works are preserved. Yet we do find a continuation from the generic conception of the traditional notion of *theoria*, that which we mentioned earlier, namely "traveling for the sake of observing something significant, perhaps divine," which runs throughout Aristotle's accounts, relying primarily on the notion of the visual apprehension of eternal, divine objects, forms. The generic notion, present also in Plato's conception of *theoria*, provides a solid basis for Aristotle's conception of philosophical *theoria*. But it is evident that Aristotle's account continues the central defining characteristics Plato develops, being a kind of visual theoretical apprehension, directed at the highest intelligible objects, possessing intrinsic value, and comprising the highest human end.[1] In fact, we find a strong similarity between the intellectual vision described in the ascent passage of *Symposium* where the lover of beauty "suddenly has something wondrous,

---

[1] Aristotle does not connect human *theoria* with circular rotation, or better, axial rotation, as Plato does; rather, in *DA* I, 3 (407a2–b11), he attacks Plato's use of rotation as an image for thought through the argument that if soul is an extended magnitude, it would imply a body moving in circular spatial motion which is inconsistent with central properties of thought like rest (cf. 407a32–b2); for discussion of the *DA* passage, see Hicks (1976, 254–60), Polansky (2007, 95–100), cf. Lee (1976, 84–86).

beautiful in nature, revealed" to him (*Symp.* 210e4–5),[2] and Aristotle's description of theoretical activity in *EN* X 7. In this chapter, Aristotle offers the most extended description of human *theoria*, naming it the activity (*energeia*) of our highest faculty (*nous*), an activity that surpasses excellent moral activity, and, perhaps most controversially, calling it "complete happiness" (ἡ τελεία εὐδαιμονία, *EN* 1177a17). Apart from *EN* X 7 comprising the most detailed look at human *theoria*, this chapter with its companion *EN* X 8, warrant close study for specific similarities they possess to Plato's account of philosophical *theoria*. In this latter regard we have a third reason for the study mentioned at the outset, the lack of scholarly attention to *theoria* itself, as present scholarship focuses almost exclusively on the relation of *theoria* to moral virtue in regard to the achievement of happiness.[3] The present chapter seeks to remedy the situation, presenting Aristotle's account of *theoria* in itself, in its relation to that of Plato, and observing, as far as possible, its relation to traditional *theoria*. In the last regard, we should note that Aristotle, like Plato, makes use of the *theor/ia/eo* family of terms in two ways, one dealing with the study of intelligible objects specifically, and another referring to the consideration of intellectual topics generally.[4]

4.2 *Theoria*, the Highest Activity, *EN* X 7–8

Keeping Plato's description of philosophical *theoria* in mind, we turn to Aristotle's account of *theoria* with the arguments presented in *EN* X 7. The chapter contains six central arguments to show the uniqueness of *theoria*, describing it, among other features, as the most complete, final, and self-sufficient of human activities (cf. *EN* 1177a13–17). In *EN* X 8, he adds that *theoria* constitutes the highest, or primary, kind of happiness (*EN* 1177a15–17, a18–19), moving to the familiar but controversial conclusion that excellent moral activity provides a secondary kind of happiness.[5]

---

[2] The partial Greek line runs: ... θεώμενος ἐφεξῆς τε καὶ ὀρθῶς τὰ καλά, πρὸς τέλος ἤδη ἰὼν τῶν ἐρωτικῶν ἐξαίφνης κατόψεταί τι θαυμαστὸν τὴν φύσιν καλόν (*Symp.* 210e4–5).

[3] As we noted, the exception to the present dearth in scholarship is Walker's study (2018).

[4] Thus, Aristotle often employs *theoreo* and related terms in non-theoric contexts outside the *EN* as, for example, in the scientific works such as *De Part. An.* I 5, where verbal forms signify "looking" in the sense of investigating something as in the method of conducting empirical or logical research; the two uses are discussed in Ch. 4. On the two senses of *theor/ia/eo* in Plato, see Des Places (1970, 262–63).

[5] For reasons of space this chapter does not enter the debate about the constituents of happiness and their worth, on which consult, e.g., Achtenberg (1995), Burger (1995), Cooper (1986), Kraut (1989, 1995), Lear (2004, 2014), Roche (1988, 1995), Rorty (1980).

In summary, the interlocking arguments are: (1) *theoria* is the highest activity since it is a function of the intellect; (2) *theoria* apprehends the highest intelligible objects (1177a20–21); (3) *theoria* is the "most continuous" activity (συνεχεστάτη, 1177a21); (4) *theoria* is the most pleasant of all virtuous activities (1177a23–25); (5) *theoria* is the most self-sufficient activity (1177a27–28); (6) *theoria* is loved for its own sake, not for the sake of anything else (1177b1–2). In addition, it is worth noting that Aristotle also describes *theoria* as "divine" (*theion*, 1177a15) on the grounds that it is the activity of *nous*, which is the "divine or most divine part of us" (*EN* 1177a13–16), an idea that recalls Plato's notion of *theoria* as involving vision of the divine (e.g., *Rep.* VII, 516b; *Phdr.* 250b; *Symp.* 212a), a point to which we return in this chapter. For the present, let us work slowly through Aristotle's discussion in *EN* X 7, subsequent to which we will give some attention to Aristotle's passing remarks about the theoretical activity of the gods in *EN* X 8.[6]

In the chapter's opening, we see Aristotle's interest in connecting the activity of *nous*, the highest faculty, with the activity of happiness: "if *eudaimonia* consists in virtuous activity (*kat' areten energeia*), it is reasonable that it should be [activity] in accordance with the highest one (*krastiste*) and this will be of the best" (*tou aristou*), (1177a12–13).[7] Aristotle clarifies that he equates the "best" faculty with our intellect (*nous*), explaining that this is the faculty that "rules and guides us," giving us "ideas of the noble and divine" (ἄρχειν καὶ ἡγεῖσθαι καὶ ἔννοιαν ἔχειν περὶ καλῶν καὶ θείων, *EN* 1777a14–15). Reaching a first conclusion about the nature of *theoria*, he says that the activity of the intellect, namely, *theoria*, is identical with "complete happiness" (*teleia eudaimonia*), which he claims has been stated (cf. *EN* 1177a17–18). While the link between theoretical activity and complete happiness has not been stated or not stated clearly, Burnet notes that the connection between theoretical wisdom (*sophia*) and happiness is suggested in *EN* VI 7 where *sophia* is described as the highest form of goodness.[8] We might suggest that since *sophia* implies *episteme* (*EN* VI 7, esp. 1141b2–4), and *episteme* implies *theoria*, by transitivity, we reach the implication that *theoria* is integral to

---

[6] Despite Aristotle's mention of divine *theoria* in *EN* X 8, this chapter does not demonstrate or analyze divine *theoria*, rather, he concludes it is the activity proper to the gods from an informal argument based on rhetorical appeal; see discussion in sec. 4.6.

[7] The Greek runs: Εἰ δ' ἐστὶν ἡ εὐδαιμονία κατ' ἀρετὴν ἐνέργεια, εὔλογον κατὰ τὴν κρατίστην· αὕτη δ' ἂν εἴη τοῦ ἀρίστου (1177a12–13).

[8] Burnet (1900, 461 fn. 1177a18); cf. his discussion at *EN* VI 7, 1141a18–b3.

the highest goodness, an implication that does not, of course, imply that the highest good is nothing but *theoria*.

The remaining portion of *EN* X 7 (*EN* 1177a18–1177b26) develops several arguments about the nature of *theoria*, showing its superiority to the activity of moral virtue. The long middle section of the chapter concludes with a complex conclusion, ending with the claim that the life of theoretical activity, or *theoria*, will comprise "complete happiness" (τελεία εὐδαιμονία, 1177b24), thus enlarging on the claim of forty-two lines earlier that the activity of *nous* is complete (cf. *EN* 1177a17). The central premise supporting this second conclusion is that *theoria* is identical with the best activity (1177a19), and Aristotle presents several linked characteristics to support this idea. First, he finds it is the activity of the highest faculty, intellect (*nous*), (1177a20); second, the objects of the faculty are most intelligible (1177a20–21); third, its activity is the most continuous (συνεχεστάτη) for "we can study (*theorei*) more continuously than perform any action" (1177a21–22).[9] To these arguments, he adds four more reasons for its elevated status: (i) the activity of *theoria* is the most pleasant (1177a23–24), (ii) it has the most self-sufficiency (αὐτάρκεια), (1177a27–28); (iii) it is the only activity loved for its own sake (1777b1–2); (iv) it is leisurely (σχολαστικὸν) (1177b23).

While all the arguments highlight features belonging to the nature of *theoria*, the feature of being loved for its own sake seems to be prior and other features, like being leisurely and self-sufficient, are posterior to it. The feature of being loved, or valued, for its own sake is distinguished by Aristotle in contrast to being valued for an end extrinsic to the activity, such as being useful to something else. This feature is one he finds characteristic of the practical virtues, those exercised in pursuit of political or military ends, which he states are chosen for the sake of an advantage beyond the virtuous actions themselves (*EN* 1177b2–4). He frequently cites military actions as chosen for the sake of victory or political actions for the sake of a political advantage, like honor; *theoria*, however, we do not choose for something that results from it. Rather, we engage in *theoria* for the activity itself: "nothing else comes to be apart from the activity of studying (*to theoresai*)" (οὐδὲν γὰρ ἀπ᾿ αὐτῆς γίνεται παρὰ τὸ θεωρῆσαι, 1177b2). The larger passage at *EN* X 7 (1177b1–15) that contains this line of thinking can be laid out as follows:

---

[9] The Greek is: θεωρεῖν γὰρ δυνάμεθα συνεχῶς μᾶλλον ἢ πράττειν ὁτιοῦν (1177a21–22).

(1)   An activity chosen for the sake of something else is not chosen only for its own sake.[10]
(2)   The practical virtues are chosen partly for the sake of something else.
(3)   So, the practical virtues are not chosen only for their own sake.
(4)   The activity of *theoria* is chosen only for its sake and not for anything else.
(5)   [An activity pursued for its own sake and not for anything else has greater value than one pursued for the sake of something else.]
(6)   So, *theoria* has more value than the activity of the practical virtues.

The previous argument reflects the position that *theoria* possesses a quality that the practical virtues do not, namely, that of being valued, or loved, exclusively for its own sake (cf. *EN* 1177b1–2). Of course, being valued for its own sake does not confer intrinsic worth, as we can imagine something valued for its own sake that is not intrinsically good, such as Midas prizing gold for its own sake. Alternatively, we may conceive something being intrinsically good that is not desired by anyone. Thus, we need an argument that supplies the qualification about what is able to be loved or valued rightly to distinguish which things valued are properly valued: Aristotle supplies such arguments at points in *EN* X 4 through *EN* X 6.

The basic premise for the winnowing argument arises from a notion about the natural faculties, e.g., seeing, hearing, desiring, or thinking, which reflect a teleological framework in that the specific activity is good if it preserves the exercise of the relevant capacity. The teleological principle applied to the present case of correct desiring yields the result that desiring something good is desiring something that is proper to desire, not just desiring anything. We know that Aristotle intends a teleological framework in *EN* X 7 from his remark at the close of the chapter: "What was stated before will fit together with what is said now; for what is naturally proper to each thing is best (*kratiston*) and most pleasant for that thing" (*EN* 1178a4–5).[11] Thus, Aristotle supplies the needed constraint for our argument about pleasure and goodness, namely, what is best for something (e.g., a substance, sense-organ, or capacity) is achieving what is naturally proper to it. This teleological principle agrees with "what was stated before" (*EN* 1178a4–5), the likely references including *EN* X 4

---

[10] So, if we pursue something for the sake of something else – even if we also pursue it for itself – we do not choose it for itself alone, although here he is not considering an activity being pursued both for its own sake and for something else.
[11] The Greek runs thus: τὸ λεχθέν τε πρότερον ἁρμόσει καὶ νῦν· τὸ γὰρ οἰκεῖον ἑκάστῳ τῇ φύσει κράτιστον καὶ ἥδιστόν ἐστιν ἑκάστῳ (*EN* 1178a4–5).

about sense-experience and pleasure (1174b20–31), *EN* X 5 about good and bad pleasures (1175b36–1176a22), and *EN* X 6 about the decent person being the standard for what is good and pleasant (1176b24–27).[12] Well in advance of *EN* X 7, then, he has argued that the good person is the standard for what activity is deemed good in itself; it does not follow that what is good and desirable in itself is identical with something that is desired by anyone, but only with what is desired or desirable by the good person (cf. *EN* 1176b24–26). As he adds in *EN* X 6, adults do not value the same things as children nor good men the same things as bad men (*EN* 1176b23–24). So, with respect to assessing what is intrinsically valuable, we should look to the judgment of an adult, not a child, and a good person, not a bad one. Our standard in respect of what is good and pleasant is, therefore, the good person, for: "as we have said many times, what is worthy and pleasant to a good man actually is of such a nature" (*EN* 1176b24–26).[13]

While this text and others (e.g., *EN* 1095b14–1096a5; 1143b33–1144a6, 1145a6–11) praise theoretical wisdom, and by implication, the activity of *theoria*, they do not mention its nature as a complete activity, the proper text for which is *EN* X 4. Thus, we turn briefly to Aristotle's discussion about complete activities in *EN* X 4 as this provides a better link for the conclusion about *theoria* and complete happiness.[14] Consequently, Aristotle's ranking of *theoria* as the best and most pleasant activity depends, first, on a teleological principle about kinds of activities that establishes that what is "naturally proper to each thing is best and most pleasant for that thing" (*EN* 1178a4–5). Second, it requires the notion that pleasures differ in relation to the activities they complete, and since "the activities of thought (*dianoia*) differ in kind from those of the senses, and from one another, so, the pleasures that complete them also

---

[12] Aristotle frequently uses a normative standard for his discussions about friendship and pleasure: see *EN* IX 9 (1169b30–1170a4), *EN* X 6 (1176b26–27), respectively.

[13] The Greek runs: καθάπερ οὖν πολλάκις εἴρηται, καὶ τίμια καὶ ἡδέα ἐστὶ τὰ τῷ σπουδαίῳ τοιαῦτα ὄντα (*EN* 1176b24–26). Other passages on the similar point about having a standard set by nature include: *EN* I 9, 1099a13; III 4, 1113a23–33; IX 4, 1166a12–13; IX 9, 1170a13–16; X 5, 1176a15–22.

[14] My reasoning is that *EN* VI 7 is concerned with elucidating the intellectual virtues, making the point that the intellectual virtue called *sophia* consists two faculties, intelligence (*nous*), and scientific knowledge (*episteme*), (1140a19–20); it is not concerned with further explaining the nature of the noetic activity, which is the needed end point. So, even if *EN* VI 7 allows us to connect *theoria* to *nous* by observing that *theoria* is an exercise of *nous*, the chapter does not advance our understanding about its nature qua activity; so, the connection of *theoria* to complete activity said to have been stated in *EN* X 7 (*EN* 1177a18) refers to a passage other than *EN* VI 7.

differ" (*EN* X 5, 1175a26–28).[15] For Aristotle, then, some activities are base and their pleasures are, correspondingly, base, whereas "the pleasure proper to a good activity is good, and to a bad activity is bad" (1175b27–28).[16] Consequently, if *theoria* is the highest among natural human activities, a conclusion supported by several grounds, its pleasure is the best. So, what determines whether an activity, and thus, a pleasure, is good or bad? As before, Aristotle defers to the notion of an evaluative limit, namely, the morally good person. Such a person provides a standard for what will count as a good activity and what for a good pleasure. So, he states: "in all cases, what appears to the good man (*ho spoudaios*) is good ... and if virtue and excellence are the standard, then the things that seem to him to be pleasures are pleasures" (*EN* X 5, 1176a15–19).[17] In addition, we note that: "the pleasure proper to a (morally) good activity is good, the pleasure proper to a bad activity is bad" (*EN* 1175b27–28).[18] Consequently, when trying to determine which activities are good and pleasant in themselves, we look to what the good person finds good and pleasant, and here Aristotle reports that the good person chooses *theoria*: "of all the activities in accordance with virtue, the most pleasant is the activity in accordance with theoretical wisdom" (*EN* 1177a23–25).[19]

Returning to the argument about *theoria* being loved for itself in *EN* X 7, it is understandable why Aristotle moves from claiming that *theoria* is something we desire and choose for its own sake to concluding that it has more value than practical pursuits like politics. For he thinks that *theoria* is the highest human activity on the ground that it is characteristically human. He states that "what is by nature proper to each thing is best" (*EN* 1178a5–6) and "our intellectual faculty (*nous*) is most of all human" (μάλιστα ἄνθρωπος) (*EN* 1178a6–7).[20] Since we know that the activity of *nous* that has *episteme* is *theoria*, it is reasonable to conclude, first, that *theoria* is most distinctively human, and second, that the activity of *theoria* is best. Generalizing to what comprises the best way of life (*bios*) at the end of *EN* X 7, he claims that "a life guided by *nous* is best and most

---

[15] The Greek runs: διαφέρουσι δ' αἱ τῆς διανοίας τῶν κατὰ τὰς αἰσθήσεις καὶ αὐταὶ ἀλλήλων κατ' εἶδος· καὶ αἱ τελειοῦσαι δὴ ἡδοναί (1175a26–28).

[16] The Greek runs: ἡ μὲν οὖν τῇ σπουδαίᾳ οἰκεία ἐπιεικής, ἡ δὲ τῇ φαύλῃ μοχθηρά (1175b27–28).

[17] The full Greek line: δοκεῖ δ' ἐν ἅπασι τοῖς τοιούτοις εἶναι τὸ φαινόμενον τῷ σπουδαίῳ. εἰ δὲ τοῦτο καλῶς λέγεται, καθάπερ δοκεῖ, καὶ ἔστιν ἑκάστου μέτρον ἡ ἀρετὴ καὶ ἀγαθός, ᾗ τοιοῦτος, καὶ ἡδοναὶ εἶεν ἂν αἱ τούτῳ φαινόμεναι καὶ ἡδέα οἷς οὗτος χαίρει (1176a15–19).

[18] The Greek is: ἡ μὲν οὖν τῇ σπουδαίᾳ οἰκεία ἐπιεικής, ἡ δὲ τῇ φαύλῃ μοχθηρά (1175b27–28).

[19] The Greek is: ἡδίστη δὲ τῶν κατ' ἀρετὴν ἐνεργειῶν ἡ κατὰ τὴν σοφίαν ὁμολογουμένως ἐστίν (1177a23–25).

[20] See note 21 for the Greek.

pleasant to humans," and therefore, "this kind of life is the happiest" (*EN* 1178a4–8).[21] He closes *EN* X 7 having reached two central conclusions, one concerning the comparative value of *theoria* as an activity and the other, the comparative value of *theoria* as a way of life, which are supported by his reasoning about specific qualities that *theoria* possesses, such as being complete, self-sufficient, leisurely, and most pleasant. Of these features, that of leisureliness (*scholastikon*) merits more attention to meet some standard criticisms, one being its appeal to elitism, and another, its irrelevance to *theoria*.

4.2.1 Theoria *and Leisureliness*

In *EN* X 7, Aristotle's conclusion that *theoria* is chosen for its own sake, not for an external end (cf. *EN* 1177b1–4) is reached by an extended contrast between kinds of activities that he qualifies as leisurely or unleisurely (cf. *EN* 1177b1–b24). In the argument, Aristotle comes to describe *theoria* as "leisurely" (*scholastikon*, *EN* 1177b22) as he differentiates it from practical pursuits like political or military actions which aim at something outside the activity (*EN* 177b6–8). These actions are performed for the sake of further ends, such as engaging in warfare for the sake of peace (*EN* 1177b8–9) or in politics for the sake of power or honor (*EN* 1177b12–15); hence, they are not leisurely. So, Aristotle's purpose in qualifying practical pursuits as "unleisurely" (*ascholos*, *EN* 1177b8, 1177b12) is in service of distinguishing them from *theoria* which he calls leisurely, or *scholastikon* (*EN* 1177b22). So it seems natural to wonder what precisely the distinction between leisureliness and unleisureliness comes to. To begin the reply, the difference is not temporal: the notion of being done in a "leisurely" fashion does not imply taking one's time to do something, but rather, analytical or conceptual, in the following sense. Each of the two kinds of activities possess different interrelated features: first, consider the activities springing from military or political pursuits. These display the characteristics of being "unleisurely" (*ascholoi*), "aiming at an end," and "not being chosen for their own sake" (*EN* 1177b16–18). These features are not synonymous but are logically related in the following sense: an activity that aims at an extrinsic end is one pursued for the sake of the end and so, it is not chosen for itself; it is thus not leisurely. On

---

21 The full Greek passage is: τὸ λεχθέν τε πρότερον ἁρμόσει καὶ νῦν· τὸ γὰρ οἰκεῖον ἑκάστῳ τῇ φύσει κράτιστον καὶ ἥδιστόν ἐστιν ἑκάστῳ· καὶ τῷ ἀνθρώπῳ δὴ ὁ κατὰ τὸν νοῦν βίος, εἴπερ τοῦτο μάλιστα ἄνθρωπος· οὗτος ἄρα καὶ εὐδαιμονέστατος (*EN* 1178a4–8).

this analysis, the feature of being pursued for an external end (viz., its effect) implies two others, namely, being unleisurely and not being chosen for itself. As Aristotle observes, while political and military pursuits have the highest nobility and rank, they aim at ends other than these activities, and are not only chosen for themselves (*EN* 1177b16–18). In contrast, consider the activity of *theoria*, which he describes as: "the activity of the intellect" (*nous*), theoretical, and having "no end beyond itself" and "its own proper pleasure" (*EN* 1177b19–21).[22] So, we see that *theoria* has the necessary features of being chosen and loved for itself, aiming at nothing beyond the activity, being leisurely, and being pleasant. To these, he adds that the activity of *theoria* is self-sufficient and free from fatigue (*EN* 1177b21–22).

Aristotle's attribution of leisureliness to *theoria* has, nevertheless, given rise to some criticism which seems to center on two closely related points. One consists in the objection that in valuing leisureliness, Aristotle unknowingly reiterates his privileged class, and the other, that linking *theoria* with leisureliness to praise this as the best life reflects class inequality.[23] These criticisms appear to stem from the general Marxist view about the origin of values, namely, that values espoused by members of privileged classes merely reflect the prejudices and interests of that class. While I am not entirely unsympathetic to this line of argument, in the present context – Aristotle's praise of *theoria* as leisurely – there is some reason to think the criticism misses the mark. First, even if some central features that *theoria* possesses coincide with activities that non-laboring classes engage in, this coincidence does not provide the ground for their value for the reason that Aristotle chooses to provide several grounds for *theoria*'s value that stand entirely independently of class interest.[24] So, in what follows, we provide a counterargument to the standing criticism, adding a brief discussion of the background of the term *scholē* by way of supporting Aristotle's choice of the feature for *theoria*.

The basic reply to the two criticisms about leisureliness turns on the observation that Aristotle's distinction between leisurely and unleisurely pursuits in *EN* X 7 is not cast as a distinction between those of aristocratic and laboring classes, but as a distinction between kinds of pursuits of the same class, namely, by members of the middle or the upper classes,

---

[22] The Greek line runs: ἡ δὲ τοῦ νοῦ ἐνέργεια σπουδῇ τε διαφέρειν δοκεῖ θεωρητικὴ οὖσα καὶ παρ' αὐτὴν οὐδενὸς ἐφίεσθαι τέλους, ἔχειν τε ἡδονὴν οἰκείαν (1177b19–21).
[23] See, for example, lines of criticism mentioned in Nightingale (2004, 191), Burger (1995, 90–91).
[24] Unless these critics have the view that all philosophical reasoning can be shown to reduce to class bias, in which case, they ought to provide an analysis to support this view.

specifically, those who engage in military or political activity. As we recall, while Aristotle describes such pursuits as noble, he finds they are unleisurely insofar as they aim at something outside the activity, like military victory or honor (cf. *EN* 1177b12–18). In contrast, he finds that *theoria* is not similarly described for its aim lies within the activity itself (cf. *EN* 1177b17–20). In this regard, the distinction between leisurely and unleisurely activities depends on different pursuits followed by the privileged class, not on the distinction between the unleisurely work of farmers or artisans, say, and the leisurely activity of aristocrats. Since warfare and politics are unleisurely pursuits and since these are activities performed by Aristotle's own class, it does not appear that being unleisurely is identified simply with lower-class labor. Rather, it seems to follow generally that being leisurely or unleisurely does not coincide precisely with the work of any class, but with some particular aspect of the work, or activity, that one performs.[25] To further the point, a brief discussion about the term *scholē* and its range of application is useful. The background also proves instrumental in understanding Aristotle's use of the term in relation to *theoria*, as well as explaining why its appearance need not merely reflect class bias.[26]

Leaving aside the details of its history, the term *scholē* undergoes changes in meaning over the Classical period from a negative to a positive kind of possession that is related to citizen freedom.[27] Roughly speaking, the positive sense of the term signifies something that enables someone to have the time to follow one's pursuits, say, to engage in public discussion. Examples of the positive meaning are found in both Plato and Euripides. In *Theaetetus* and *Laws*, we find Plato using *scholē* in connection with the idea of having adequate time to pursue philosophical discussion. So, in the *Theaetetus*, Theodorus mentions the interlocutors having the leisure (*scholē*) for more discussion to which Socrates contrasts their *scholē* for philosophical discussion with the time limits imposed on speakers in the law-courts (cf. *Theaet.* 172c–d, 187d).[28] A similar comment arises in *Laws* I, where the Athenian states that having *scholē* allows the interlocutors to

---

[25] However, it is admitted that the work of a household slave or an unfree artisan, say, cannot be considered to fall into the realm of leisurely work at all, but my larger point remains.

[26] For, I take it, the force of these criticisms (cf. Burger 1995) does not amount merely to the claim that Aristotle's ideas (or some of them) reflect his class identity, as it would be surprising if they did not reflect it in some way.

[27] The range includes the positive idea mentioned to the value-neutral notion of having enough time to the negative notion of having time to do nothing, or wasting time; for discussion, see Anastasiades (2004, 62–67).

[28] Here Socrates explains that their lack of leisure is imposed by the water-clock used in the law-courts that limits their speech, so they are "always in a hurry" (*ascholia*) (*Theaet.* 172d–e).

consider the laws from all points of view (cf. *Laws* 781d). In a similar vein, Euripides' *Ion* reflects the notion of *scholē* as being free time in which one chooses one's pursuits: in the passage, the temple attendant Ion speaks about his leisure (*scholē*) as "most dear" to him (1. 634), the context showing that what he values is being free to carry out his temple duties (as treasurer and attendant), not that he values having nothing to do.[29] Lastly, Plato gives Socrates an ironical comment about leisure in *Apology* when he complains that his lack of leisure (*ascholia*) is due to his pursuit of wisdom (*Apol.* 23a–b) for by pursuing philosophy, he is deprived of the leisure (*scholē*) to pursue public affairs or profit, which has led him to poverty (*Apol.* 23b–c). The high comedy of the remark lies partly in its confuting our expectations about leisure being conjoined with philosophy, for surely, we assume, philosophy pairs with leisure, it does not drive it away. More seriously considered, the comment is significant for undercutting the criticism about a class-biased preference for leisure: Socrates' claim about pursuing philosophy and lacking leisure cannot be seen as reflecting elitist class preferences for obvious reasons. First, Socrates is hardly a member of the aristocratic class and so, is free of the charge of elitist bias.[30] Second, the criticism has no material basis given the content of Socrates' remark which shows the lack of leisure is an effect of pursuing philosophy, thus presenting philosophy as the impediment to leisure (cf. *Apol.* 23b–c).[31] In consideration with other sources, it appears that, in general, both poor and rich citizens can refer to having or lacking leisure, and so, the term is not indexed to a single, elite class.[32]

Taking the above-cited passages into consideration, it is evident that Aristotle follows the positive interpretation of leisure as the ability to choose one's activities. Seen from this perspective, Aristotle's qualification of *theoria* as a leisurely activity in *EN* X 7 coincides with the dominant classical view of *scholē*, and more particularly, with Plato's view about the connection between leisure and philosophical discussion. As we have noted, Aristotle thinks that *theoria* is leisurely (*scholastikon*) in the sense that it is an activity one may choose if one has *scholē*, i.e., the time to

---

[29] Thus, what Ion rejects is not work, but "the demands of public, mainly political, life," so we see that he values *scholē* as "the voluntary disposal of one's time" (Anastasiades 2004, 66).

[30] Leaving aside further assumptions about false consciousness, which are not persuasive in this situation, anyway.

[31] Socrates' comment in *Apol.* 23a–b implies that *scholē* may apply to the same class members at different times since he complains that he has lost his leisure, not that he never had it.

[32] There is, however, one unfortunate class for which having or lacking leisure is never applied, the class performing exclusively manual labor, slaves (Anastasiades 2004, 63); Xenophon also describes craft labor as reflecting a lack of leisure (*ascholia*) (*Cyr.* 4.3.12).

pursue something one chooses.[33] Consequently, he reasons that a moral
agent who has leisure will choose a worthwhile, or virtuous, activity aiming
at nothing beyond itself (cf. *EN* 1177b19), and so, chooses *theoria*. The
condition of having leisure allows the moral agent to choose freely, apart
from the constraints imposed by practical pursuits that aim at external
ends (*EN* 1177b12, b17–18), and so, the agent may elect *theoria*. Broadly
speaking, then, by connecting theoretical activity with leisure (*scholē*),
Aristotle continues Plato's view of leisure as a necessary condition for
philosophical investigation. As we see the conjunction developed in *EN*
X 7, *theoria* requires *scholē*, but is not co-extensive with it; rather, *theoria* is
an activity valued for itself and chosen when we have leisure. In the
descriptive context, he contrasts *theoria* with practical pursuits on the
ground that we expect an advantage from them whereas with *theoria*,
"nothing comes apart from the activity" (*to theoresai*), (*EN* 1177b2–4).
Thus, for Aristotle, leisure may be considered one of several jointly
necessary conditions for the activity of *theoria* along with, say, moral virtue
considered as habitual. So, the attribution of leisure to *theoria* does not
reduce to the aiming at nothing beyond itself (cf. *EN* 1177b19). The two
do not name the same property; if I am correct, being leisurely is a
necessary condition for choosing something for its own sake, but they do
not have the same meaning. In the *Protrepticus*, a work that gives some
attention to *theoria*, we see the text emphasizing primarily its lack of utility
from which we may infer its leisureliness, but this feature remains implicit.

4.3   *Theoria* in *Protrepticus*

The feature of being chosen for its own sake that we find emerging
strongly in the discussion of *theoria* of *EN* X 7 also appears in
Iamblichus' *Protrepticus*.[34] First, a brief word about the work: while the
scholarship concerning the authorship of this work is long and vexed,
suffice it to say that dominant scholarly opinion holds that the work
preserves Aristotle's views.[35] So considered, it seems reasonable to consider
the account of *theoria* in Iamblichus' version for purposes of comparison

---

[33] If we also assume the moral virtue of the agent, the choice of *theoria* as the leisure activity in *EN* X 7
is all but determined.
[34] Some semblance of Aristotle's eponymous work is preserved in Iamblichus' text, which, minimally,
provides knowledge about what the Neo-Platonist writer held about Aristotle's view of *theoria*.
[35] For the controverted history of the authentication of Iamblichus' account, esp. on the 19th to 20th
centuries, see Chroust (1965); for more recent views, see Hutchinson and Johnson (2005, 2017),
Nightingale (2004, 18), and Walker (2010, 2018).

with the key account of philosophical *theoria* in *EN* X 7–8. A recent study by Walker (2018) proves essential in this regard, providing an analysis of the differing features of *theoria* found in the various sections of *Protrepticus* that will allow the comparison with Aristotle's discussion in *EN* X 7–8. Let us brief summarize the features of *theoria* this work develops, focusing on one, namely, being chosen for its own sake, that is common to both *Protrep.* 9 and *EN* X 7. But first we need to contend with an initial problem about apparently conflicting features of *theoria* in *Protrep.* 9–10. As Walker points out, in *Protrep.* 9, *theoria* is described as having no practical use by virtue of it aiming at nothing beyond the activity, whereas in *Protrep.* 10, *theoria* is suddenly found to be useful. The solution that Walker correctly proposes involves describing the manner in which an activity that is chosen for itself alone can nevertheless provide benefits to other human faculties. More specifically, Walker argues that while *theoria* aims at nothing beyond itself, it also provides knowledge of moral boundary points about the good (Walker 2018, 145–70. Walker's solution to the problem of the conflicting features of *theoria* arising from *Protrep.* 9–10 is useful in itself, and also as means of indicating a broader position about how Aristotle values *theoria*. As we develop the topic about Aristotle's valuation of *theoria* more fully in Chapter 6, it is necessary to state that when Aristotle says that *theoria* is chosen for its own sake, he does not rule out that good results may flow from it. Rather, what he excludes by speaking about *theoria* "being chosen for itself" and "being loved for its own sake" (*EN* X 7, 1177b1–4, b16–20) is the idea that we prize *theoria* for some end apart from the activity itself. According to Aristotle, we do not do so. Yet, as we noted, nothing precludes the possibility that good effects spring from the activity of *theoria*. In fact, Chapter 6 develops my position that beneficial effects supervene on the activity of *theoria*, a view that departs slightly from Walker's position, providing a better interpretation for Aristotle's statements about the nature and value of theoretical activity. At present, let us return to the account of *theoria* as chosen for its own sake that is developed in *Protrep.* 9.[36]

The dominant feature of *theoria* that emerges in *Protrep.* 9 (53.15–26) turns on the striking image it presents comparing the activity of philosophical *theoria* to viewers at a festival. More specifically, it likens those engaged in *theoria* to spectators at festival events who are present simply for the viewing – the implication being that the viewing itself is the end of the

---

[36] For full analysis of both features of *theoria* in *Protrepticus*, I refer readers to Walker's excellent monograph (2018).

activity. Since philosophical *theoria* is pursued for its own sake, not as means to something else, it is implied that *theoria* has no utility. The passage thus recalls the analogy between *theoria* and festival spectators we found in other texts, such as the three lives account in Heraclides fr. 88, and even a reference to the theoretical life in *EN* I 5 (1095b15–19). The passage of *Protrep.* 9 runs:

> It is not a terrible thing at all, then, if it [*theoria*] does not seem to be useful (*chresimon*) or beneficial (*ophelimos*); for we do not claim that it is beneficial but that it is good in itself and it is appropriate to choose it for itself and not for the sake of some other thing. For, just as we travel to Olympia for the sake of the spectacle itself (*autes heneka tes theas*) even if there were nothing more to get from it (for *theoria* itself is superior to lots of money), and as we observe (*theoroumen*) the Dionysia not in order to acquire anything from the actors (rather than actually spending), and as there are many other spectacles (*theas*) we would choose instead of lots of money, so, too, *theoria* of the universe (*ten theorian tou pantos*) should be honored above everything that is thought to be useful (*chresimon*). For, surely one should not travel with great effort for the sake of beholding (*theasasthai*) people imitating women and slaves or fighting and running and not think one should behold (*theorein*) the nature of existing things, that is the truth, for free. (*Protrep.* 9, 53.15–26/B44, tr. Hutchinson and Johnson)[37]

The central claim being advanced is that *theoria* (considered as philosophical *theoria*) is valuable "in itself," chosen "for itself," and not chosen "for any other thing." So, *theoria* is not valued for being useful or profitable. We note that the argument assumes an exhaustive distinction between being valued for itself and for something else: there is no alternative allowing something to be both. For this reason, the author reasons from *theoria*'s lack of practical utility to it being valued for itself, stating that it "does not seem to be useful (*chresimon*) or beneficial (*ophelimos*) . . . but it is good in itself" (*Protrep.* 9, 53.15–16). After mentioning the features of being valued and chosen for itself, the author illustrates these with an analogy to spectators who attend festivals solely for the sake of the visual experience. The passage mentions two festivals, the Olympic and Dionysiac, for the purpose of stressing that the spectators travel there only "for the sake of the spectacle" (*autes heneka tes theas*) itself, not for anything else. Before we discuss other aspects of the analogy, it is worth noting similarities between *Protrep.* 9 and other texts, for example, the parallel to

---

[37] On translation and comments, see Hutchinson and Johnson (2017, 51–52); for the non-specialist, the preceding reference is by H. Pistelli (1888) citing ch., p., l., followed by "B" numbering from the reconstruction by Düring (1961).

claims in *EN* X 7 regarding *theoria* being good and choiceworthy in itself, or that between the three lives mentioned in *EN* I 5 (1095b15–19) and Heraclides fr. 88.[38] These texts have common ground in the parable about three kinds of visitors and three kinds of life, and specifically, in the way that they describe *theoria* as perceptual and an activity valuable in itself, features that are connected through the analogy to festival spectators. Thus, *Protrep.* 9 makes clear that the spectators seek an activity that is self-contained, having no end beyond itself and we see a parallel to the idea in *EN* X 7 that *theoria* is valued for its own sake, not sought for anything beyond the activity.

Let us pause for a moment to consider the abovementioned feature of *theoria* being good in itself. First, if we interpret the distinction between being chosen for itself and for the sake of something else as being exhaustive, then the claim in *Protrep.* 9 about *theoria* as valued for itself implies it lacks instrumental value. In my view, the passage demands that we take the distinction as exhaustive. Yet Walker's response seems to reject the exhaustive reading as he argues that the feature of lacking an end external to an activity is not by itself a "good-making feature" but rather only a necessary condition for *theoria* being complete (Walker 2010, 137, fn. 4).[39] While I concur that the feature of being chosen for itself, considered abstractly, need not confer goodness, the distinction is not apt for the argument in *Protrep.* 9 where the reasoning clearly implies an exhaustive reading of the distinction between being chosen for itself and being chosen for an end outside the activity. For example, the *Protrep.* passage begins by stating *theoria* is not useful or beneficial, but that it is "good in itself," from which it is argued that *theoria* is "chosen for itself" and "not chosen for anything else." Hence, its line of argument reinforces the exclusive distinction between being good in itself and good for an external end.

What we have left out until this point concerns the perceptual aspect of the analogy offered in *Protrep.* 9 (53.15–26) in which *theoria* is compared to the activity of spectators observing (*theoreo/theoroumen*) at festivals. As we noted, the three lives parable compares the three types of visitors at festivals to followers of different kinds of life. From the fuller Heraclides'

---

[38] This text recalls the Pythagorean account given in Iamblichus (*Vit. Pythag.* 58); see also Plato's analysis of three lives in *Rep.* IX where he introduces three psychological types and their pleasures correlated with three ways of life: money-loving, honor-loving, and learning-loving (cf. *Rep.* 581a–e).

[39] Walker goes on to argue that this provides only a necessary condition for *theoria* being complete, or *teleion* (Walker 2010, 137), a topic I take up below in regard to complete activities.

passage, we recall that the festival visitors are distinguished as follows: the athletes attend aiming at glory, the traders aiming at profit, and the spectators, solely for observing – with the first class being compared to the political life, the second class to the mercantile life, and the third to the philosophical life. While *Protrep.* 9 does not give us as complete a version of the parable as Heraclides fr. 88, in both texts the activity of *theoria* is described as: (i) chosen for its own sake, (ii) comparable to the activity of spectators, and (iii) not chosen for an external end. These features overlap with those we find in the account of *theoria* in *EN* I and X 7; however, there are differences as well, two relating to content, one, to language. We have noted one minor difference concerning the incompleteness of the spectator analogy in *Protrep.* 9, namely, it omits mention of the athletic competitor seeking glory who represents the political life and barely mentions the money-maker seeking profit who represents the business life and focuses entirely on the spectator representing the philosophical life. The main difference in *Protrep.* 9 involves extending the comparison of *theoria* from the festival spectator to one engaging in observation of the whole universe (*ten theorian tou pantos*) which is absent in the other accounts. In fact, the phrase "*theoria* of the whole universe" recalls Anaxagoras, who mentions that *theoria* of the sun, moon, and heavenly bodies comprises the end of human life (cf. *DK* 59A1; *DL* 2.6.10). So, there are certain differences in terminology and style between the accounts of *theoria* in *Protrep.* 9 and *EN* X 7–8 that I note briefly.[40] First, in relation to terminology, the *Protrep.* passage employs four different terms including two nouns *theoria* and *thea* (sight), and two verbs *theoro* and *theaomai* eight times in a section of eleven lines which comes to a higher frequency than for *EN* X 7–8. Second, and most atypically for Aristotle, in *Protrep.* 9 we find *theoria* being used with reference to festival observation, a use that is entirely absent in Aristotle's standard works. Third, in *Protrep.* 9 we find the verb *theaomai* employed in reference to a study of the heavens and this use is wholly distinct from Aristotle's use of observation terms in his scientific works.[41]

---

[40] Some evidence tends to complicate the issue of authenticity, which is not discussed by Walker's work (2018, 139–45); as we have noted, Hutchinson and Johnson (2005) maintain its authenticity.

[41] In sum, these points reduce to: (i) the absence of *theoria* as observing at festivals outside *Protrep.*; (ii) no genuine work employs *theoria* referring to festival-attendance; one related exception is that of *architheoros* (embassy-leader) in *EN* IV 2 in conjunction with the virtue of *megaloprepeia* for the financial outlays of *leitourgia* (cf. *EN* 1122a22–25); (iii) Aristotle does not use *theaomai* in place of *theoreo*, as Plato does.

4.4 *Theoria*, Complete and Loved for Itself

Two central features of philosophical *theoria* that the three texts, *Protrep.* 9 (53.15–16), *EN* I 5 (1096a4–9), and *EN* X 7 (1177b1–2, 1177b20, 1178b18) mention, in various phrasing, are being chosen, or loved, "for its own sake" (*di' hauten agapasthai*, 1177b1–2), and "not aiming at an end beyond itself" (*par' hauten oudenos ephiesthai telous*, 1177b20). While the immediate sense of these phrases seems to imply that *theoria* has no practical utility, this is not fully correct. Rather, it is more correct to state that since *theoria* is the activity of a theoretical faculty, its proper aim is to reveal metaphysical truth. Consequently, it does not aim at anything practical, namely, it does not seek to illuminate actions or to produce things. The conception of theoretical activity and *theoria* as being directed at divine, not human, objects has a distinct history, from Anaxagoras' mention of *theoria* of the heavenly bodies being the end of human life (*DK* 59A1; *DL* 2.6.10) to Plato's elevated description about "*theoria* of the whole of time and of existence" in *Rep.* VI (*Rep.* 486a8–9).[42] These lines reveal an underlying notion of *theoria* that calls to mind Aristotle's description of an activity directed at "the highest objects of intellect" (*EN* 1177a20–21).[43] Hence, it is unsurprising that theoretical activity is directed at metaphysical truth and not at the useful; in this notion, Aristotle follows Plato. Also, like Plato, Aristotle assumes these aims are exclusive of one another. However, an activity that does not aim at something useful and outside itself may, nonetheless, have practical application; in fact, it would be surprising if the achievement of scientific truth did not have practical application as a secondary result. Consequently, having the "good" of an activity reside in the activity itself implies only that its aim is non-utilitarian. From this perspective, it is perfectly reasonable for *Protrep.* 9 to claim that *theoria* is not chosen for profit or advantage, but for its own sake (cf. *Protrep.* 53.15–18).

We can appreciate, then, how the so-called "aristocratic conception" of *theoria*, a common but somewhat misconceived view, arises.[44] The conception would seem the inevitable result of texts like those just canvassed where Aristotle contrasts activities having no external end, and in effect, being useless in relation to an external end, like gaining wealth or power.

---

[42] The Greek phrase is: ... θεωρία παντὸς μὲν χρόνου, πάσης δὲ οὐσίας (486a).
[43] The full Greek line runs: κρατίστη τε γὰρ αὕτη ἐστὶν ἡ ἐνέργεια· καὶ γὰρ ὁ νοῦς τῶν ἐν ἡμῖν, καὶ τῶν γνωστῶν, περὶ ἃ ὁ νοῦς (1177a20–21).
[44] For discussion of the aristocratic view, see Walker (2010).

Of course, such ends arise in the context of discussing things that humans pursue as good, as when, in *EN* I 5 Aristotle correlates the common ends of pleasure, honor, and knowledge with the life of enjoyment, the political life, and the theoretical life (βίος θεωρητικός) (1095b17–19). The *Protrep.* 9 passage differs slightly from this one in its sketch of the three lives by distinguishing the lives of glory, money-making, and *theoria* (*Protrep.* 53.15–21). But in *EN* I 5 Aristotle tries to show that pleasure and honor fail the test of being stable, complete goods, or goods in themselves, not in being useless. In *EN*, he demonstrates that neither pleasure nor honor meet the standard for genuine goods for living: first, the life aimed at pleasure is "slavish" (*andrapododeis*, 1095b19–20) while that aimed at honor depends on those bestowing it and so, is unstable; in addition, since honor is desired for the sake of virtue, honor is incomplete in itself (cf. 1095b26–30).[45] Thus, while he defers proving the superiority of the theoretical life (*ho theoretikos*) until later than *EN* I 5 (cf. 1096a4–5), he returns to finish the proof in the last section in *EN* X 7 (1177b24–1178a8). Here he returns to the notion of complete happiness (*teleia eudaimonia*, 1177b24) raised in *EN* I 7 (1097a28–1097b6) to accomplish the task. Throughout the discussion, Aristotle's strategy consists in measuring the proposed ends, namely, pleasure, honor, and contemplation (*theoria*) against the standard of completeness set by *eudaimonia*, for any successful good must be shown to be complete and lacking in nothing (cf. *EN* 1097a28–1097b1). Thus, since we have seen that in *EN* I 5 Aristotle shows that pleasure and honor fail on account of being incomplete in different ways, this leaves the theoretical life as the only defensible candidate (cf. 1096a4–5).

The arguments about completeness comprise species of a general kind that depend on the logic of something being complete, or final (*teles/teleia*). In brief, his argumentative strategy turns on the idea that one end is more final than another if it is that for sake of which other ends are sought. In *EN* X 7, Aristotle employs the premise from *EN* I 5 to establish the senses in which *theoria* is the highest activity by showing it is the most complete activity. More specifically, in *EN* X 7, Aristotle explains the way in which *theoria* comprises a more complete activity than others by showing it is chosen for its own sake: it is pursued for itself and not for anything beyond the activity. As we have discussed, being chosen, or loved, for its own sake

---

45   The full Greek line runs thus: ἔτι δ᾽ ἐοίκασι τὴν τιμὴν διώκειν ἵνα πιστεύσωσιν ἑαυτοὺς ἀγαθοὺς εἶναι· ζητοῦσι γοῦν ὑπὸ τῶν φρονίμων τιμᾶσθαι, καὶ παρ᾽ οἷς γιγνώσκονται, καὶ ἐπ᾽ ἀρετῇ. δῆλον οὖν ὅτι κατά γε τούτους ἡ ἀρετὴ κρείττων (1095b26–30).

implies that the aim of *theoria* is contained in the activity, not in anything beyond it. The other key features of *theoria* mentioned in *EN* X 7, namely, being self-sufficient (*autarkes*), continuous (*suneches*), and pleasant (*hedone*) are logically related to being complete (*teleia*). In my view, these three features are necessary accidents of *theoria*, and its most fundamental feature is being a "complete activity" (ἐνέργεια τέλεια), a term that indicates its generic property. Since it signifies a generic quality, it is not identical with what is unique to *theoria*; it does not name its defining quality. In conjunction with the generic description, we need to add the defining characteristic described in *EN* X 7, namely, being an active exercise of intellect (*nous*), (*EN* 1177a19–21).[46] In my view, the generic feature explains its other qualities, such as being continuous or pleasant, in the sense that they follow from that which is a complete activity (*energeia teleia*). As well, the fact that *theoria* belongs to the genus of complete activity explains it being pursued for its own sake (cf. *EN* 1177b1–20) on the grounds that, in so belonging, it is paired with other natural activities, such as seeing and hearing, which are also complete activities. To understand the connection between *theoria* and completeness, we might investigate what kinds of things activities (*energeiai*) as such are, and what the distinction is between "complete" and "incomplete" activities.

4.5   The Nature of Complete Activities

Understanding the connection between *theoria* and completeness requires that we clarify, first, the notion of an activity, or *energeia* (ἐνέργεια), and then explain that of a complete activity (ἐνέργεια τέλεια) for those who may be unfamiliar with the notions. An activity (*energeia*) is the exercise of some potentiality (*dunamis*), as, for example, motion (*kinesis*, κίνησις) is the activity of what can move, seeing (*horasis*) is the activity of what can see, and thinking (*noesis*, νόησις) is the activity of what can think, namely, intellect (*nous*).[47] For the present discussion, we should also distinguish between a complete and incomplete activity: this difference maps onto the difference between fulfillment (*entelecheia*) and motion (*kinesis*).[48] The

---

[46] As Burnet notes on *EN* 1177a20–21 in reference to the description of *theoria* as an activity of *nous*, "*theoria* is the *energeia* of a *dunamis* which is so high as almost to be an *energeia*" (Burnet 1900, 461).

[47] For a fine-grained discussion of the *dunamis/energeia* distinction in Aristotle, see Menn (1994, esp. 87–95).

[48] For discussion about the status of the potentiality involved in the distinction between *energeia* and *kinesis*, see Heinaman (1994): Heinaman challenges Kosman's view (1984) that in *kinesis*, the

latter refers to the state of undergoing change over time, such as walking or building; the former refers to a state continually reaching its end, such as seeing or thinking, which is the category in which he places *theoria*. As we recall at the close of *EN* X 7, Aristotle links *theoria* to completeness by relating this activity to happiness itself. He states that the activity of *nous*, namely, *theoria*, is to be identified with "complete" happiness (*teleia eudaimonia*, *EN* 1177b24–25). The conclusion in *EN* X 7 about *theoria* and complete happiness depends on Aristotle's earlier discussion about pleasure and complete activity in *EN* X 4 and 5.

In the discussion in *EN* 4–5, Aristotle explains the completeness of pleasure by analogy to seeing (*horasis*), an activity which is also complete (1174a14–15). He does so by means of four conjoined premises. First, he explains that seeing is "complete at any moment" (1174a14–15) in the sense of "not lacking anything that develops later to complete its form" (*EN* 1174a15–16),[49] and second, it is something "whole" (ὅλον, *EN* 1174a17) by nature. Thus, third, pleasure, like seeing, is an activity whose form is complete throughout the activity: like seeing, pleasure is not something whose form is completed by lasting longer (*EN* 1174a17–19). Therefore, fourth, as with seeing, pleasure is not something that takes time to develop; it does not come to be what it is, rather, its "form is complete at each moment" (*EN* 1174b5–6). He underscores the difference between motions and complete activities by noting the temporal aspect of motion: motion extends over time, whereas complete activities have no temporal extension as such, but happen in a moment (*EN* 1174b7–9). So, to take any of his examples of motions (*kineseis*), such as building, walking, or flying, we find that any one of these, like building, for example, takes place over time and is directed at an end outside the activity (*EN* 1174a20–21). For this reason, then, a motion like building is only "complete" when its aim is reached – in the case of building, when the structure is built (cf. *EN* 1174a21). In contrast, Aristotle holds that complete activities such as seeing, hearing, feeling pleasure, or thinking are non-temporal, whole, do not have an external end, and are complete at each moment (cf. *EN* 1174b5–6). So, we see that complete activities comprise an exceptional class, to which it may be added that they belong to the higher species of living things, namely, non-rational animals, humans, and god.

---

dunamis is destroyed, but in *energeia* preserved, mentioning the case of god's activity, thinking, which is not an actuality of any *dunamis* (Heinaman 1994, 209); this claim holds true for the gods' *theoria* but not human *theoria*, an *energeia* which preserves and completes its *dunamis*, like seeing.

[49] The Greek line runs thus: οὐ γάρ ἐστιν ἐνδεὴς οὐδενός, ὃ εἰς ὕστερον γινόμενον τελειώσει αὐτῆς τὸ εἶδος (1174a15–16).

Let us complicate the account of complete activities by enlarging the kinds of activities we include from seeing, hearing, and feeling pleasure, to add two kinds of thinking, namely, reasoning (*dianoia*, διάνοια) and *theoria* (*EN* 1174b20–21). In *EN* X 4, he claims that these activities, too, afford us pleasure by their exercise, stating: "the activity of sense-perception is pleasant, and similarly, that of reasoning (*dianoia*) and study (*theoria*), and the most pleasant is the most complete (*teleiotate*)" (*EN* X 4, 1174b21–23).[50] Combining this statement with the those he makes about complete activities in *EN* X 7, we may now conclude that such activities: (i) are non-temporal wholes, (ii) are complete at each moment, (iii) have forms that undergo no process of coming to be (cf. *EN* 1174a15–19), (iv) have their end in the activity, (v) possess a specific pleasure (*EN* 1177b19–21). So, the two kinds of thinking he mentions in *EN* X 4, namely, reasoning (*dianoia*) and *theoria* also exhibit the features that characterize complete activities like seeing, hearing, and feeling pleasure.[51]

4.5.1   Theoria, the Most Pleasant, Complete Activity

For Aristotle, there is a necessary connection between a complete activity and its pleasure: so, in *EN* X 5 we find: "every activity is completed (*teleioi*) by pleasure" (*EN* 1175a21). Without going into detail, suffice it to say that Aristotle employs a naturalistic, teleological framework to determine which capacities belong to a thing's nature, and these, in turn, circumscribe the range of its complete activities. In regard to pleasure-producing activity, Aristotle holds that when an activity is the exercise of a natural capacity, the pleasure that completes the activity is good (*EN* 1175b26–31, 1176a1–3). According to this line of reasoning, sight, for example, is a natural capacity belonging to most animal life and its exercise, the activity of seeing, is both good and pleasant to the animal.[52] Keeping this claim in mind and leaving aside the subsequent argument about distinguishing

---

[50] The Greek line runs: κατὰ πᾶσαν γὰρ αἴσθησίν ἐστιν ἡδονή, ὁμοίως δὲ καὶ διάνοιαν καὶ θεωρίαν, ἡδίστη δ' ἡ τελειοτάτη (1174b21–23).

[51] In *EN* X 4, Aristotle claims that pleasure, like seeing, is a complete activity having the same generic characteristics (cf. 1174a14–1174b10); in *EN* X 5, he argues that not all pleasure is similar since good and bad pleasure is not the same in kind, and good pleasure completes the activity (*EN* 1175a20–21).

[52] In *EN* X 5, it is implied that the kind of activity that would tend to degrade the natural faculty, for example, staring at very bright objects in the case of sight, would count as improper, and so, this activity is not completed by pleasure but pain; for similar discussion, see *DA* II 12 on how excesses in the sensibles destroy the balance of the sense-organs (424a26–32), and *DA* II 10 on what is destructive of the sense of taste (422a30–33).

good and bad pleasures (*EN* X 5, 1175b1–36),[53] we may anticipate the conclusion in *EN* X 7 that *theoria* is an activity that is both complete (*EN* 1177b24) and most pleasant (*EN* 1177a23). The argument leading up to this conclusion presupposes his ranking of good activities with those in accord with virtue as being the highest. And since good activities are completed by pleasure (which is good), he reasons that "among the activities in accord with virtue, that of theoretical wisdom is most pleasant" (*EN* 1177a23–25). Thus, we note that the assertion about *theoria* being the most pleasant activity in *EN* X 7 has roots in the naturalistic account of human nature with its connection between complete activities and good pleasures from *EN* X 5.

Yet, while its roots lie in the naturalistic account of human capacities, its branches stretch up to one theological in character. For, when he comes to declare *theoria* as the best and most pleasant activity in *EN* X 7, he appeals not only to human but to divine capacities for measure. Thus, at the outset of *EN* X 7, he supports the claim that *theoria* is the "best" (*kratiste*) activity (*EN* 1177a19–20) by connecting it to human intellect (*nous*) which is qualified as divine (θείων) in virtue of it giving us "ideas of what is noble and divine" (ἔννοιαν ἔχειν περὶ καλῶν καὶ θείων) (*EN* 1177a14–15). From this point, he reasons that since *nous* is "divine in itself or the most divine in us" (*EN* 1177a15–16), this is the activity that affords "complete happiness" (τελεία εὐδαιμονία) (1177a17). In *EN* X 8, he adds a second line of support for his claim that human *theoria* is the best and highest human activity by arguing that it resembles the activity proper to the gods (*EN* X 8, 1178b21–22). This line of argument appears to imply that he is taking the gods' best activity as the standard for humans' best activity, and this invites certain objections.[54] However, these need not prove overly troublesome; for example, to the objection that posing a divine standard is impractical insofar as it prescribes an unattainable standard for humans, we may reply that the objection misses the mark.[55] After all, Aristotle

---

[53] It may be worth noting that in *EN* X 5, Aristotle uses the decent man (*ho spoudaios*) as the standard for distinguishing good and bad pleasures in the sense that a good pleasure is what the decent man finds pleasant, which comprises what is pleasant absolutely (*haplos*).

[54] Another standing objection about *EN* X 8 concerns Aristotle's comparison of excellent moral and intellectual activity, where, it is claimed, Aristotle tips the scales in favor of *theoria* to diminish the value of moral activity, on which see Achtenberg (1995), Ackrill (1980), Cooper (1986), Kraut (1995), Nagel (1980), Roche (1988, 1995), Rorty (1980), Tuozzo (1992).

[55] It may be argued as well that the analogy between human and divine *theoria* in *EN* X 8 is flawed on the grounds that differences between human and divine nature prevent the basis for the comparison, to which we reply that the differences in nature are not relevant to the analogy about *theoria*, which, as Aristotle conceives it, has the same formal features in both cases.

recognizes that humans cannot engage in *theoria* continuously or for the entirety of a life, as such "would be more than human" (*EN* 1177b26–27). Rather, what he seeks to clarify at the close of *EN* X 7 (cf. 1177b26–1178-a8) and in *EN* X 8 (cf. 1178b8–b32) concerns the special status of the activity of *theoria*: viz., its nature is such that we ought to yearn to possess it so we become divine-like.

In summary, Aristotle's praise of *theoria* as the best human activity in *EN* X 7–8 contains two central lines of argument that we consider separately. The first line in *EN* X 7 consists in several short arguments about human *theoria* that reflect its connections to our faculties and nature: *theoria* is an activity of our intellect (*nous*), concerned with the highest objects, a complete activity, one desired for its own sake that is leisurely, self-sufficient, continuous, and most pleasant (cf. *EN* 1177a14–1177b24). As we have analyzed these features and their arguments at length already, we may leave this section aside, only noting that its general line of argument makes no comparison to the gods' *theoria*; rather, this section stands on independent grounds by demonstrating the essential features of human *theoria*. This section uses the term "divine" (θείων, 1177a15) only in relation to human intellect: the specific reference is to *nous* being "divine or the most divine thing in us" (*EN* 1177a15–16); in this regard, the term reflects a focus fixed on human *theoria*. The second line of argument appears at the end of *EN* X 7 (1177b26–1178a3) where Aristotle seems to offer a prescriptive line of reasoning based the nature of our *nous*: he argues we should engage in *theoria* and "try to become as immortal as we can" (*EN* 1177b33) on the ground that "our intellect (*nous*) is the best part of us" (*to kratiston ... en hautou*, *EN* 1177b34).[56] This line of argument can be read as an aspirational appeal: "Engage in *theoria* to attain the highest level of humanity you can." This line of approach to *theoria* – in effect, by encouraging us to adopt a higher perspective than a merely mortal one – is developed in *EN* X 8 which takes gods' *theoria* as its initial focus. In this regard, in *EN* X 8 we find Aristotle first showing that the gods engage in *theoria* as their proper activity, and subsequently, offering an analogy between divine and human *theoria* to underscore the idea that humans who participate in *theoria* have the happiest life. This conclusion is supported by two linked claims: (i) the gods are "the most blessed and happy" (*EN* 1178b8–9), and they engage in *theoria* (*EN* 1178b21–22), and (ii) human activity that is "most similar to

---

[56] The Greek line is: ἀλλ' ἐφ' ὅσον ἐνδέχεται ἀθανατίζειν καὶ πάντα ποιεῖν πρὸς τὸ ἦν κατὰ τὸ κράτιστον τῶν ἐν αὑτῷ (*EN* 1177b33–34).

divine activity will be the happiest (*EN* 1178b23). By combining premises from sections of *EN* X 7–8, we have the following argument:

(1)   The gods are most blessed and happiest.
(2)   The gods engage only in *theoria*.
(3)   Humans have a capacity for *theoria*.
(4)   The human activity most similar to divine activity is the happiest.
(5)   [A human life characterized by the happiest activity is the happiest life.]
(6)   Therefore, a human life devoted to *theoria* is the happiest.

A few notes are in order. First, we see that the concluding premise in the argument from *EN* X 8 extends the idea expressed in the closing lines from *EN* X 7 to the effect that "we should try to make ourselves immortal as far as is possible ..." (*EN* 1177b33–34), based on having the capacity of *nous*.[57] In addition, premise 4 of the argument relies on an analogy between human and divine *theoria* but it does not imply that the two are identical in their nature, since elements comprising the activities differ.[58] But using this premise, we can infer that the kind of life that gives priority to theoretical activity is the happiest human life.[59]

4.6   *Theoria* and Divine Activity

EN X 8 continues the discussion about *theoria* in connection with divine activity, where the term "divine" refers to the activity that gods perform, as opposed to referring to an aspect of human *theoria*. The upward direction of thought in *EN* X 7–8 continues that in the prior discussions about pleasure and happiness in *EN* X 4–8 where his analyses of related capacities move upward toward those of greater abstraction, like the hierarchy of faculties in *Meta.* I 1.[60] It is predictable, then, at the end of *EN* X 7 that after stating that a life directed by one's intelligence (*nous*) is "divine" (*EN* 1177b32), he turns our attention to the gods' *theoria* in *EN* X 8. Yet, his argument about the gods' *theoria* is purely negative, not demonstrative.

---

[57] The Greek is: ἀλλ' ἐφ' ὅσον ἐνδέχεται ἀθανατίζειν καὶ πάντα ποιεῖν πρὸς τὸ ζῆν κατὰ τὸ κράτιστον τῶν ἐν αὐτῷ (*EN* 1177b33–34).

[58] It is reasonable to infer that human *theoria* contains residual elements derived from sense-perception, *phantasia*, and *epagoge* that are wholly absent from divine *theoria*.

[59] Further discussion of the implications this has for the practical life are developed in Ch. 6, sec. 6.3.3.

[60] See *Meta.* I 1, 980a23–981b12, or *DA* II 3, 414a28–415a12 for the consecution of faculties in the soul.

For it shows that this activity is theoretical simply by showing that the gods' nature would not allow any other kind of activity. Aristotle finds it is inconsistent with the gods' natures to engage in any other kind of activity: since the gods have no need that would require morally virtuous acts, they do not engage in moral actions but only in *theoria*. But the conclusion that the gods do not engage in virtuous activity is unexpected, even shocking: on what grounds would it be plausible to argue this? The argument in *EN* X 8 is an indirect, eliminative argument that opens with the premise that the gods are living beings capable of activity, from which he shows that since it is not proper for gods to engage in excellent moral activity, they must engage in *theoria*, the sole activity remaining to them (*EN* X 8, 1178b21). He then concludes that: "the activity of the gods that is the most blessed is theoretical (θεωρητική); and the human activity most similar to it is the happiest" (*EN* X 8, 1178b21–23).[61] Furthermore, since the activities of *theoria* and *eudaimonia* are co-extensive (διατείνει, 1178b28–29), the more theoretical activity one has, the happier one will be (cf. *EN* 1178b29–30), and so "it follows that *eudaimonia* is some kind of *theoria*" (*EN* 1178b32).[62] The argument about the gods engaging in *theoria* may be represented as follows:

(1)   Among living things, only gods and humans share in happiness (*EN* 1178b26–27).

(2)   Among the activities that comprise happiness, humans share in both moral and theoretical activity.

(3)   Gods share in theoretical activity but not in moral activity (*EN* 1178b20–21).

(4)   So, the activity of the gods that constitutes happiness is theoretical (*EN* 1178b21–22).

(5)   The human activity that is most like divine activity must comprise the highest happiness (*EN* 1178b23–24).

(6)   So, human theoretical activity constitutes the highest happiness (*EN* X 8, 1178b7–b32).

Premise 3 and its supporting argument is worthy of note being most crucial to determining the outcome of the larger argument. The supporting argument for premise 3 lies at *EN* 1178b8–b18, in a section couched in rhetorical language consisting of interrogatives. The reasoning consists

---

[61] The Greek is: ὥστε ἡ τοῦ θεοῦ ἐνέργεια, μακαριότητι διαφέρουσα, θεωρητικὴ ἂν εἴη· καὶ τῶν ἀνθρωπίνων δὴ ἡ ταύτῃ συγγενεστάτη εὐδαιμονικωτάτη (1178b21–23).
[62] The Greek is: ὥστ' εἴη ἂν ἡ εὐδαιμονία θεωρία τις (1178b32).

in an indirect argument (if we interpret the questions as statements) in which he argues to the gods engaging in *theoria* by eliminating their activity in moral virtue. He makes no reference to the gods' essential properties to demonstrate that their proper activity is *theoria*. Rather, he structures the informal reasoning by posing several questions that point to the conclusion that the gods cannot exercise any activity but *theoria* (*EN* 1178b10–18). After stating that we agree that the gods are "most happy and blessed" (*EN* 1178b8–9), he asks whether we can attribute any moral actions to them, such as acts of justice. He replies that doing so would imply that the gods need acts of justice, such as keeping contracts, paying back debts, and so on, which is absurd; the same situation results when we consider whether the gods engage in brave or generous acts, as we see that being concerned with actions is "petty (*mikra*) and unworthy (*anaxia*) of the gods" (cf. *EN* 1178b10–b18).[63] This statement provides the explanation for gods forbearing from moral actions: unlike fallible humans, gods have no need for moral virtue. In effect, he argues that having to exercise character virtue is inconsistent with the gods being "most blessed" (*EN* 1178b8–9), and, as such, having no need for justice, courage, moderation, and the like. Yet the gods can engage in the intellectual activity of *theoria* without this feature posing an inconsistency with their nature. In answer to the natural question concerning why the activity of *theoria* does not contradict their divine nature, we can do no better than to recall the difference between complete and incomplete activities.

We should first recall that Aristotle's defining condition for a complete activity consists in the end and the activity being the same (cf. *EN* 1174a14–21). Let us assume that in virtue of their nature as most blessed and happiest living things, the gods engage in complete activities, and if there is more than one such activity, they engage in the most complete. Now also consider the case of excellent moral activity: while it is desired for its own sake, it is also desired for the sake of something else. For, as we have seen in section 4.2, excellent moral activity also brings an advantage: "we derive a greater or smaller advantage from practical pursuits beyond the action itself" (*EN* X 7, 1177b2–4).[64] Aristotle offers examples of the advantages of excellent moral activity: (1) for military actions, which we suppose involve the virtue of courage, the advantage is victory; after all, as

---

[63] The last Greek line is: διεξιοῦσι δὲ πάντα φαίνοιτ' ἂν τὰ περὶ τὰς πράξεις μικρὰ καὶ ἀνάξια θεῶν (*EN* 1178b17–18).

[64] The full Greek line is: οὐδὲν γὰρ ἀπ' αὐτῆς γίνεται παρὰ τὸ θεωρῆσαι, ἀπὸ δὲ τῶν πρακτικῶν ἢ πλεῖον ἢ ἔλαττον περιποιούμεθα παρὰ τὴν πρᾶξιν (1177b2–4).

he says, "no one chooses to wage war for the sake of war" (*EN* 1177b9).[65]
(2) For political actions, the advantage is political power or prestige;
hence, these are also performed for something other than the activity itself
(*EN* 1177b12–15). So, while military and political actions surpass others
in terms of their nobility, they are unleisurely aim at ends outside themselves, and are not chosen only for their own sake (cf. *EN* X 7,
1177b16–18). Given these results, if we assume the gods only engage in
complete activity, or in the most complete activity, it follows that the gods
cannot engage in excellent moral activity. If a more complete kind of
activity exists, then it is not inconsistent for the gods to engage in
that activity.

In fact, there is a more complete activity than morally virtuous activity:
it is *theoria*. Contrasted with moral activity where we derive something of
advantage, he says that: ". . . from study, we derive nothing from the
activity of studying" (τὸ θεωρῆσαι, *EN* X 8, 1177b2).[66] We can appreciate
this aspect recalling the defining features of *theoria* in *EN* X 7, namely, that
it is an activity of the intellect (*nous*) (1177a14–15); an activity of the
greatest value insofar as this activity is the highest (1177a19–21) because it
is theoretical (*theoretike*, 1177b19); it aims at nothing beyond itself; it is
continuous (*suneches*, 1177a21),[67] it is the most pleasant (1177a23–25),
self-sufficient (*autarkes*), leisurely (*scholastikon*), and free from fatigue
(*atruton*, ἄτρυτον) (1177b21–22). In the list of these by now familiar
features, let me emphasize the third: that it aims at nothing beyond the
activity itself. As we noted, some excellent moral activity is chosen not only
for its own sake but also for the sake of something else, such as military or
political ends. So, this activity is not as final, or complete, as one chosen for
itself and not for anything else. This conclusion follows from a principle
about finality we find Aristotle using in *EN* I 7 (1097a25–30) which states
that one activity is more complete (*teleion*) than another if it is chosen only
for its own sake. So, if some activity is chosen for itself and not for the sake
of anything else, this activity will be what is "absolutely complete" (*haplos
teleia*, ἁπλῶς τέλεια) (*EN* 1097a33). Aristotle tells us there is such an

---

[65] The Greek is: οὐδεὶς γὰρ αἱρεῖται τὸ πολεμεῖν τοῦ πολεμεῖν ἕνεκα (1177b9).

[66] The Greek is: οὐδὲν γὰρ ἀπ' αὐτῆς γίνεται παρὰ τὸ θεωρῆσαι (1177b2).

[67] On the "continuity" accorded study: "we are able to think more continuously (*sunechestate*) than we
are able to perform any action" (θεωρεῖν τε γὰρ δυνάμεθα συνεχῶς μᾶλλον ἢ πράττειν ὁτιοῦν, *EN*
1177a21–22); the suggestion that *theoria* being "most continuous" concerns its being an activity of
a non-composite faculty, the intellect, seems reasonable, as Gauthier and Jolif (1970, 879) suggest.
It may be related also to Aristotle's comment about activities being more and less complete
depending on the object and condition of the faculty, cf. *EN* X 4, 1174b21–23.

activity, and it is *theoria*, or study. Therefore, the activity the gods engage in will be *theoria*, as this activity is the most complete. Furthermore, since happiness was initially agreed to be an activity, the happiness that the gods enjoy will comprise the activity of *theoria*.

While Aristotle is not unaware that looking to the gods to provide a standard for the best human activity sets a high bar for us – as he concedes, "such a life (*bios*) would be more than human" (*EN* X 7, 1177b26–27)[68] – this admission does not diminish the uniqueness of the highest activity. From a human perspective, he agrees that we cannot engage in *theoria* continuously; we cannot live a life of *theoria*.[69] The reasons supporting this admission are obvious, including that humans have physical, material needs, as well as psychological, affective needs for friends, family, and community. Nonetheless, he recommends the activity of *theoria* both for its own qualities and also as an aspirational goal, stating, "we should try to become immortal as far as possible, and to do all we can to live according with what is best in us" (*EN* X 7, 1177b33–34).[70] Yet, here Aristotle is endorsing the way of life that is directed at intelligence (*nous*), not simply praising the activity of *theoria*, for, as we know, *theoria* itself cannot comprise a full human life as humans have other needs such as family, friends, and political life. In this sense, the human best life, directed by intelligence, is one that must include excellent moral activity, and other good things.[71]

In *EN*, Aristotle's affirmation of *theoria* as the highest activity emerges from several different lines of reasoning including the discussion in *EN* X 4 about complete and pleasant activities, like seeing, the unique epistemic grounds for *theoria* in X 7, and the argument from the gods' theoretical activity in X 8. Having completed the discussion about *theoria* from both the human and divine angles, he returns in X 9 to the starting point of the work[72] by admitting that "in matters of action, the end is not to study (*to theoresai*) and to know (*to gnonai*) the specific things to be done, but to

---

[68] The Greek runs thus: ὁ δὲ τοιοῦτος ἂν εἴη βίος κρείττων ἢ κατ' ἄνθρωπον (1177b26–27).

[69] The reference to *bios* at *EN* 1177b27 needs to be taken as referring to a whole life, not a part, as some interpreters, like Gauthier (1958), and Gauthier and Jolif (1970, 893–96) have done; see also Cooper (1986, 157–63).

[70] The Greek runs thus: ἐφ' ὅσον ἐνδέχεται ἀθανατίζειν καὶ πάντα ποιεῖν πρὸς τὸ ζῆν κατὰ τὸ κράτιστον τῶν ἐν αὑτῷ (1177b33–34).

[71] In this regard, the argument has been made that being a good person, or having moral excellence, is the only way in which we are able to perform complete activities like *theoria*, on which see Olfert (2014).

[72] For the familiar claim about seeking the practical, not the theoretical, good, see *EN* I 6 (1096b35–1097a13), VI 7 (1141b5–23, passim).

do them" (*EN* X 9, 1179a35–b2).[73] With these words, he returns to the
starting point with which the *Ethics* begins: "let us discuss the aim of
politics . . . the highest good attainable by action" (*EN* I 4, 1095a15–16).[74]
While the return to the same topic with which the work begins has
occasioned some comment about it displaying a kind of chiasmus, in my
view, the referral to the topic comprises more a rhetorical figure than it
closes a ring composition.[75]

4.7 Comparison of *Theoria* in Plato and Aristotle

In concluding the analysis about the nature of *theoria* in *EN* X 7–8, let us
take stock of the key similarities between Platonic and Aristotelian *theoria*.
With respect to Aristotle's account, it has been suggested that the generic
definition of *theoria* consists in being a complete activity, to which we may
add that its specific feature is being the activity (*energeia*) of the intellect
(*nous*). More specifically, *theoria* for Aristotle consists in an exercise of the
highest intellectual faculty, *nous*, that involves apprehending the highest
objects of knowledge (*EN* 1177a20–21). In this description, we find an
account of *theoria* that closely resembles that which Plato gives in *Rep.* VII
and *Symp.* 210a–211d with reference to three points, briefly described as
activity, objects, and way of life. First, Plato's account reflects the elevated,
apprehensive nature of the activity by the use of the verbs *theaomai* and
theoreo, and more specifically, that its objects are the highest theoretical
entities, Platonic Forms. In reaching these objects, the dialogues also show
that the activity of *theoria* requires an "ascent" that involves both a
cognitive and an affective change in the thinking subject, as the knower
progresses from a mundane, perceptually-fixated state of awareness to an
intellectually-oriented state of beholding immaterial essences which the
knower then desires to imitate.[76] The cognitive and affective aspects of the
ascent are well described in Plato's *Symposium*, where the lover of beauty,
"beginning from beautiful bodies, is always climbing upwards for the sake

---

[73] The Greek runs thus: οὐκ ἔστιν ἐν τοῖς πρακτοῖς τέλος τὸ θεωρῆσαι ἕκαστα καὶ γνῶναι, ἀλλὰ
μᾶλλον τὸ πράττειν αὐτά (1179a35–b2).

[74] The Greek runs: τί ἐστιν οὗ λέγομεν τὴν πολιτικὴν ἐφίεσθαι καὶ τί τὸ πάντων ἀκρότατον τῶν
πρακτῶν ἀγαθῶν (1095a15–16).

[75] The *EN* has not escaped notice as being a ring form composition, largely in its similarity to Plato's
Republic, as, for example, Sparshott argues about the two works (1982); Keaney (1992, 72–95)
similarly argues that the Aristotelian work *Ath. Con.* reflects ring form and chiasmus.

[76] The description of the knower, the philosopher, trying to imitate the forms comes out vividly in
Rep. VII 514a–516b; the notion of the change in perspective is marked elsewhere as *Symp.* 210a–e,
211c–d, *Phdr.* 249b–c; see also Kraut (1997), Vlastos (1997).

of the beautiful, just as one ascends a flight of stairs, from one to two, and two to all beautiful bodies ... at last to that particular study which is nothing other than the study of the beautiful itself, so that finally he knows what beauty itself is" (*Symp.* 211c1–d1).[77] While Aristotle does not detail the epistemic stages of an ascent to *theoria* in his account of human *theoria* in *EN* X 7 as Plato does, two texts may be mentioned in a similar regard. First, Aristotle describes the progressive unfolding of cognitive faculties culminating with *nous* in *An. Po.* II 19 (100a3–a14), where, beginning with sense-perception (*aesthesis*), we have a capacity to retain perceptual images in memory (*mneme*) that are initially unified in experience (*empeiria*), providing the universal for art (*techne*), and finally, for scientific knowledge (*episteme*). This account of cognitive faculties, broadly similar to the description of cognitive abilities in *Meta.* I 1, resembles that of *Symp.* (210a–212a) and *Rep.* VI (509d–511d) in naming an upward progression of intellectual abilities culminating with *nous*, intellect.[78] For example, in the ascent passage, Plato details stages of cognitive apprehension in the lover, beginning with sense-perception of beautiful bodies (210a5–6) followed by that of souls (210b6–8), the beauty in activities and laws (210c3–4), followed by beauty in knowledge (*episteme*) (210c7); finally, after seeing the "ocean of beauty" (210d4–5), the lover "suddenly, catches sight of something wonderfully beautiful in its nature" (210e4–5), the form of beauty itself.[79] The point in the ascent passage indicating the stage of noetic apprehension of the form of beauty is the description that the lover is "beholding (*theomenos*) beautiful things in the right order and correctly" (210e3). I think we must understand the activity of *nous* here as tantamount to *theoria*, that which Aristotle defines in *EN* X 7 (1177a16–18) as being the activity of *nous*. So, the consideration of these texts provides a sketch of faculties that culminate in *nous*, the activity of which we see Aristotle define as philosophical *theoria* in EN X 7, a sketch which overlaps with Plato's description of cognitive stages in *Symp.* 210a–211a.

---

[77] The full Greek passage runs: τοῦτο γὰρ δή ἐστι τὸ ὀρθῶς ἐπὶ τὰ ἐρωτικὰ ἰέναι ἢ ὑπ' ἄλλου ἄγεσθαι, ἀρχόμενον ἀπὸ τῶνδε τῶν καλῶν ἐκείνου ἕνεκα τοῦ καλοῦ ἀεὶ ἐπανιέναι, ὥσπερ ἐπαναβασμοῖς χρώμενον, ἀπὸ ἑνὸς ἐπὶ δύο καὶ ἀπὸ δυοῖν ἐπὶ πάντα τὰ καλὰ σώματα, καὶ ἀπὸ τῶν καλῶν σωμάτων ἐπὶ τὰ καλὰ ἐπιτηδεύματα, καὶ ἀπὸ τῶν ἐπιτηδευμάτων ἐπὶ τὰ καλὰ μαθήματα, καὶ ἀπὸ τῶν μαθημάτων ἐπ' ἐκεῖνο τὸ μάθημα τελευτῆσαι, ὅ ἐστιν οὐκ ἄλλου ἢ αὐτοῦ ἐκείνου τοῦ καλοῦ μάθημα, καὶ γνῷ αὐτὸ τελευτῶν ὅ ἔστι καλόν (*Symp.* 211c–d).

[78] The progression of cognitive states in *Meta.* I 1 differs from that in *An. Po.* II 19 in one aspect, that concerning a focus on the theoretical-practical distinction of knowing.

[79] Trans. *Symp.*, Nehamas and Woodruff (1989).

Returning to the previously mentioned features of *theoria* common to both accounts, the primary one consists in the nature of the activity itself: like Plato, Aristotle holds that the activity is the exercise of our highest faculty, and comprises an intellectual vision described as "divine" (*EN* X 7, 1177a14–15, a27, a30; cf. *Rep.* VII, 516b4–7, 532b6–c6). In this respect, both hold that engaging in the activity of *theoria* comprises an activity that allows humans to approach divinity.[80] Here a cautionary note is needed: while it may seem reasonable to infer from these lines that in exercising *theoria*, humans engage in the very same activity as the gods, this is not true, primarily for reasons connected to humans' composite nature.[81] To be more precise, first, Plato and Aristotle find that the path to human *theoria* is arduous, requiring extensive discursive thought with its requisite errors and discontinuities; second, both thinkers consider *theoria* as performed by embodied human intellects as intermittent at best, exercised in episodic bursts and interspersed with mundane and perhaps errant lines of thought. Neither of these limitations pertains to the *theoria* of the gods, whose eternal thought is effortless and continuous, as made clear by Aristotle's descriptions of god's thinking in *Meta.* XII 7 (1072b18–30) and XII 9 (1074b25–35). Consequently, when we find Plato or Aristotle qualifying human *theoria* as "divine" (*theion*), we should proceed cautiously, taking the attribution to imply there is a basis for similarity between human and divine *theoria*, not that humans and gods engage in the same activity as such.[82] Notwithstanding the differences between the two forms of *theoria*, describing human *theoria* as "divine" is, indeed, significant, reflecting the elevated status and uniqueness of *nous* among our intellectual faculties. Additionally, the aspects of *theoria* that incline Aristotle to qualify it as divine also direct him to recommend its practice for humans (cf. *EN* X 7, 1177b27–1178a2, 1178b7–23). Specifically, by identifying the formal features of *theoria* – being an activity, continuous, self-sufficient, chosen for itself, and most pleasant – with those of happiness, Aristotle concludes that theoretical activity affords us "complete happiness" (*EN* 1177b19–25; cf. 1178b21–22). These same claims about *theoria* and divinity in *EN* X 7 recall Plato's description, perhaps best

---

[80] In *EN* X 7, Aristotle makes clear that the proper activity of the god or gods is "theoretical," hence, *theoria* (cf. *EN* 1178b8–22).

[81] That is, the abstract thinking exercised by the embodied human intellect, not by the disembodied intellectual soul Plato describes, at times metaphorically in terms of its circular motion, cf. *Phdr.* 246b, 247c1–2, 249c3–4, *Tim.* 90c8–d1.

[82] The most plausible option thus appears to be a relationship of similarity; this relation does not meet the conditions for genus-species or type-token relation, in my view.

expressed in *Symposium* where he states: "In that way of way of life above all others . . . one finds human life worth living in studying beauty itself" (*Symp.* 211d1–3), adding that the one who "brings forth true virtue and has raised it up" becomes "loved by god" (*theophilei*) and "immortal" (*athanatos*) (*Symp.* 212a3–7).[83] For both thinkers, then, exercising theoretical insight, *theoria*, requires moral virtue, affording humans complete happiness and a measure of the divine.

---

[83] The full second passage is: ἢ οὐκ ἐνθυμῇ, ἔφη, ὅτι ἐνταῦθα αὐτῷ μοναχοῦ γενήσεται, ὁρῶντι ᾧ ὁρατὸν τὸ καλόν, τίκτειν οὐκ εἴδωλα ἀρετῆς, ἅτε οὐκ εἰδώλου ἐφαπτομένῳ, ἀλλὰ ἀληθῆ, ἅτε τοῦ ἀληθοῦς ἐφαπτομένῳ· τεκόντι δὲ ἀρετὴν ἀληθῆ καὶ θρεψαμένῳ ὑπάρχει θεοφιλεῖ γενέσθαι, καὶ εἴπέρ τῳ ἄλλῳ ἀνθρώπων ἀθανάτῳ καὶ ἐκείνῳ (*Symp.* 212a2–7).

CHAPTER 5

Theoria *and Its Objects*

[A]t first, he would see shadows most easily, and then images of
humans and other things in water; later on, the things themselves . . .
Finally, the sun, not images in water . . . but the sun itself in its own
place and be able to study (*theasthasthai*) what it is.

(*Rep.* 516a4–b5)

5.1 Objects of Traditional *Theoria*

According to accounts of traditional *theoria*, which includes attendance at
healing sanctuaries as well as at designated festivals, one of the constituent
activities consists in visitors observing images of gods as part of the
experience. The images, called *agalmata* (ἀγάλματα), are sculpted statues
or other representations of the deities to whom the sites are dedicated. In
the case of the panhellenic festivals (i.e., Olympian, Pythian, Isthmian, and
Nemean festivals), the sites contain temples with statues of the designated
deities, Zeus, Apollo, and Poseidon, in the four abovementioned sites. For
example, the site at Olympia includes temples to Zeus and to Hera, with
the temple to Zeus having a famed statue of Zeus by Pheidias inside, and
outside, flanking the pediments and metopes, agonistic scenes of chariot
races between two heroes, Pelops and Oenomaus, labors of Herakles, and
battles of Lapiths and Centaurs.[1] The temple to Apollo at Delphi, the site
of the leading sanctuary as well as a major festival, displays a number of
statues for the visitors as well, if we consider the description by Euripides
in his play *Ion*.[2] In addition to the sites of the panhellenic festivals like
Olympia and Delphi, perhaps that most familiar is the Athenian Acropolis,

---

[1] For discussion of the temple decoration, see Dillon (1997, 106–107).
[2] While Euripides' account in *Ion* is fictive, the description is taken as useful to highlight the role of
images, or *agalmata*, in a visitor's theoric experience at sanctuaries and temples.

where Athens hosts two festivals, the greater and lesser Panathenaea.[3] The colossal bronze statue of Athena Promachos by Pheidias is situated on the Acropolis between the Parthenon, dedicated to the city's eponymous deity, Athena, and the Propylaea. As well, the temple itself contains statues of Athena and is adorned with *agalmata*, statues of gods, goddesses, and heroes along its sides.

Before we look at how these *agalmata* are used in traditional *theoria*, it may be useful to offer a few notes about etymological connections involving the term *agalma* and connecting them to the verbs *theoreo and theaomai* that we have remarked on. First, the noun *agalma*, from the verb *agallo* (ἀγάλλω) meaning "to glorify," "exalt," is used with the accusative case of the noun "god" (*thelos/a*) to signify "to give honor to a god." Second, the viewing of *agalmata* is expressed using the core verbs *theoreo* and *theaomai* as well as the noun *theoria*. In fact, the viewing of cult statues comprises a specialized use of the verbs *theoreo* and *theaomai* as is reflected in accounts by a Pythagorean philosopher, Parmeniskos of Metapontum, and by Democritus in the fifth century. Both accounts describe experiences of viewing statues using *theoreo* verbal expressions.[4] For a general use, we may mention Plato's employment of the noun *agalma* in *Protagoras* and *Symposium*. In the former, Protagoras provides a mythic account of animal creation that details humans as the only created animals who worship gods, and "set up altars and images of gods" (ἐπεχείρει βωμούς τε ἱδρύεσθαι καὶ ἀγάλματα θεῶν) (*Prot.* 322a5). In the *Symposium*, we find the famous simile about Socrates and Silenus in Alcibiades' speech where he compares Socrates to a status of Silenus, which in being pulled apart ". . . contains inside images of the gods" (ἔνδοθεν ἀγάλματα ἔχοντες θεῶν) (*Symp.* 215b3). There are other, frequent references in Plato conjoining *agalma* and *theos* (god) or *theion* (divine)[5] in addition to those where we find *agalma/agalmata* as signifying "image" or even "likeness," in which case the term is synonymous with *eikon* as in *Rep.* VII, 517d10, where the term is used as a metaphorical allusion to laws of a city.[6]

---

[3] These, like the panhellenic festivals, were established well before the 4th century, according to Rutherford (Rutherford 2013, 41–42).

[4] The Pythagorean is reported as seeing "a statue remarkable to contemplate" (*agalma ti theorein axiologon*) in Athenaeus 14.614b, and Democritus employs *theoreo* in conjunction with *eidola* (DK, *VS* B195), cf. Rutherford (2013, 143, 143, fn. 5).

[5] For other Platonic references to "images of the gods" (ἀγάλματα τῶν θεῶν), see *Tim.* 37c7, *Laws* XI, 931d4, *Ep.* 984a1.

[6] The use of *agalmata* at *Rep.* 517d10 is said to refer to the laws of the city, or more precisely: "the enacted laws of the city" while the representations or misrepresentations are "the shadows" (*skiai*) that come from them, according to Adam (1965, vol. 2, 96 fn.); cf. Shorey (1895, 287).

Provided with this data and returning to the issue concerning the objects of traditional *theoria*, we know, first, that statues, or images, of the deities are erected at shrines and temples where they are observed by the visitors, and second, it is suggested that the statues are frequently presented as to be seen in a certain order, typically, a circular or semi-circular fashion, which repeats the circular motion central to the practice of *theoria*.[7] The second point raises an issue that may require elaboration by means of a few examples that suggest the kind of movement visitors are considered to have followed in viewing some specific sites. The first concerns aspects of viewing of the Parthenon while the second example arises from a textual account of visitors looking at statues in the temple to Apollo at Delphi. Beginning with the Parthenon, we may note that the large pathway ringing the Parthenon allows the attending visitors to view the sculptures adorning the tympanum and triglyphs depicting mythic scenes, like the battles between Greeks and Amazons; it also allows visual engagement with the inner frieze that represents scenes from Athenian civic life, and specifically, a festival procession of the Panathenaea.[8] Since visitors to the Parthenon ascend the hill from the west, and the main entrance to the temple is on the east, they must walk around the building in a circular direction.[9] More central evidence that the sculpted images are intended to be seen in a circular manner arises from the fact that the figures of the sculptures on the building have a directional orientation, moving around the building in a sequence of imagistic narratives. Thus, there is no doubt that the sculpted figures comprising the scenes in the decoration are intended to be seen in circular (or semi-circular) fashion, moving from the western side of the temple to allow visitors to follow the narrative scenes sculpted on the northern, then the eastern, sides. This matter concerning the circular motion of viewing of sculpted images of gods is raised in relation to another set of secular images, but let me postpone that discussion while we look to another example of viewing images of gods, this time made in relation to the viewing experience at Delphi presented in Euripides' *Ion*.

In the *Ion*, we find an extended description of female visitors looking at the sculpted images of gods, *agalmata*, and discussing their reactions. In the scene in question, the speakers are servant women who are

---

[7] See Goldhill (1996, 19–21), and below (this chapter), for further discussion.
[8] Scholarship about the Parthenon frieze has a long record, but for recent discussion, see, for example, Boardman (1999), Marconi (2009), Neils (2001), Stillwell (1969).
[9] It appears that, after entering the Propylaea on the west, the *theoria* likely would be following a semi-circular path to the altar on the east via the northern side of the temple owing in part to its greater expanse of land (suggested by Dr. Laura Gawlinski in conversation).

accompanying Creusa, the Queen of Athens, on her *theoria* to the sanctuary at Delphi. Creusa and her husband Xuthus have traveled from Athens to Delphi on a private *theoria* seeking to remedy their lack of children. In this focal scene, the female attendants walk around the temple looking at the statues, making remarks to one another about them: it is worth noting that the images cause them to remember other sculpted images – like those of Athena and other deities at Athens, their home city. Euripides fills the scene with their sense-perceptions, recollections, and the associated stories of the gods. The passage runs:

> So holy Athens is not the only place
> Where the gods have pillared courtyards
> And are honored as guardians of the streets.
>
> Apollo's temple, too, has the twin pediments,
> Like brows on a smiling face.
> Look—look at this! The Lernian snake
> Being killed by Herakles with his golden falchion—
> Do look, friend!
> —Yes, I see.
> But who is this other next to him
> Waving a flaming torch? Is it the man
> Whose adventures we are told at weaving-time
> The brave fighter Iolaus,
> Who went with Herakles on his labours
> And stayed with him to the bitter end?
> —Oh! And look here
> At Bellerophon astride his winged horse
> Killing the monster with three bodies
> And fire belching from its nostrils!
> —I am looking eagerly on every side.
> See, carved on the marble wall,
> The Giants overcome by the Gods in battle!
> —Yes, we can see it from over here.
> Ah! But behold her there,
> Brandishing her Gorgon shield over Enceladus—
> —I see her, my own Pallas Athene! [λεύσσω Παλλάδ᾽, ἐμὰν θεόν]
> —And the thunderbolt, smoldering and irresistible
> which Zeus holds ready to hurl from heaven!
> I see huge Mimas fiercely raging,
> Charred with the flame of the thunderbolt.
> —Here's yet another earth-born giant
> Destroyed by Dionysus with no weapon
> But his thyrsus wreathed with ivy-shoots.
>
>   (*Ion*, ll. 184–218, tr. Vellicott)

The discussion among the female attendants[10] develops a scene with some characteristic features of standard *theoria*: first, the strongly visual nature of the scene; second, the role played by *agalmata*, sacred images, in their perceptions; third, the rotational figure of their walking and looking. Regarding the type of viewing described, we note that the women are walking around, looking at the statues in the pediments, and their perceptions lead them to another kind of visual experience, their recollections of seeing deities in prior temple visits. As we follow their speech, we hear them recollecting seven or eight stories of gods and heroes, brought to their mind by the statues they see, namely, Herakles, Iolaus, Bellerophon, Athena, Zeus, Mimas, and Dionysus – and, in addition, Apollo, whose temple is adorned "with twin pediments, like brows on a face" (ll. 188–89). The second feature concerns the fact that their conversation contains several verbs signifying visual sense-perception, namely, "look at," "see," "gaze at," "behold." In one section, the passage uses the verb *leusso* (λεύσσω) meaning "to behold" or "gaze," which is used in repetition between two attendants. Thus, one attendant exclaims with reference to seeing the image of Athena, "Behold her there, brandishing her Gorgon shield ..." (λεύσσεις οὖν ἐπ' Ἐγκελάδῳ / γοργωπὸν πάλλουσαν ἴτυν ...) (ll. 209–10), and another replies using the same verb: "I see her, my own Pallas Athene!" (λεύσσω Παλλάδ', ἐμὰν θεόν) (l. 211).[11] The use of visual perception verbs nine times in the short passage emphasizes the theoric elements of the scene, some of which we touched on above, but may be further enumerated as follows. First, the female attendants are attending Creusa on her *theoria* to Delphi, and moreover, in entering the sanctuary, they are themselves engaged in a *theoria* as they are actively looking at the statues of gods (*agalmata*) on the temple; third, their collective *theoria* is augmented by sharing their visual perceptions as recollections of the stories about the gods, goddesses, and heroes.

After reflecting on the women's shared, visual experience at the sanctuary, we return to consider the nature and objects of this kind of *theoria*. It is worth noting, initially, that Nightingale finds the viewing of sacred images an essential feature of the practice. In her view, the *agalmata* are central to the religious experience of visitors to festivals and sanctuaries alike: since images of

---

[10] In the list of dramatic persons, the term for the female attendant is *therapaina*, normally used to signify "female servant," or "handmaid," but one who is not a slave; Vellacott renders the term as "slave," which seems incongruous with their speeches reflecting fidelity to Athens and to Creusa (*Ion*, ll. 185–220).

[11] Their remarks reflect the extent to which they as servants or handmaids identify with Athens and Athena, her patron deity, so much as to exclaim "my city" (l. 719), and "my goddess" (l. 211); concerning their identification with these symbols and with their mistress, Creusa, see Loraux (1993, 190–92).

the gods are "housed in temples and sacred precincts," they appear "in every religious festival," comprising "one of the most important 'spectacles' that are seen"; they also play an essential part in what she terms "the 'ritualized visualization' that characterizes theoric viewing at religious sanctuaries" (Nightingale 2004, 163). Taking the concept of viewing religious icons as central to *theoria* allows us to appreciate more fully the activity represented through the verbal exchanges of the women attendants (*Ion*, ll. 184–213). Specifically, we can understand the pivotal role played by *agalmata* in the Chorus' shared experience in viewing the statues on the temple pediments and metopes. The visual aspect of the whole scene is emphasized by the ensuing lines between the Chorus and Ion, the chief attendant. For example, when Ion appears in the courtyard, the women inquire whether they may enter the sanctuary, to which he answers they may not unless they have made offerings of sacrifice (ll. 226–29). They reply they have not and since they do not wish to do what is "not allowed," they tell him they will remain where they are, as they "like looking around outside" (cf. ll. 229–31). To this statement Ion replies they "may look at everything that is permitted" (πάντα θεᾶσθ', ὅ τι καὶ θέμις, ὄμμασι) (l. 232); they then state that their mistress gave them permission "to look upon (*eisidein*) the temple of the god" (... θεοῦ γύαλα τάδ' εἰσιδεῖν, l. 233).[12] Thus, we find that lines 229–33 are filled with verbs of visual perception: Ion uses the verb *theaomai* (to observe) in l. 232, and the female attendants employ perceptual terms in ll. 231, 233. Both passages exhibit the visual aspect of the women's activity at the sanctuary as well as the central role played by the religious images they are observing.

After considering the use of images in *theoria* related to sanctuary visitation, it is worth remarking on what we may consider the objects of secular *theoria*, if only briefly. As background for this point, classical scholars connect traditional *theoria* with the notion of spectatorship, specifically, that taking place in a public arena, like the theater or the city assembly, where, they maintain, the specifically political function of *theoria* is played out. In this regard, public spaces in Athens are deemed the necessary backdrop against which political *theoria*, which one scholar describes as "the participatory attendance of the spectator in the political ... rites of the city," is carried out.[13] If political *theoria* takes place in the assembly where citizens are acting as spectators, it seems reasonable to

---

[12] It may be noted that when the attendants say they have permission "to see" (*eisidein*) the temple (*Ion*, l. 233), the verb *eisorao* signifies "to look upon," "behold," and with accusative (as here), "to pay regard to, respect."

[13] Goldhill (1996, 19) quoted by Ker (2000, 304) about the political role of *theoria* in Athens.

conclude that the immediate objects of such viewing are simply one's fellow citizens (Ker 2000). Yet, as Goldhill points out, inanimate objects also may be involved in political *theoria* in the sense that citizens may be performing a kind of secular *theoria* by engaging in certain public forms of observation that have meaning as political activities. For example, he suggests that citizens walking along the *Stoa Poikile* are observing statues of civic figures lining the colonnade that borders the Athenian Agora (Goldhill 1996). In walking around the Agora, then, citizens can view the statues of political figures, like Solon, that are placed along the portico. The visual experience of observing statues of civic figures is complemented by viewing wooden pieces on which Solon's laws are inscribed (called *axones*) that are set up so that, in effect, the citizens can visualize both the lawgiver and the laws he gave (Ker 2000, 305).

Using the above descriptions of Goldhill and Ker, it seems reasonable to suggest a parallel between political and religious *theoria* on two points: first, in political *theoria*, citizens may "theorize," in the sense of "contemplate," images of their lawgivers who represent Athenian law in a fashion similar to the attendants on a religious *theoria* who look at the temple statues and reflect on their gods. The latter kind of *theoria* is, of course, well exemplified in the activity of the female attendants in the *Ion* passage discussed in which the women servants walk around the sanctuary observing the statues and recollecting stories of the deities represented. A second point of intersection concerns a more abstract feature: the circular motion underlying *theoria* when it is performed in situ, at a specific shrine or site. For example, consider attendants at a Panathenaic festival visiting the Parthenon: they first pass through the Propylaea and then follow the Via Sacra along the north side of the Parthenon. In doing so, they are walking parallel to the long, northern side of the temple containing sculptures in the metopes and more importantly, the frieze that depicts a festival procession, perhaps, that of the Panathenaic festival. This portion of the viewing thus allows the observers to re-enact in public the same activity that is represented by the figures in the frieze in that the public procession of the festival curves around the temple to the main entrance on eastern side. So, in following the direction of the procession, visitors repeat the direction of figures of the bas relief composing the frieze: in effect, following a semi-circular path in walking. This motion appears to be the same kind followed by visitors to the Agora who move along the colonnade in the Stoa that Goldhill has described.[14] In both cases, the visitors

---

[14] For discussion about the viewing of images in Athenian public spaces, including the Acropolis, see Goldhill (1996, 19–21); for analysis of the role of motion involved in observing public architecture, see As and Schodek (2008, 27–33).

follow a presentation of sculpted figures, or images, in a certain order that results in a circular or semi-circular direction as they move around the temple or colonnade from a beginning to a focal point, and then back.

Returning to the visual element at work in religious and political *theoria*, we see that whether one is viewing bas reliefs of mythical and historical figures or observing wooden slabs with inscribed laws of the city, the activity involves looking at theoric objects that function as culturally "sacred" images. Therefore, the feature of observing *agalmata* holds across secular and religious *theoria* despite differences among theoric objects, whether images of deities or of political figures. Again, the differences among the immediate objects of *theoria* may imply different mediate objects as well, namely, the deities in the case of traditional *theoria* or the laws in the case of political *theoria*. But despite differences in the mediate and immediate objects of religious and political *theoria*, two general conclusions seem well-supported. First, both religious and political *theoria* require images for their exercise, for example, using sacred images of gods or representations of politicians for their active performance. Second, political *theoria* possesses features that distinguish it from religious *theoria*, such as its role in preserving democratic institutions, which is not clearly the case with religious *theoria*.[15] In the transition from religious to *Platonic* – that is, to philosophical – *theoria*, it becomes evident that Plato chooses to connect *theoria* with the standard objects, *agalmata*, but for Plato, the latter are secular images or representations that nonetheless play a similar role to that in traditional *theoria*. However, the difference consists in the fact that in Platonic *theoria*, the images observed, or *agalmata*, have less importance than the mediate objects to which these images give rise.[16]

5.2 Objects of Platonic *Theoria*

5.2.1 Comparing Objects in Platonic and Traditional Theoria

Nightingale offers a persuasive case that connects the use of *agalmata* in traditional *theoria* and the way in which Plato employs the term *agalma* as "divine image" in his account of philosophical *theoria*.[17] Yet in addition to

---

[15] The mutual support between Athenian democratic institutions and political *theoria* is reflected, for example, in Cleon's description of Athenians as "spectators of speeches" (θεαταὶ μὲν τῶν λόγων) (Thucydides, *Hist*. III, 38), according to Goldhill (1996, 19).

[16] In advance of the discussion about Platonic *theoria*, we should note that it is being restricted to the objects of human *theoria* and does not include consideration of the *theoria* of the gods.

[17] See Nightingale's discussion of *agalmata* in Plato's thinking (Nightingale 2004, 37, 87, 139, 157–68).

the continuity she finds, I suggest there are differences that Plato exploits to his advantage for developing the notion of philosophical *theoria* by redefining certain characteristics of the image and its role in relation to contemplative activity. Plato enlarges the conventional idea of what counts as an *agalma*: he expands the term to cover items from carved Silenus-statues containing images of gods (*Symp.* 215b3) to perceptual visions leading the observer upward to the divine. For example, in *Phaedrus*, we find that the perception of a young man's beauty by a lover carries the philosophical soul upwards to recollect its experience with beauty in its pre-incarnated state of knowledge of the form (*Phdr.* 250b). In the well-known analogy of the charioteer, Plato describes the soul's ascent using the metaphor of charioteer and twin horses that represent the rational and irrational parts of the human psyche such that, when the lover sees the beautiful face of his beloved, it causes desire and conflict in the soul and so, between the horses. While the lustful horse drags the philosophical soul toward sexual contact, the charioteer sees in a flash the beauty of the boy's face which reminds the rational soul of the form of beauty it knows already (*Phdr.* 254b1–4).

For purposes of comparing the objects in Plato's account to those in traditional *theoria*, we begin with Plato's description of the experience: "As the charioteer looks upon [him], his memory (*mneme*) is brought back to the nature of beauty (*ten tou kallous physin*), and he sees it again, standing with moderation (*sophrosune*) on a pedestal of purity" (*Phdr.* 254b5–7).[18] The language of this passage reinforces the earlier analogy of the young man revering the beautiful image to that in which "he would sacrifice to his beloved as to an *agalma* and a god" (θύοι ἂν ὡς ἀγάλματι καὶ θεῷ τοῖς παιδικοῖς, *Phdr.* 251a6–7). Thus, the act of beholding the beautiful image is likened to religious *theoria*. In regard to the visual element, the larger passage about the image in *Phaedrus* (roughly 249d–251b) may be compared to the scene of the female attendants visiting the shrine in Euripides' *Ion*. More specifically, the elements of visual perception, sacred images, pedestals of statues, memory, recollection, honoring and sacrificing to the gods are all common in both passages. Taking some of the features individually, first, the visual experiences of the charioteer and the female attendants are prompted by the sculpted objects they see to which they react with awe. In the play, the female attendants are looking at *agalmata*, sculpted images of gods, as they walk about the temple recollecting other images of deities they have seen. In similar fashion, Plato chooses certain

---

[18] The Greek runs thus: ἰδόντος δὲ τοῦ ἡνιόχου ἡ μνήμη πρὸς τὴν τοῦ κάλλους φύσιν ἠνέχθη, καὶ πάλιν εἶδεν αὐτὴν μετὰ σωφροσύνης ἐν ἁγνῷ βάθρῳ βεβῶσαν (*Phdr.* 254b5–7).

words to describe the way the charioteer sees the form of beauty "standing ... on a pedestal (*bathron*) of purity" (*Phdr.* 254b6), creating a phrase that invites comparison to a sculpted statue standing on a base (*bathron*) for purposes of worship. As Nightingale has pointed out, the image of the beautiful youth that Plato describes plays the role of a traditional *agalma* in the ritualized viewing of a visitor to a sanctuary (Nightingale 2004, 163).

The comparison between sanctuary *theoria* and Platonic gazing might be further enlarged, in my view, by comparing the two epistemic levels. For, in Plato and Euripides, the active looking at sacred images comprises what we may consider the lowest epistemic stage which, for Plato conduces to philosophical *theoria*, but for both, consists in a visual apprehension leading to thought about the divine. Having stated this, we should be aware of the differences: in Euripides, perceptions of statues of gods lead to the recollections of prior perception of gods, whereas in Plato, perception of a beautiful face awakens the intellect to an imperceptible, intelligible object. Plato thus conceives the perceived image as a pathway by which the rational soul recollects some image of beauty that it knew prior to being incarnated. In so doing, the visual perception of a particular, beautiful thing successfully stirs the soul's recollection of the form, and the soul moves upwards towards the intelligible object.[19] For Plato, then, the role of the perceived sensible *agalma* in relation to the epistemological ascent of the knower cannot be underestimated, for without the visual perception of the *agalma*, the soul does not ascend to the intelligible form.

Keeping in mind the differentiating factor that the mediate object in Platonic *theoria* is an intelligible form, it is evident that the perception of a sacred statue and the perception of a sensible quality, such as beauty in a face, play analogous roles in traditional and Platonic *theoria*, perhaps in the sense of providing causes in the process of knowing.[20] As Euripides describes the experience in the *Ion*, the visitors to the temple behold sculpted images representing gods, goddesses, heroes, and the like that function as the immediate objects of traditional *theoria*. In addition, the attendants' perceptions lead them to recollect previous perceptions of

[19] The ascent of the rational soul using recollection described here is to be identified with the fully conscious knowledge of Forms that Ferejohn (2006, 221) recognizes as represented by the top half of the divided line or the upper world of the cave, and not with "pre-philosophical cognition" of the ordinary person that is defended by Bostock (1986, 72).

[20] I suggest it is not unreasonable to consider the perceptual element involved as "the that out of which" or "the that by which" (cf. *Physics* II, 4) a person comes to know something; compare Bolton on the role of incidental perceptions as causes of thinking (Bolton 2005, 217–22).

images they have seen of the gods.[21] So, too, in *Phaedrus* where the perception of a beautiful particular thing, like the beauty of a specific face, functions in a similar way: the image, like a traditional *agalma*, stimulates the recollection of something other than perception – for Plato, something far greater – which has the potential to lead the philosophical soul upwards to the knowledge of the form of beauty (*Phdr.* 251e3). The epistemic process Plato describes coincides with the activity described in sanctuary *theoria*, at least at the initial stages. The visual experience of *agalmata* had by the female attendants in *Ion* shows them recounting their recollections of gods from other statues, and thus far, their process corresponds to the ascent that Plato describes in *Phaedrus*. As we recall, in *Phaedrus*, the lover's perception of beauty in the face of the beloved "kickstarts" a process of recollection, which – if all goes well – culminates in the recognition of the form of beauty (cf. *Phdr.* 254b5–6). So, the *Phaedrus* passage leads us to two conclusions: first, the perception of a beautiful face functions as an *agalma*, and second, the perception functions as both material and efficient cause in an epistemic sequence leading to the apprehension of a form. While no such epistemic ascent is envisioned by Euripides in his play, the analogy between his description and Plato's lies in the lowest epistemic level, the starting point of *theoria*, namely, visual experience and its connection to recollection. Hence, the role played by the image in both kinds of *theoria* provides a common point of reference; yet those reading Plato's lines about the lover looking at an image and honoring a deity (cf. *Phdr.* 249d–251b) may interpret them but half-seriously in the sense that, from the standpoint of Platonic *theoria*, traveling to a sanctuary to achieve knowledge of the divine by viewing images of the gods seems at best misguided. Consequently, Plato clearly employs the notion of *agalma* common to traditional *theoria* in his account of philosophical *theoria*, and yet, he also retools the notion to complete his own account of *theoria*.

5.2.2   Platonic Objects in Four Dialogues

Having sketched the common background between traditional and Platonic *theoria* concerning their respective objects, closer analysis of the

---

[21] In this regard, the female attendants' epistemic level remains tethered to the perceptible realm (*Ion*, ll. 184–218) and may be identified with what Plato identifies as *eikasia*, reasoning through images (*Rep.* 511e2, 510a1–3) or perhaps *pistis*, reasoning about sensible objects (*Rep.* 511e1, 510a3–5), both of which comprise lower levels of apprehension than that reached by Meno's slave, for example (cf. *Meno* 85a–d), whose final epistemic state is not yet full knowledge, but perhaps is what Bostock describes as "ordinary ... knowledge that everyone has as a result of being reminded" (Bostock 1986, 70).

role of the objects in four dialogues, namely, *Phaedrus, Phaedo, Republic,* and *Symposium,* reveals that the immediate objects of *theoria* can provide the initial, upward direction toward apprehension of forms. So, perception of the quality of beauty in an individual's face has the function of revealing the divine to the philosophical soul, the account of which recalls, in some ways, the route taken by visitors on a *theoria* to a shrine in some traditional descriptions. In the four dialogues, Plato provides the epistemological and metaphysical theories to substantiate the experience of the theoric traveler which reveals a certain degree of reliance on the objects of sense-perception. For example, in *Phaedrus,* Plato explains the way in which perceived images from sensation are collected into the capacity for memory which, ultimately, has the role of revealing contents of the immortal, rational soul to the embodied soul. To begin, Plato describes the process by which reason "collects into a unity the many perceptions of the senses," and so, forms a general notion which can be recollected by memory (cf. *Phdr.* 249b7–c2). Given the immortality of the rational soul, our minds retain the memory of intelligible objects seen in our travels with God, and this retained storage of memory is what the philosopher can access through recollection (cf. *Phdr.* 249c2–5). So, the passage conjoins Plato's theories of immortality (*Phdr.* 245c–e), recollection (*Phdr.* 249b–c), and perception to furnish the metaphysical backdrop for the experience of Platonic *theoria.* In the genetic account of the process, Plato maintains that perception of a single beauty is that which partly causes the philosophical soul to recollect the form of beauty, the vision of which is known by the pre-incarnated, rational soul. Furthermore, through the visual sensation of beauty, the rational soul desires the form of beauty, an experience that Plato compares to the philosophical soul growing wings (cf. *Phdr.* 249d, 251b–d). In this account, the visual experience of beauty is not operating alone, but rather, the recollection of the form occurs in a moment of visual perception when the philosophical soul sees an individual beauty and simultaneously, in a flash, recalls another beauty, beauty itself.

It should be noted that the passage framing the ascent in *Phaedrus* (249b–254e) is replete with verbs of sense-perception, especially visual perception (including *theaomai*), such as the disembodied rational soul "seeing the vision of Beauty" (250b5–8, 250c8–d1) and "beholding the realities" (*tetheatai ta onta,* 249e5); recollection is described as re-envisioning things "which the soul once beheld (*eidein*) when it journeyed with the divine" (249c1–3), the philosophical soul described as seeing earthly beauty (250d7–e1, 250e3, 251c6), and the charioteer as seeing (*eidein*) the face of the beloved (253e5, 254b4–5, 254e7–8).

The overwhelming dominance of visual terms throughout the passage is primarily accounted by the philosophical-allegorical framework that explains the significance of perceived beauty. According to the account, the pre-incarnate soul has visions of things in its travels, and among these, the sight of beauty is "the most shining and clear" (cf. *Phdr.* 250d1–3), being perceived through "the sharpest of our senses, sight" (*opsis*) (*Phdr.* 250d3–4). So, Socrates concludes, "beauty alone (*kallos monon*) . . . is the most clearly seen and most beloved" (*Phdr.* 250d7–8) of the things perceived.[22] While such perception, of course, is not wisdom (*phronesis*) as "wisdom is not seen by it" (*Phdr.* 250d4), it is possible for the prepared philosophical soul "to look upon its namesake" and be led upwards "to Beauty itself (*auto to kallos*)" (*Phdr.* 250e2–3).[23] Here the term "namesake" (*ten eponumian*, 250e3) refers to the perceived image of beauty, something the initiated philosophical soul is tempted to treat "as an *agalma* or a god and offer sacrifice" (θύοι ἂν ὡς ἀγάλματι καὶ θεῷ, *Phdr.* 251a6), but which, if taken correctly, has the effect of bringing the soul upwards to the mediate object of *theoria*, beauty itself. Hence, while evident that the simple perception of a sensible quality, like the beauty of a face, is not adequate to realize the form of beauty, through recollection, sense-perception may stir the rational soul's prior apprehension of the form, moving the soul in an upward direction. The figure of the ascent is, of course, common to all four works, namely, *Phdr.* 250b–253c, *Phd.* 73d–75d, *Rep.* 514a–516b, and *Symp.* 210a–212a, in which it is generally understood as an epistemological development from a lower to a higher state of cognition with objects correlative to the faculties. More significantly for present purposes, these four passages exhibit the learner or budding philosopher moving from an initial state of sensory-based cognition to a developed state of rationally-based cognition. In this respect, perceptual elements play central roles in the initial levels of the process, which accounts for Plato's reliance on verbs of visual apprehension in describing the ascent, as well as *theoreo* and *theaomai* at the final levels.

While the four passages are compatible regarding the fact of visual perception in the upward epistemic process, they seem to differ in the strength of the causal role played by the perceptual faculty and the objects perceived. For example, the ascents in *Phaedrus* and *Phaedo* are initiated by

---

[22] The Greek runs: νῦν δὲ κάλλος μόνον ταύτην ἔσχε μοῖραν, ὥστ' ἐκφανέστατον εἶναι καὶ ἐρασμιώτατον (*Phdr.* 250d–8).
[23] The Greek runs: ὁ μὲν οὖν μὴ νεοτελὴς ἢ διεφθαρμένος οὐκ ὀξέως ἐνθένδε ἐκεῖσε φέρεται πρὸς αὐτὸ τὸ κάλλος, θεώμενος αὐτοῦ τὴν τῇδε ἐπωνυμίαν (*Phdr.* 250e1–3).

a visual perception of a sensible quality that ultimately leads, through the activity of recollection, to the grasp of something non-sensible. So, in *Phaedrus*, the perceiver initially sees a beautiful face, and by a process of recollection, grasps the form of beauty that is called to mind by means of the perceptual image. The significant point is that in *Phaedrus* and *Phaedo*, the perception of a sensible quality has the effect of motivating the perceiver "upwards" through the activity of recollection to the abstract object of thought. As Plato explains the capacity of recollection in *Phaedrus*, while it arises from sense-perception, it requires an abstractive step, such that "a human being must comprehend a general notion (*eidos*) by collecting many perceptions into one by reasoning; this is a recollection (*anamnesis*) of those things which our soul once saw when it journeyed together with god" (*Phdr.* 249b6–8).[24] This account of recollection resembles its appearance in *Phaedo*, where Socrates argues that the soul must be immortal based on the logic of recollecting something absent, an inference that assumes the fact of a present perception acting as catalyst (cf. *Phd.* 73c–76e).[25] In more detail, let us suppose that we have seen equal sticks and, in grasping the notion of equality as "the capacity neither-to-exceed-nor-be-exceeded" (Sedley 2006, 322), we then see that the sticks fall short of the character since, undoubtedly, they are unequal in certain respects, and simultaneous with this perceptual cognition, our mind is catapulted to the form equality with the sensible projectile falling away. For Plato, then, since our grasp of certain *a priori* concepts, e.g., equality, beauty, goodness, justice, and piety (*Phd.* 75c10–d2), cannot be explained by a process of abstraction, we postulate an eternal subject of knowledge, the intellective soul, which recollects these concepts by way of perceiving their imperfect instantiations, and in so doing, recalls their perfect correlates (cf. *Phd.* 76a1–7).[26]

---

[24] The Greek runs: δεῖ γὰρ ἄνθρωπον συνιέναι κατ᾽ εἶδος λεγόμενον, ἐκ πολλῶν ἰὸν αἰσθήσεων εἰς ἓν λογισμῷ συναιρούμενον· τοῦτο δ᾽ ἐστὶν ἀνάμνησις ἐκείνων ἅ ποτ᾽ εἶδεν ἡμῶν ἡ ψυχὴ συμπορευθεῖσα θεῷ (*Phdr.* 249b6–8); contrast Aristotle, *DM* 451a20–b6: recollection is not the recovery of any memory, although both presuppose sense-perception (cf. *Meta.* 980a28–30).

[25] Regarding the apparent tension between this argument and the earlier *Phd.* passage concerning the philosopher's need to reject perceptual experience, see Bedu-Addo (1991) who argues for two kinds of recollection, one kind being "a gradual process of learning" (cf. *Meno*), the other, "the immediate recollection of Forms by true philosophers" (cf. *Republic*), which presupposes the first kind of recollection (Bedu-Addo 1991, 30).

[26] It may be suggested that the forms of justice or piety are less amenable than equality as candidates for perception in the recollection account in *Phd.* sketched, but whether the quality of "neither exceeding nor being exceeded by" is more easily grasped by perception than, say, the beauty of a particular sculpture remains unclear.

So considered, the ascent described in *Phaedo* requires that sense-perception and sensible objects play significant roles at two distinct stages, the first involving an initial sense-perception, and the second, what I consider a complex, or combinatory, perception that also involves recollection of a past perception.[27] More specifically, the first stage consists in an initial apprehension of a sensible quality, as, for example, seeing sticks equal in length: we may call this uncontroversial, or naïve, perception. The second stage occurs when we see the sticks as only roughly equal in length, a stage where, for Plato, we recognize that they are not perfectly equal in length. For, we now see that they "fall short of being equal" (*Phd.* 74d6–7), a cognition that we reach as the result of a complex, perceptual awareness consisting in partly a perceptual element, and partly a rational element, namely, a recognition of the sensible object as "falling short" of the form in respect of some specific characteristic.[28] Overall, the sensation cum recollection account in *Phaedo* transcends that in *Phaedrus* in its detail, yet, the two accounts are compatible regarding the contributory role of perception in the epistemic ascent. In both, the initial perception of a specific kind of sensible property spurs the rational soul to investigate further, ultimately attaining knowledge of the relevant form, and in this respect, sense-perception plays a pivotal, if ancillary, role in the overall ascent to the form in both dialogues. For, while the rational soul supplies the dominant determinative cause of the ascent, it also relies on the contribution of perceptual experience, specifically, visual sense-perception, appearing, first, as naïve perception and later, as a nuanced cognitive recollection, in *Phaedrus* and *Phaedo*.[29]

For comparison, reconsider the ascent passage in *Symposium* (210a–212a) to that in *Phaedrus*, paying specific attention to the role of the

---

[27] We might refer the two-level perceptual account I am proposing as mapping onto what has been referred to as "ordinary" and then "philosophical" recollection, on which see Franklin (2005, 290–91); similarly, Bedu-Addo claims two kinds of recollection, one, a learning process, the other, "the immediate recollection of forms by philosophers" (Bedu-Addo 1991, 30) which presupposes the first.

[28] It is useful to refer the second perceptual level here to Lee's fine-grained analysis of the image in Plato as substantial or non-substantial: in *Phd.* 74d–e, Plato describes apprehending a present sensible in light of an absent form, recognizing "what the Form is perfectly, the image-phenomenon is imperfectly—*but that much, at least, it is*" (Lee 1966, 361); Lee describes this perception of a quality along with the recognition of its falling short as involving a "mental reference to a Form that remains extrinsic to our apprehension of the sensible phenomenon," which reflects an ontology of the "substantial image," whereas *Tim.* 48e–52d presents all phenomenal being as having the status of the "insubstantial image" (Lee 1966, 361).

[29] See *Phdr.* 249b7–8 on recollection as reliant on sense-perception, on which *Phd.* 74c13–d2 concurs; as well, *Phdr.* 254b5–6 makes clear that perception of beauty brings about *mneme* of beauty itself.

perceived image specifically, and that of visual experience generally. As Diotima's speech makes clear, the soul of the potential philosopher does not remain at the level of corporeal beauty, but is drawn to study its more abstract expressions, first, in the beauty of many bodies, later, in that of souls, or minds (*Symp.* 210a5–b8), and in the beauty of practices, laws, and sciences (*Symp.* 210c3–d1), before apprehending the vision of beauty itself.[30] Over the course of the ascent, the potential philosopher is exercising *theoria* in relation to two kinds of objects, one is a sensible object presenting an inchoate form, the other is an intelligible object. So, for example, in *Symp.* after perceiving the beauty in one body and then in several bodies, Plato uses *theaomai* to describe the way of seeing the quality of beauty in its abstract form. At this intermediate stage, as Plato explains, the student "studies (*theasasthai*) the beautiful in practices and laws" (*Symp.* 210c3), and subsequently, "studies" the beauty among the sciences (cf. 210c5–6). Finally, at the highest stage, the student, "turning toward the great ocean of beauty in contemplation (*theoroun*), brings forth many fine arguments" (*Symp.* 210d3–4). Ultimately, the student who is exercising *theoria* is able to grasp the form of beauty, which comprises the final object of *theoria*. Following the proper sequence of objects ensures that the one who contemplates (*theomenos*) has the form of beauty revealed to him (*Symp.* 210e2–3),[31] at which time the student comes to know the beautiful itself and to achieve the best human life in contemplating beauty itself (*theomeno auto to kalon*) (*Symp.* 211d2).[32] In general, then, while sense-perception has a causal role in the ascents in *Symposium* and *Phaedrus*, the account in *Symposium* seems to accord it a lesser place, as indicated by perception being superseded by the rational faculty in striving to clarify the nature of beauty.[33] In this regard, we may conclude that in Platonic dialogues, the perceived images of beauty comprise the immediate, sensible objects that are typically described using sense-perception verbs, whereas the forms of beauty, justice, piety, equality, goodness, and others, constitute the final, proper objects of *theoria*, signaled with the verbs *theoreo* and *theaomai*.[34]

[30] The ascent from the cave, in *Rep.* VII, and in *Symp.* appear to concern that of potential philosophers rather than ordinary learners, while the status of learners in *Phd.* and *Phdr.* is less clear, some evidence supporting an ordinary learner, some a philosophical one, see Franklin (2005, 290–91).
[31] The Greek line runs: Ὃς γὰρ ἂν μέχρι ἐνταῦθα πρὸς τὰ ἐρωτικὰ παιδαγωγηθῇ, θεώμενος ἐφεξῆς τε καὶ ὀρθῶς τὰ καλά, πρὸς τέλος ἤδη ἰὼν τῶν ἐρωτικῶν ἐξαίφνης κατόψεταί τι θαυμαστὸν τὴν φύσιν καλόν (*Symp.* 210e2–3).
[32] The Greek phrase: θεωμένῳ αὐτὸ τὸ καλόν (*Symp.* 210d2).
[33] Noting an absence of the recollection account in the ascent in *Symp.*, and *Rep.* VII.
[34] We have noted, as well, Plato's use of *theaomai* or *theoreo* in regard to seeing festival "sights," as at *Rep.* I, 327a2–b1, but again, these verbs do not refer to "garden-variety" seeing.

Some differences concerning the role of perception can be discerned among the four ascent passages in that, for example, those in *Phaedo* and *Phaedrus* seem to reflect a greater reliance on perceptual experience than those in *Symposium* and *Republic*. More specifically, in the former two works, sense-perception conjoins with recollection to constitute a cognitive-perceptual power, able to assist the rational soul in its goal to attain the knowledge of forms. In contrast, the ascent passage in *Symposium* is notable for its absence of recollection theory; in fact, neither *Symp.* (210a–212a) nor *Rep.* VII (514a–516c) relies on the mechanism of recollection to play a critical role in moving the soul toward the form. While both ascents in *Republic* and *Symposium* require the activity of sense-perception, its activity is not described as having adequate motive power to enable the first level of ascent in the cave. Rather, the nature of the cause behind the prisoner's bonds being released, enabling him to stand up and turn his head around (*Rep.* 515c5–6) is not given; the passage describes a necessity, or force, compelling the prisoner to stand, rather than him achieving this on his own by perception or thought. In fact, various stages of the ascent are framed using the language of compulsion: the chained prisoner "is compelled" initially to look only in one direction toward the shadows (*Rep.* 515a9–b1), he is suddenly released and "compelled" to turn from the shadows toward the light (*Rep.* 515c6), he is "compelled" to look directly at the light (*Rep.* 515e1).[35] So, whatever force is moving the prisoner upward out of the cave does not appear to be identified with perception, whether naïve perception or recollection; we find no *agalma* equivalent to the beauty of a beloved's face moving the prisoner upward to the form.[36] Similarly, the ascent in *Symposium* is made possible by "a guide" (*hegoumenos*, *Symp.* 210a7) who instructs the potential philosopher in the process, leading him from one beautiful body to many, and one beautiful soul to many (*Symp.* 210b–c).[37] Subsequently, at the intermediate stages of the ascent in *Symposium*, the potential philosopher is "constrained (*anakasthe*) to contemplate (*theasasthai*) the beautiful in practices and laws" (*Symp.* 210c3–4). It may be admitted that the reference to "a guide" may be benign, and the use of compulsion language need not imply coercive influence (as noted below), but these appear along with the

---

[35] The Greek line runs: αὐτὸ τὸ φῶς ἀναγκάζοι αὐτὸν βλέπειν (*Rep.* 515e1).
[36] As well, the lack of sunlight (form of the good) in the cave implies that the prisoner is not led upward by a desire for the good.
[37] The identity of the "guide" (*Symp.* 210a7) remains unclear, although Nehamas and Woodruff claim it is Love (Nehamas and Woodruff 1989, 57 fn. 90).

absence of an account concerning complex perception and the activity of recollection. In contrast, the accounts of ascent in *Phaedo* and *Phaedrus* emphasize sense-perception and recollection as "that by which" the end goal is attained; those in *Republic* and *Symposium* do not. Rather, the upward, epistemic progress in *Rep.* VII and *Symposium* is achieved without the budding philosopher's perception or recollection but, seemingly, by direction outside the agent. So, for example, even in the stages after the ascent from the cave in *Rep.* VII, Socrates notes that the prisoner needs educational habituation to be able to perceive even the lowest of "the things we call real" (*Rep.* 516a3–5). However, despite the presence of what appears as external compulsion in the initial and middle stages of the ascent in *Republic* and *Symposium*,[38] such compulsion is absent at the final stage where the philosopher can directly study the chosen objects, including the form of the good. So, in *Rep.* VII, after the intermediate stages of ascent, the nascent philosopher appears to move upwards to the forms by his own curiosity (cf. *Rep.* 515a5–b7).[39] Thus, finally, the philosopher can see the sun itself, ". . . not in water or images (*phantasmata*) in an alien medium but look at the sun itself (*auton kath' hauton*) in its own place and be able to study (*theasasthai*) its own nature" (*Rep.* 516b4–7).[40]

5.2.3   *Conclusion on Platonic Objects in Four Dialogues*

In general, the four dialogues employ sensible images functioning as *agalmata* as the initial perceptual objects in their respective ascents. Yet, in contrast to passages in *Phaedrus* and *Phaedo* which rely on recollection as providing the impetus in arriving at the knower's apprehension of form, the ascents in *Republic* and *Symposium* do not rely on the mechanism of recollection to "kickstart" the process, although in both the upward process of learning presupposes an element supplied by sense-perception.

---

[38] The distinction between external and internal forms of compulsion is complex, but for present purposes, let us assume that vivid sense-perception or perceptual experience taken broadly might count as an internal, non-noxious kind (e.g., "It was unbelievable, but I saw it with my own eyes"); a teacher instilling moral values as an external, non-noxious kind; police coercion on a witness as an external, noxious kind; for a comprehensive discussion of compulsion in Plato, see Shields (2007).

[39] Hence, in the stages immediately following the cave, Socrates claims the prisoner needs educational habituation to be able to perceive even the lowest of "the things we call real" (*Rep.* 516a3–5); after this stage, the knower moves upwards to the forms by his own curiosity (cf. *Rep.* 515a5–b7).

[40] The full Greek line: τελευταῖον δὴ οἶμαι τὸν ἥλιον, οὐκ ἐν ὕδασιν οὐδ᾽ ἐν ἀλλοτρίᾳ ἕδρᾳ φαντάσματα αὐτοῦ, ἀλλ᾽ αὐτὸν καθ᾽ αὑτὸν ἐν τῇ αὑτοῦ χώρᾳ δύναιτ᾽ ἂν κατιδεῖν καὶ θεάσασθαι οἷός ἐστιν (*Rep.* 516b4–7).

Perhaps significantly, both these works include an external source of motion independent of perception: for example, the knowing guide in the *Symposium* or the undetermined force applied to the prisoner within the cave, that lead or, perhaps better, assist, the nascent philosopher in reaching the final objects of *theoria*, the forms. Setting aside the difference concerning recollection among the four works, it is safe to conclude that while sensible images may play the role of *agalmata* in traditional *theoria*, similar to what we see described by the female attendants in Euripides' *Ion*, they are not the final objects of *theoria* for Plato, for these are reserved for the highest objects of theoric study, the forms. Moreover, the four works fully coincide concerning the goal of the ascent of *theoria*, namely, seeing and knowing forms. They further concur concerning the effects of such apprehension: for Plato, grasping the highest objects of *theoria* implies permanent epistemic change in the knower. In *Rep.* VII, for example, following the stage of apprehending the form of the good, the philosopher is enabled to infer conclusions (*sullogizein*) about the visible world based on his knowledge of the form of the good. As Socrates explains to Glaucon: "it seems to me that in the knowable realm, the form of the good is the last to be seen and reached with difficulty; once it is seen, one must conclude (*sullogistea*) that it is the cause of all that is correct and beautiful in anything" (*Rep.* 517b8–c3). It is worth noting that according to this passage, after apprehending the form of the good, the philosopher has the cognitive capacity to use her knowledge to draw her own inferences correctly without external assistance. So, once in possession of the forms as objects of *theoria*, the philosopher is epistemically free, able to move "downwards" in the application of the first principles to seek the causes of phenomena in the visible realm (cf. *Rep.* 516b9–c2). The downward use of one's philosophical knowledge is exemplified, then, in the application of the forms of the good, the just, the pious, and so on, to the domain of human law, as Socrates describes in *Rep.* VII (517d4–e2). In this regard, it may be accurate to claim that in the *Republic*, while forms constitute the highest proper objects of *theoria*, it is also reasonable to consider the downward phase of philosophical activity, what we may call the "applied" phase of *theoria*, as directed at lower objects; for example, in the case of the philosopher-rulers, part of their activity is to construct specific laws to preserve justice in the city.[41] Since such activity would employ knowledge

---

[41] It may be useful here to compare the activity of the philosophers as rulers with the functions of the traditional *theoros*, such as acting as the city's formal representative, taking part in festival rituals, making observations, reporting back to the city council (see Ch. 1, sec. 1.3).

of forms, it would not be identical with the kind of reasoning Socrates terms *dianoia* (*Rep.* 511e1), the kind of reasoning that uses hypotheses as starting points that is characteristic of the sciences in the third level of the line (cf. *Rep.* 511a2–d5).

5.3 Celestial Objects of Study in Plato

One may wonder whether for Plato anything other than intelligible forms are proper objects of *theoria*: my analysis leads me to answer negatively, but some qualification must be added here. In the four dialogues canvassed above, the nature of the highest objects of *theoria* remains unequivocally clear, namely, intelligible forms. However, in additional works, we seem to find Plato endorsing the view that humans can engage in *theoria* of the heavens, specifically, of celestial bodies, in which case planets and fixed stars may be numbered along with the forms as the proper objects of *theoria*. There are two initial difficulties in assessing the proposal about celestial bodies as objects of *theoria*: the first is that the suggestion is briefly raised in just three works, *Phaedrus*, *Republic*, and *Timaeus*, and the second, two of these passages involve cosmological myths, which adds a further layer of difficulty in reaching a conclusion.[42] Let us work through these passages taken together to evaluate this claim.

We may find a suggestion about heavenly bodies being objects of *theoria* in part of *Phaedrus'* cosmological myth involving the charioteer-soul analogy (cf. 246a–256b) where Plato refers both to the perceptible heavens in which souls of divinities travel and a *huperouranian* realm "above the heavens" (*Phdr.* 247c3) in which forms subsist (cf. *Phdr.* 247c–e). Here we find a reference to the heavenly realm containing "many blessed sights" (*pollai makariai theai*, πολλαὶ μακάριαι θέαι, *Phdr.* 247a4), which might refer to heavenly bodies. An explicit claim about studying the heavens is made in *Timaeus* (37c–39e) concerning the created universe in which the heavenly bodies move according to mathematical principles, like time which is described as the number of motion (*Tim.* 37d), in a universe described as reflecting divine intellect (cf. *Tim.* 37c–d). As part of the visible heavens, it appears that Timaeus considers the heavenly bodies as among the things he terms "visible gods" (*Tim.* 40d), and as counted among "the necessary causes" (*Tim.* 68e) that must be grasped "to comprehend (*katanoein*) the divine causes" (*Tim.* 69a). The *Republic* offers two

---

[42] The difficulty in part concerns the view formulated by Nightingale (2004, 168–78) that Plato in *Timaeus* holds that *theoria* of the heavens is necessary to philosophical *theoria*.

passages that are less definitive than those in the *Timaeus*, both occurring in *Rep*. VII. The first is where Socrates states that the prisoner will be able "to study (*theaomai*) the things in the heavens and the heaven itself more easily by night, looking at the light of the stars and the moon" (516a6–b2), and the second, where Socrates details the philosopher's regimen of studies, listing astronomy, if this is studied in the right way, as useful for turning the soul upwards towards intelligible forms (cf. *Rep*. 528e3–529e).[43] From this perspective, the texts in *Timaeus* and *Republic* suggest the idea that the heavenly bodies may serve as genuine objects of intellectual study, or *theoria*, a position that I find defensible. However, a different view of the texts concerns the idea that Plato holds that philosophers must study celestial objects, like planets, prior to grasping the highest intelligible objects, forms.[44]

This latter, stronger version of the connection between studying planets and forms seems rather weakly supported by the texts, for two reasons. One involves a conceptual problem and the other, a linguistic detail. The linguistic matter concerns the fact that while the cited *Republic* passages employ verbs commonly linked to *theoria*, namely, *theoreo* and *theaomai*, the use of either verb need not imply the presence of philosophical *theoria* insofar as it may refer to looking at a sensible object *as* a sensible object. Thus, for example, the passage in *Rep*. VII (528e–529e) about "studying" the heavenly bodies displays a perceptual use – but also a philosophical one, as when at *Rep*. 529b1–3, Plato uses *theoreo* twice in a critical account of astronomy. Socrates' point is that, as astronomy is currently practiced, it involves the observer falsely believing that he is going to learn something about the heavenly bodies simply by looking at them, as if one "is staring at decorations on a ceiling" (*Rep*. 529b1–3).[45] Instead, Socrates states, we should regard "the embroidered heaven as patterns that are useful to the study of the other things," by which he clearly is referring to the forms (*Rep*. 529d6–7).[46] Thus, according to Plato, the error in the current practice of star-gazing consists in studying the heavenly bodies to gain knowledge of them as perceptible bodies, and not as studying them as

---

[43] The wrong way of doing astronomy, according to Socrates, is the method of studying heavenly bodies as objects of real knowledge, since they are sensible; the correct manner is considering them "as patterns to aid in the study of those realities" (*Rep*. VII, 529d6–7).

[44] As, I take it, Nightingale interprets the texts mentioned (cf. Nightingale 2004, 168–78).

[45] The Greek line runs: ἐν ὀροφῇ ποικίλματα θεώμενος ἀνακύπτων (*Rep*. VII, 529b1–3).

[46] The Greek line runs: οὐκοῦν, εἶπον, τῇ περὶ τὸν οὐρανὸν ποικιλίᾳ παραδείγμασι χρηστέον τῆς πρὸς ἐκεῖνα μαθήσεως ἕνεκα (*Rep*. VII, 529d6–7).

stepping-stones to knowledge of the intelligible forms themselves.[47] The citation of the error in current star-gazing leads to the primary reason for doubting that the planets are logically prior objects of study: the three texts cited above support the idea that the value in looking at the planets is instrumental, namely, as a means of apprehending "the divine causes" (*Tim.* 69a), which are, obviously, forms.[48] So, while some passages show that we may engage in observational study of the heavenly bodies, the value of this study lies in its instrumentality to apprehending forms, the proper objects of *theoria*, the forms. Hence, it does not follow that the apprehension of forms presupposes or requires the study of celestial objects, and perhaps it is fairer to find them instrumental to apprehending the final objects, forms. Consequently, it appears that we lack adequate evidence to overturn the view that for Plato, philosophical *theoria* is exercised, properly speaking, only with regard to intelligible objects, forms, which are its proper objects.[49]

5.4   Aristotle and the Objects of *Theoria*

When we come to discuss the objects of *theoria* as Aristotle conceives them, it is natural to cast a backwards glance to Plato: while their analyses converge in many respects, specifically, in relation to the nature, scope, and aim of the activity, the issue regarding objects reveals some differences. Let me preface this discussion by noting that, as with Plato, the analysis is restricted to the objects of human *theoria*. This restriction may be initially surprising for textual reasons: first, in *EN* X 8 Aristotle argues the gods also engage in *theoria*, and second, divine *theoria* is explored at some length in *Meta.* XII 7 and 9, leading one to question the restriction to human *theoria*. Two kinds of consideration may be mentioned in response, one philosophical and the other interpretive. The philosophical reasons rest, first, on the fact that Aristotle's central discussions of *theoria*, such as *EN* X 7–8 and *DA* III 4–5, focus squarely on human *theoria*, leaving the nature

---

[47] Some support for thinking of study of heavenly bodies as instrumental to study of forms is suggested in *Tim.* 47b6–c4; see Ch. 6, sec. 6.2.2.
[48] On a related issue of revolution of the heavens, see *Tim.* 47b–c about how these motions can be used to order the soul.
[49] There are, I think, two potential objections to my conclusion, one concerning whether Plato thinks we study heavenly bodies as perceptible or as theoretical objects; the other that my defense of Platonic *theoria* is too narrow and invites circularity. The former raises a complex matter that exceeds space for proper attention, see Gill (1971), Lee (1966), Silverman (1992), Zeyl (1975); the latter objection mistakes my view as dogmatic, but it is, rather, skeptical concerning the strength of the textual evidence for the competing view.

of divine *theoria* unexplored.[50] This omission is reasonable given that while human *theoria* is open to our investigation, divine *theoria* is not similarly accessible to human investigation. If we look to arguments of *Meta.* XII 7 and 9 about divine *theoria* to clarify the objects of our human activity, we find there is only one, God, or more precisely God's thinking as object, and this revelation is surely irrelevant to determining the objects of human *theoria.*[51] So, it appears that an investigation about the objects of human *theoria* must proceed as if it were *sui generis*, as I argue it in fact is. The other reason for keeping a focus on human *theoria* is related to the overall interpretive theme, examining the influence of traditional *theoria* on philosophical thinkers. Since the defining features of such *theoria* belong to humans alone (despite the orientation of the practice to deities), consideration of the gods' *theoria* becomes peripheral.

5.4.1   Two Views of the Objects of Aristotelian Theoria

Aristotle opens his discussion of human *theoria* in *EN* X 7 with an ambiguity about the classification of its objects in a line that mentions the activity (*EN* 1177a18–21). At *EN* 1177a19–21, Aristotle states that *theoria* is the "highest," or "best" (κρατίστη) activity, for, as he explains, it is an activity of *nous*, and *nous* apprehends the highest of the knowable, or intelligible objects (γνωστῶν) (*EN* 1177a20–21). In brief, *EN* X 7 1177a19–21 tells us that in being an activity of *nous*, *theoria* is the highest (or best) activity (*energeia*), and that it deals with the highest of intelligible objects. As the text does not state precisely what the highest of the intelligible objects are, it invites a certain ambiguity about the members of this class. The phrasing of the text at *EN* X 7 1177a19–21 seems to allow two different readings leading to distinct views about the objects of Aristotelian *theoria.*[52] In broad terms, we might call one the "ontological" view of objects in that it gives priority to their ontological status: what Aristotle describes as the "highest" objects of knowledge (cf. *EN* 1177a19–21) is taken to imply the highest, or most elevated, in being.[53]

---

[50] For example, in *EN* X 8, divine *theoria* is mentioned in reference to establish the fact that the gods engage in *theoria*, not to describe its nature.

[51] There are, of course, substantial arguments in *Meta.* XII 7 and 9 about the fact of God's existence and about divine properties, including thinking, but these are better considered part of Aristotle's theology; for discussion of divine *theoria* in *Meta.* XII 7, 9 see Norman (1969).

[52] I note a parallel ambiguity between views of the objects of *theoria* and the subject matter of being qua being as mentioned in *Meta.* IV 2; on the latter kind, see Patzig (1979).

[53] Thus, Reeve assumes the proper object of *theoria* is God (Reeve 2012, 275–78).

As to the range of objects included under this description, we might suggest the Prime Mover of *Meta.* XII 7 and 9, and perhaps eternal, supra-lunar heavenly bodies. Another view of the objects studied by *theoria* consists in what we might term the "epistemological" view in that it gives priority to their intelligibility. On this reading, the objects described as the "highest" (*kratiste*) objects (*EN* 1177a20–21) are "the most intelligible" of objects.[54] On an epistemic reading of the phrase, the highest objects of *theoria* would include the forms of sensible, perishable substances (biological natural kinds), forms of sensible, imperishable substances (i.e., heavenly bodies), and metaphysical principles such as laws of logic and mathematical axioms.[55] One difference of the two views, one making knowability primary, the other making ontological status primary, is that the two classes of objects signified overlap but do not precisely coincide. On the epistemic view, the proper objects of *theoria* are co-extensive with the most intelligible objects. Since formal entities, like substantial forms, are epistemically independent, they qualify as objects of *theoria* unlike their composite counterparts.[56] To pause for a moment, we should mention Aristotle's familiar distinction between being knowable "in itself" and "to us" raised in *Phys.* I 1 (184a16–18) and elsewhere.[57] The initial problem concerns the fact that *EN* X 7 (1177a19–21) does not clarify whether the intelligible objects of *theoria* stated as "the highest," are supposed to be intelligible "to us" or "in themselves." However, in the lines immediately preceding *EN* 1177a19–21 Aristotle states that *theoria* is the activity (*energeia*) of "the best part of us," which is a reference to *nous* (*EN* 1177a13–14), immediately after described as "the most divine thing in us" (*EN* 1177a16). Since in its precise sense *nous* apprehends intelligible things farthest from sense-experience, such objects cannot be described as more knowable "to us" but knowable "in themselves." Thus, whatever the scope, the precise objects of *theoria* must belong to things knowable, or intelligible, in themselves.[58]

---

[54] This reading results from taking "highest" at *EN* 1177a19 as an intensive modifying "intelligibles" (genitive plural, *gnoston*) at *EN* 1177a21.

[55] We may include here the principles of non-contradiction and excluded middle as well as mathematical axioms, such as "equals added to (or taken from) equals leave equals."

[56] For example, *Meta.* VII 17 considers what is most knowable, identifying the formal cause of the thing (*Meta.* 1141a27–30).

[57] Additional passages mentioning the distinction include *An. Po.* 71b33–72a5, and *EN* I 4, 1094b2–4.

[58] For this reason, I do not follow Walker (2018, 170–82) in arguing that one's own self is an object of *theoria*; while Aristotle claims in *EN* IX 9 that we may "study" (*theorein*) our friends (*EN* 1169b33), clearly, the verb is not being used in the precise sense as related to *episteme*.

Now let us consider the problems attendant upon the two views described, taking each one in turn. For the ontological view, the first problem concerns how to take Aristotle's description of the objects of *theoria* being "the highest" of intelligible objects (*EN* 1177a20–21). As we mentioned, the class of things that are arguably the highest ontologically would include, maximally, the Prime Mover and supra-lunar celestial entities. Yet here we pause, for supra-lunar, eternal substances are not absolutely the highest ontologically, and so, they might be excluded from the class of objects *theoria* studies. If we were to exclude them, it would be by considering the phrase in an absolute, or exclusive, sense, with the result that the reference is restricted to a single highest substance: this narrows the scope to the Prime Mover, or God. So, taking the ontological view and its phrase "the highest" in an absolute sense, the proper object of *theoria* is the Prime Mover alone.[59] However, if the phrase is taken in an inclusive sense, *theoria* may be thought to include celestial objects such as the planets and stars as well as the Prime Mover. One suggestion would be to turn to additional texts for clarification about the objects of *theoria*. For, while *EN* X 7 (1177a19–21) does not distinguish which intelligible objects *theoria* studies, in fact, *EE* VIII 3 seems to claim precisely that engaging in *theoria* of God is part of the highest moral standard. Specifically, the lines of *EE* VIII 3 state: "whatever way of choosing and acquiring things good by nature that best promotes *theoria* of God (τὴν τοῦ θεοῦ θεωρίαν 1249b17) is the best" (*EE* 1249b16–17), adding that any practice that "prevents us from serving and studying god is bad" (*EE* 1249b20–21).[60]

While it might be supposed that the lines in *EE* VIII 3 (1249b17–21) provide incontrovertible evidence for taking God as the single proper object of *theoria*, the matter requires analysis. For, as Woods points out, commentators are hardly unanimous on the interpretation of *EE* VIII 3, 1249b16–23: we can distinguish two groups disputing the reference of the phrase "the *theoria* of god" (*ten tou theou theorian*, 1249b17). One view, favored by Dirlmeier and During, holds that "god" in the phrase

---

[59] Burnyeat seems to support this move, identifying Aristotle's recommendation to engage in *theoria* as the highest activity as recommending us to become like God "as far as we can" in *EN* X 7 (1177b33), which he thinks implies we are "to make ourselves immortal, to enjoy for a while the same understanding as God has" (Burnyeat 2008, 43), presumably, by thinking about the highest object, God, to which I counter that we cannot become similar to God in our understanding since the two kinds of intellect are fundamentally different.

[60] The full Greek line is: ἥτις οὖν αἵρεσις καὶ κτῆσις τῶν φύσει ἀγαθῶν ποιήσει μάλιστα τὴν τοῦ θεοῦ θεωρίαν, ἢ σώματος ἢ χρημάτων ἢ φίλων ἢ τῶν ἄλλων ἀγαθῶν, αὕτη ἀρίστη καὶ οὗτος ὁ ὅρος κάλλιστος (1249b17–18); a phrase similar to "the *theoria* of god" occurs a line later in "... from serving and studying god" (*ton theon therapeuein kai theorein*, *EE* 1249b20–21).

"the *theoria* of god" (*EE* 1249b17) refers to the highest element in the human soul, so that the whole phrase should be taken to refer to divine speculation, or the activity of the intellect (Woods 1992, 183–84). The alternative view, held by Verdenius and Rowe, maintains that "god" in this phrase refers to the supreme being, God, and that the phrase implies that *theoria* explicitly takes God as its proper object (Woods 1992, 184). On the latter view, the word "god" both in the phrase "the *theoria* of god" at *EE* 1249b17, and in the phrase "to serve and contemplate god" at *EE* 1249b20 have God as their grammatical objects.[61] While Woods points to an inconsistency in Dirlmeier's reading, giving the edge to the view of Verdenius and Rowe, he does not clearly prefer it; rather, he interprets the passage at *EE* VIII 3 (1249b16–23) broadly as showing that "the good man's choice and possession of natural goods should be made with regard to the activity of speculation" (viz., *theoria*) and that "whatever promotes it is good, whatever hinders it is bad" (Woods 1992, 183), with which I cannot disagree. Woods' description is fully consistent with Aristotle's position in *EN* X 7 that *theoria* is the highest activity (1177a19–20) and that the intellectual way of life is the happiest (1177b24–25), and is, moreover, a description that does not require us to infer that the single object of such activity is the Prime Mover. In this regard, then, Woods' view is perfectly agreeable to the position I have been supporting regarding the non-exclusive reading of the objects of *theoria* for Aristotle.

An additional, less decisive reason for taking a more cautious (i.e., a non-exclusive) reading of *EN* X 7 (1177a19–21) and *EE* VIII 3 (1249b16–23) concerning the objects of *theoria* stems from Aristotle's complex usage of the *theor/ia/eo* family of terms.[62] If we reconsider this use, specifically of the verb *theoreo*, we find it allows for a dual application, with one of these referring to the elevated activity of *nous* spelled out in *EN* X 7. The other, more inchoate use refers to an activity of investigating a subject matter in a quite different manner than that described as *theoria* in *EN* X 7. On the second use, Aristotle employs *theoreo* in contexts to signify an activity of studying that resembles an empirical investigation, perhaps like that appearing in the recommendation of *theoria* of plants and animals in *De Part. An.* I 5. In the text, he famously contrasts two kinds of inquiry,

---

[61] In their view, in the case of "to serve and study god" at *EE* 1249b20, "god" is the grammatical object of the verbs used, namely, *therapeuein* and *theorein* (Woods 1992, 184); the Greek line runs: εἴ τις δ' ἢ δι' ἔνδειαν ἢ δι' ὑπερβολὴν κωλύει τὸν θεὸν θεραπεύειν καὶ θεωρεῖν, αὕτη δὲ φαύλη.

[62] Like Plato, Aristotle employs two principal uses of *theor/eo/ia* terms, one concerned with the activity of contemplation, the other with the study, or observation, of things associated with learning (cf. Des Places 1970, 262–63).

one comprises the elevated study of divine things, and the other, less elevated, offers more opportunity for extended observation and learning, and is equally worthy of our esteem, he finds. Here Aristotle observes that it is not right to infer that the close study of plants and animals, though lacking the status of the elevated study, is wanting in epistemic worth and intrinsic pleasure: as he mentions, "There are gods here, too" (cf. *De Part. An.* 644b24–645a19).[63] Aristotle's dual use of *theor/eo/ia* terminology carries implications for his use of phrases employing it, especially when it comes to phrases stating *theos* as the object of *theoria* – as we find in *EE* VIII with "the *theoria* of god" (*EE* 1249b17), and "to serve and contemplate (*theorein*) god" (*EE* 1249b20). Here the meaning of the whole phrase depends as much upon the *theor*-term as it does upon the meaning of *theos*, in that the phrases may signify "divine study" in a sense that includes studying forms as much as studying one entity, God. Thus, despite the complexities involved in interpreting the larger passage of *EE* VIII 3 (viz., 1249b6–23),[64] it does not appear that *EE* 1249b16–23 must be read in support of the notion that the primary object of *theoria* is the Prime Mover, a result which leaves undetermined the nature of the "highest" intelligible objects grasped by *theoria* in *EN* X 7 (1177a19–21).

One conclusion for the ontological view of the objects of *theoria* involves the relative indeterminacy of the class, namely, that it may refer to sensible, imperishable substances like heavenly bodies, as well as to the Prime Mover; there seems to be no reason to prefer the exclusive reading of "highest" with regard to its potential objects to restrict the field. However, this conclusion is an unwelcome result for adherents of the view that God is the single proper object of *theoria*. For proper consideration of both sides, we should also study whether the epistemological view of the objects of *theoria* fares better conceptually and textually than the ontological view. Does this view admit the same kind of indeterminacy concerning the nature of the highest intelligible objects? There are, to begin, two issues that need to be addressed in coming to answer this question, both concerned with the notion of being knowable, or intelligible. The first concerns what object or set of objects should be understood if the term "highest" (*kratiste*) is understood as modifying "the intelligible objects" mentioned at *EN* X 7 1177a19.[65] As we have noted, if the term "highest"

---

[63] For discussion of Aristotle's rhetoric calling on the scientist to examine nature, see Poulakos and Crick (2012).

[64] The complexities of *EE* 1249b6–25 are well discussed by Woods (1992, 181–84).

[65] It is so taken in various translations, e.g., Ostwald (2000) and Rackham (1926).

implies being most intelligible, it would seem that substantial forms must be counted among the objects of *theoria*, which is a reasonable conclusion.[66] Nevertheless, we find that the problem of scope concerning the meaning of "highest" mentioned at *EN* X 7 (1177a19–21) arises once again: are we to consider the "highest" of knowable objects to be understood in an exclusive sense as referring to a single entity or as referring more broadly to a class of highly intelligible objects? So here again we find that the kinds of objects *theoria* apprehends seems underdetermined: it is possible that they cover a range, including substantial forms and logical laws, or they comprise a narrow class, only God. A second issue concerns the ambiguity of something being knowable: as Aristotle frequently reminds us, there is a distinction between something known "to us" and known "in itself."[67] So, if we interpret the reference to the "highest" of intelligible objects in *EN* X 7 (1177a19–21) as signifying what is most knowable, we need to consider in which sense this phrase is used. While the context of the passage in *EN* X 7 seems to suggest it is being knowable in itself, the matter is not easily resolved. We return to discuss the problem momentarily; since we have uncovered certain difficulties with both the ontological and epistemological readings of the objects of *theoria*, more work remains to be done to determine which view is better supported.

5.4.2   Problems with the Ontological View

There are three areas of difficulty for the ontological view of the objects of *theoria*; two of these arise from taking the exclusive, or absolute, reading of these objects as this generates problems of consistency internal to *EN*. Discussion of the third issue, that concerning scientific knowledge of God, is deferred as it pertains to the second (i.e., epistemic) view of objects. So, with regard to the problems directly impacting the ontological view, if *EN* X 7 (1177a19–21) is taken as emphasizing what is highest in being in an exclusive sense, *theoria* has only one object, God, and this result lacks consonance with central claims made in Aristotle's prior discussion. Specifically, prior to *EN* X 7 he has not prepared us for the notion that the study of a single object, God, comprises the aim of ethics; in fact, the contrary is true. From the perspective of a practical work, the reading of

---

[66] The qualification of being "highest" among the intelligible objects implies an intensifier to the property of being knowable, so that the highest of the intelligible objects is the most intelligible; however, this need not imply there is numerically one such object.

[67] On the distinction between known in itself (*haplos*) or to us, see *Phys* 184a16–23, *An. Po.* 71b33–72a5, and *EN* I 4, 1095b2–4.

lines in *EN* X 7 (1177a19–21) which direct us to pursue *theoria* of God as an object of study either contradicts the notion that human happiness is a good attainable by virtuous action in *EN* I 1 or it appears extraneous to it. Without opening the present discussion to the perennial problem about the competing ends of happiness in *EN*, the point is that nothing leading up to the passage in *EN* X 7 supports taking the exclusive reading of the ontological view of objects. Rather, we find that Aristotle's praise of *theoria* in *EN* X 7 as the "highest activity" (EN 1177a19–20) leaves undetermined the object or objects of such activity; hence, *EN* X 7 (1177a19–21) does not require taking God as the single, proper object of *theoria*.

A second internal problem for the exclusive reading of the ontological view arises with the tension between *EN* X 7 (*EN* 1177a19–21) and an earlier passage concerning the non-synonymy of the good in *EN* I 6. Given Aristotle's arguments in *EN* I 6 against the notion of a transcendent good, i.e., a Platonic form of goodness, it is difficult to see how he can be referring to a wholly good, transcendent entity as the object of *theoria* in *EN* X 7, inasmuch as the latter appears to contradict his thesis about good being homonymous. To recall Aristotle's familiar phasing in *EN* I 6, "good is said in as many ways as the term 'is' is" (*EN* 1096a23–25), and this statement, in allowing for various kinds of goods without mention of a "highest" good (which God must be counted as being), seems to rule out such a being as the basis for comparison of goods in *EN*.[68] Various texts in *EN* support Aristotle's claim about the multivocity of the good in service to his denial of a transcendent form of the Good, not only at the practical level – that knowing the form of the good cannot be useful in practicing the good (*EN* 1097a5–10) – but also in relation to denying a Socratic form of intellectualism that assumes that all the virtues belong to knowledge (*EN* VI 13, 1144b19–20).[69] The central Aristotelian view arising from such passages concerns the idea that the ability to achieve happiness turns on success in acting well and aiming at the human good. With this background, the interpretation that implies that the primary, if not the sole, object of *theoria* is God is a view ill-prepared for and inconsistent with major theses in *EN*.

---

[68] This problem holds even if one argues that the application of good across the categories is analyzed in a core-dependent homonymous fashion with God as the primary instance of the predicate goodness as this view precludes the synonymy of the good necessary for comparability; for various discussions about the good, see Ackrill (1978), Baker (2016), Gotthelf (1988), Shields (1999, 194–216; 2015), Ward (2008, 156–60).

[69] Other typical passages where we find the central rallying point of *EN* I 6 about the aim of ethics being practical, not theoretical, include *EN* II 2 (1103b26–27) and *EN* X 9 (1179a35–b4).

5.4.3   God as an Object of Aristotelian Theoria

A deeper problem attends the exclusive reading of the highest objects of *theoria*, whether it is advanced on the ontological or the epistemological view: it is one that does not arise from internal tensions within *EN* but from the definition of *theoria*. Put more precisely, if we assume with Burnet that the technical definition of *theoria* is "the activity (*energeia*) of scientific knowledge (*episteme*),"[70] we encounter a difficulty concerning the scientific knowledge of God, specifically. To put the problem briefly, if *episteme* is the scientific grasp of an object and the object is God, it follows that God is a possible object of scientific understanding (*episteme*).[71] For, having *episteme* of God implies having demonstrative knowledge of God, which, in turn, implies grasping God's essence by means of a demonstrative proof (*epideixis*). Here a difficulty arises concerning the lack of textual support for the idea that we can produce a demonstrative proof of God's essence; it seems, then, we must remain skeptical about the possibility of possessing scientific knowledge of God.[72] This conclusion requires supporting argumentation which is developed in detail in the subsequent section. For the moment, suffice it to say that the argument is directed at answering the question concerning the possible objects of human *theoria* for Aristotle – to which, the brief reply is that we cannot pose God as an object of *theoria* since we do not have *episteme* of God in the strict sense. As this conclusion may occasion disbelief, a fuller line of argument is detailed below employing two general lines of argument: one, mentioned above, depends on considerations about *episteme* itself, and the other, on considerations about the properties of God.

With regard to the first line of argument, recall that Aristotle understands *episteme* as the state of knowing the interrelation of specific propositions that are explanatory of the natural world.[73] For example, we have *episteme* about an eclipse, for example, when we can produce an argument

---

[70] For Burnet, the strict definition of *theoria* as the *energeia* of *episteme* is that which remains dominant throughout *EN* X 7 (Burnet 1900, xxviii, 258).

[71] For discussion about demonstration (*epideixis*) as the sole basis for scientific knowledge (*episteme*) see, for example, *An. Po.* 71b33–72a5, *Phys.* 184a16–23, and *EN* 1095b2–4. In general, *episteme* requires demonstrative knowledge of the subject, knowledge which reveals the reason for which an observable fact obtains; it also exhibits what is better known in itself.

[72] The problem with demonstrating God's essence differs from the usual objection concerning the inferential gap in apprehending scientific universals in that we lack the means for direct empirical confirmation or disconfirmation of some essence; see Barnes (1993, esp. 262–67), Burnyeat (1981), Irwin (1990), Upton (1981, 1987, 2004).

[73] So Burnyeat interprets *episteme* as "scientific understanding," referring to the state one has after grasping the demonstration (Burnyeat 1981), cf. Irwin (1990).

that explains the fact of the eclipse with an account of its cause.[74] As is well known, for Aristotle, *episteme* depends on knowing the why, or cause, of the item or phenomena; in the example above, it involves understanding the reason for a lunar eclipse, which is described as the lack of light from the moon, and this consists in grasping its cause as the interposition of the earth between the sun and the moon. Broadly speaking, then, we possess *episteme* when we are able to supply a demonstration (*epideixis*) of the phenomenon or thing under study; we provide a deductive argument whose middle premise states the reason for the observed fact – for example, that the moon casts no shadow – and explain the fact by means of the cause, namely, the earth intervening. What we are seeking by means of the demonstration is knowledge of the cause of the fact: this knowledge provides an account of the essence of an eclipse. By these means, we can explain why the moon casts no light although it is full; we are reasoning from a property of the lunar eclipse, namely, the lack of the moon's light, to the reason for the eclipse. So, when we have *episteme* of a lunar eclipse, we understand the essence of what a lunar eclipse is; there is nothing remaining to its essence that we fail to grasp with our intellect.

More to the point at hand, the epistemic fact just mentioned causes a problem when it comes to grasping God's essence scientifically. In effect, Aristotle's arguments about the properties of God in *Meta.* XII 7 are insufficient for constructing a demonstrative proof about God's essence, and consequently, we lack scientific knowledge of God. To the point at hand, since *theoria* implies having *episteme* of the object in question, it follows that God is not an object of *theoria* in the strict sense. The general conclusion to be noted, then, is that given the definition of *theoria* that Burnet provides, it does not appear that God can be an object of *theoria* precisely speaking. The previous conclusion need not imply that we have no knowledge of God; it is evident that he thinks we do from arguments in *Meta.* XII 7 and 9 that include empirical considerations about the causes of motion, as well as more non-empirical analyses about the causes of actuality, thought and desire. Leaving aside these arguments and their conclusions about properties of the Prime Mover for the moment, it is enough to suggest a gap between what Aristotle attributes to the deity in *Meta.* XII 7 and 9 and the epistemic conditions for scientific knowledge of a thing: we find that we possess only a limited grasp of divine nature.

[74] For discussion about the eclipse and Aristotle's account of scientific demonstration, see Goldin (1996, 15–40), Burnyeat (1981).

5.4.4   Problems with the Epistemological View

Let us consider the possibility of having scientific knowledge, or *episteme*, of God at greater length. To construct a demonstrative proof about God's essence, we need to establish "the that" (*to hoti*), or fact, of God's existence. We note that we do not follow quite the same path in showing the existence of God as we do with the eclipse, for, as mentioned, in case of the eclipse, we immediately perceive by sight the fact of the lunar eclipse by the lack of light from the moon, and then employ a rational procedure to infer its cause. We cannot grasp the fact of God by sight or another sense; rather we perceive the fact of motion or change in the sub-lunar world, including local motion, generation, and destruction, and these perceptions (or conclusions based on them) may be used as empirical premises in *a posteriori* proofs for a first cause of motion, as we find in *Meta.* XII 7. Leaving aside the details of this argument and accepting the argument as showing the need for a first cause of motion, let us consider whether we are justified in inferring God's essential properties from this or another of Aristotle's arguments about the Prime Mover in *Meta.* XII 7. We observe that the arguments establish that there is some eternal, immovable, separate substance (*Meta.* 1073a4–5) that is necessary and good (*Meta.* 1072b10–11); that it is in continuous activity of thinking itself (*Meta.*1072b19–20); it is without magnitude, without parts, indivisible (*Meta.* 1073a5–7), unaffected, and unalterable (*Meta.* 1073a11).

The problem in the proof concerns the fact that since these properties are logically distinct, we cannot know whether the properties established by the arguments for God's existence belong to the essence. So, while it appears that being a first cause of motion belongs to God as a necessary property, there is no logical connection between this and the property of being in continuous thought about thinking. So, it appears that nothing prevents a being that is the first cause of motion from existing independently from one that is continuously thinking itself (*Meta.* XII 7, 1072b19–20). Consequently, we are unable to understand why other properties of God such as being an eternal substance (*Meta.* 1073a3–4), being in continual activity (*energeia, Meta.* 1072b23–24), being alive (*Meta.* 1072b26), or being most good (*Meta.* 1072b29) belong to God. In other words, we do not know that thought thinking itself is a cause of the other properties, and so, we cannot know how these properties are related causally. For example, we do not know which properties are necessary, which are essential, and which are accidental. Furthermore, we do not even know whether what we are thinking about is one unified essence or more than one essence since the priority and relation of these properties cannot be known. So, even if we were to assume that God's essence is the continual thinking about thinking, we cannot grasp the reasoned cause, or why this is so. We may grasp some of the properties that belong to God, but we cannot know how they are united and what their causal essence is. Consequently, it appears that we can have no *episteme* of God. But if we cannot have *episteme* of God, we cannot exercise *theoria* of God, strictly speaking, insofar as we defined *theoria* as an activity of *episteme*, and as such, it is an activity that requires having a rational grasp of an essence as its precondition.[75] Again, however, nothing prevents us from exercising our intellectual powers of reasoning on the nature of the Prime Mover, such as being a first cause of motion, immovable, simple, complete, and so on, and to the extent that we produce sound, if not demonstrative, arguments, we have some knowledge of God.

Considering the difficulty in exercising *theoria* of God's essence, we need to take stock of other possible objects of *theoria*. Recalling that in *EN* X 7, Aristotle states that *theoria* is the "highest" power and apprehends "the most knowable" objects (*EN* 1177a19–20), we might also consider stressing the latter feature, being most knowable. From this angle, this list would include: (i) the forms of sensible, imperishable substances such as celestial bodies; (ii) the forms of sensible, perishable substances, which includes natural biological kinds (e.g., horses, human beings); and (iii) the forms of parts of perishable substances (e.g., hearts or legs). The argument for the revised list consists in the fact that Aristotle considers forms or formal essences as more knowable than their composite counterparts (whether sub-lunar or supra-lunar substances) because they are causes of composite entities. By considering the objects of *theoria* as forms of perishable and imperishable substances, we satisfy the condition of their being the "most knowable" (*EN* 1177a20–21) of objects. For reasons of consistency, I have excluded the laws of logic for this revised list of the most knowable objects on the ground that they are not susceptible of demonstration, strictly speaking, although we and Aristotle would concur in their being among the most knowable in themselves.[76] On the present

---

[75] While we do not have *theoria* of God's essence in the strict sense, nothing prevents an understanding of the properties mentioned, namely, continuous thinking of thinking, being a primary cause of motion or a complete activity; so, we can grasp something about a divine being thusly; compare Aquinas on problems in the comprehension of God, *Summa Theologiae*, Part 1, Question 12 (esp. Articles 1, 4, 7, 11).

[76] So, I am excluding logical laws in this revised list since we are requiring objects of *theoria* are demonstrable, and Aristotle claims they are not strictly so, although they are amenable to proof by *reductio* arguments (*An. Po.* I 11, 77a22–31) and are most certain (*Meta.* IV 3, 1005b17–24).

list of objects, then, we may exercise *theoria* with regard to anything within the class of formal entities, including forms of sensible, perishable substances as well as forms of imperishable substances. The explanation for this conception of the class resides in the fact that we have a prior grasp of these entities by means of *episteme*, and so we can exercise such knowledge in the activity of *theoria*.

Before concluding that the epistemological view of objects of *theoria* is better supported both by arguments and texts, let me mention a potential objection to the present epistemic interpretation that is concerned with linguistic ambiguity: this arises from the fact that the verb *epistamai* (ἐπίσταμαι) admits of a broad and a narrow sense. For example, at times Aristotle uses the term *epistamai* in a broad sense to mean "to know" in the sense of "to be aware of" something, and this fact might be thought to have implications for what scientific knowledge, or *episteme*, consists in. Let us suppose that, taken in a broad sense, the verb *epistamai* implies having general, non-scientific knowledge of something, not scientific knowledge of something. If we transfer this broad sense of knowing to what Aristotle terms *episteme*, it might appear that the objects of *theoria* could be described more broadly than we have done. Specifically, it might be argued that a broad reading of *episteme* would allow having non-scientific knowledge of God, given that Aristotle's arguments in *Meta.* XII 7 provide grounds for God's existence.[77] In this case, we might be able to exercise *theoria* on the objects these grounds provide, allowing for some non-scientific knowledge of God, even if we do not have demonstrations about God's essence. For, it may be conceded that the arguments in *Meta.* XII 7 provide a rational basis for the fact of God's existence, even if they fail to prove what belongs to God's essence. The objection posed thus depends on showing that we might have *theoria* of a wider range of objects if we widen the scope of what the verb *epistamai* – and thus, the noun *episteme* – signify.

However, the present objection faces a textual problem in that it is inconsistent with the notion of theoretical knowledge advanced not only in *EN* X 7, but in Aristotle's theory of demonstration in *An. Po* I. As we noted, in *EN* X 7, he is offering specific grounds for the idea that *theoria* is the highest, most complete activity, directed at specific objects. The difficulty in arguing for a broad reading of *epistamai* here in *EN* X 7 is

---

[77] I have not argued decisively against the position that the arguments in *Meta.* XII 7 provide knowledge of the necessary *propria* of God; the attributes shown by arguments may be necessary; whether they belong to the essence is another issue.

that it would necessitate a similarly broad reading of *theoria* such that it (*theoria*) would be understood as being generally aware of any object, say, of nursery rhymes as well as of mathematical proof. Yet, since in *EN* X 7 we find that *theoria*'s objects are the knowable and *theoria* is the highest activity, to suppose that the activity of *theoria* could be directed at the lowest, as well as the highest, kind of objects would be wholly inconsistent. Since the kind of *episteme* implied in *EN* X 7 is not just a "garden-variety" state of knowing, similarly, the kind of *theoria* concerned here cannot be thinking about "garden-variety" types of objects.

In sum, the textual evidence from *EN* X 7 in conjunction with that of *DA* II 1 and II 5, supports three conclusions: (i) *theoria* has objects that are different in kind from those of other cognitive faculties, like belief; (ii) the strict sense of *theoria* implies having achieved a prior state, scientific knowledge (*episteme*) which is understood in its precise sense as having reasoned comprehension of real essences; (iii) the activity of *theoria* is directed at epistemologically elevated objects, the forms of substances which are grasped by *episteme*. So, the objects of *theoria* are better considered as comprising forms, or formal abstractions, of sensible and non-sensible substances rather than the most ontologically elevated object, God. Consequently, while we may exercise *theoria* in the strict sense about the formal essences of sensible, imperishable substances like the heavenly bodies or about the formal essences of sensible, perishable substances like biological natural kinds, we do not exercise *theoria* in the same strict sense about God.[78]

5.5   Conclusion: The Objects of *Theoria*

Taking a long, comparative view across the three areas of focus, the traditional, Platonic, and Aristotelian notions of *theoria*, three general conclusions about the objects of *theoria* are worth noting. First, a reliance on sacred images (*agalmata*) in the kinds of traditional *theoria* we considered, namely, the travel to festivals and shrines, invites comparison with Plato's employment of *theoria* and its objects. For, Plato makes implicit or explicit reference to traditional *theoria* and sometimes, to its objects in specific dialogues: in *Phaedrus*, where the lover makes an "image" of the beloved (*Phdr.* 249d–251b), in *Rep.* V, with reference to "lovers of

---

[78] This claim does not bear on the intellectual activity of the god which Aristotle describes as *theoria* in *Meta.* XII 7: "and its *theoria* is most pleasant and best" (καὶ ἡ θεωρία τὸ ἥδιστον καὶ ἄριστον, *Meta.* 1072b23).

spectacles" (*philatheamones*) running to attend festivals (*Rep.* 475d–476c), in *Rep.* I, in the mention of going to the festival in Piraeus (Rep. 328a–b), or to the Delian in (*Cr.* 43c9–d1; *Phd.* 58b1–5). Secondly, we find Plato employing theoric structures, such as perception by sensible images (functioning as *agalmata*) that may lead to recollection and upward to intelligible objects, forms, as, for example, in the recollection passages in *Phd.* (73c4–77a5) and *Phdr.* (254b1–4), and the ascent passages in *Rep.* VII (514a–516c) and *Symp.* (210a–212c). While Plato's complex theoric structure gives a nod to the larger practice of traditional *theoria*, clearly, it also transcends it. Third, Aristotle's own line of thinking about the path to the apprehension of scientific first principles is indebted to Plato's in the respect that both reflect a similar reliance on sense-perception and recollection in the upward ascent to such apprehension (*episteme*); like Plato, he terms the activity of such knowing *theoria*, describing its qualities in *EN* X 7.[79] Thus, the similarity between Platonic and Aristotelian philosophical *theoria* concerns the coincidence in its objects: for both, the proper objects of philosophical *theoria* are forms, or formal essences.[80] For both thinkers, formal entities are discovered by a route that begins with sense-perception, is aided by recollection or complex cognitive perception, and eventually leads to scientific knowledge; the activity of such knowing is *theoria*, which, in essence, consists in something god-like, seeing the first causes of being, the forms. However, while Plato makes frequent references to traditional *theoria*, developing his conception of Platonic *theoria* alongside the traditional account, Aristotle, perhaps for stylistic reasons of composition, does not employ it.[81] Aristotle's extended analysis of *theoria* in *EN* X 7–8 reflects his debt to Plato's theory of philosophical *theoria* in the various respects mentioned, particularly, that the objects of *theoria* are forms, or formal essences, and its activity consists in what we may term a Platonic vision of form.[82]

---

[79] Some references to sense-perception as causally fundamental to scientific knowledge include *Meta.* I 1 (980a23–981b12), *An. Po.* II 19 (99b34–100b5), *Phys.* I 1 (184a10–b14); for discussion, see, for example, Barnes (2002, 261–71), Bolton (1991, 2005), Salmieri (2010), Tuominen (2010).

[80] Allowing for the accepted metaphysical differences between Platonic and Aristotelian form.

[81] Why not? While Aristotle is clearly not unaware of traditional *theoria*, as a reference about the cost of leading a *theoria* (in relation to magnificence) at *EN* IV 2, 1122a24–25 shows, his literary needs are not Plato's.

[82] The phrase "the vision of Form" is borrowed from Vlastos (1997, 190); on its implications, see Ch. 6, sec. 6.2.2.

CHAPTER 6

The Value of Theoria

And there in life, my friend Socrates . . . there if anywhere should a
person live his life, beholding (*theomeno*) that Beauty . . . Do you
think it would be a poor life for a human being to look there and
behold (*theomenou*) it by which he ought, and to be with it?

(*Symp.* 211d1–3, 211e4–212a2)

6.1 Reasons for Engaging in *Theoria*

The final chapter is devoted to examining a central issue concerning *theoria*
that has remained implicit in our discussion up to this point, namely, why
theoria is deemed good, or is valuable. More precisely stated, we need to
examine the reasons for which individuals and cities held traditional,
Platonic, and Aristotelian *theoria* good and pursued it.[1] For present purposes, we are employing a distinction between an instrumental and a non-
instrumental standard of value that differentiates, broadly speaking,
between something producing something else of value – as something
producing a good result – and something having value in itself by virtue of
its own quality.[2] Furthermore, since Aristotle considers *theoria* an activity
(*energeia*), let us distinguish between a good instrumental and good non-
instrumental activity as follows: (i) an instrumentally good activity is one
where its goodness depends on its effect, or what it produces; (ii) a non-
instrumentally good activity is one where its goodness depends on an
intrinsic quality of the activity itself. Following Aristotle's descriptive use
of "good" in *EN* I 1 according to which the good of an action or choice is

---

[1] For present purposes, we consider traditional *theoria* as sight-seeing in Herodotus (*Hist.* 1. 29) falling
under festival-attendance; for discussion, see Ch. 2, fn. 9, and ff.
[2] Admittedly, the instrumental/intrinsic distinction has limitations for making distinctions as to the
cause of the goodness, on which see Tuozzo (1995); in what follows, I try to clarify the source of the
value, generally following the formulations suggested by Plato *Rep.* II (357b4–358a2) and Aristotle
EN I 6 (1096b13–16).

synonymous with its aim or end (*EN* 1094a1–5), we may infer that the good of an instrumental activity depends on its effect whereas the good of a non-instrumental activity resides in the nature of the activity rather than anything arising from it. In addition to the two contrasting kinds of good activities, it is useful to consider a third kind that we may describe as "mixed" in that it includes those having both instrumental and non-instrumental value.[3] This category recalls the class of goods that Plato names "the finest" (*to kallisto, Rep.* 358a1): it is that which includes justice, referring to what we like "for its own sake and also for what comes from it" (*Rep.* 357c1–2). It seems reasonable, then, to consider what the source of the value attached to *theoria* is, specifically, whether it is thought to be desired as a "mixed" good in the sense of being valuable partly for itself and partly for its effect, or as an instrumental good or a non-instrumental good.[4]

The addition of the mixed class of goods that Plato suggests in *Rep.* II is useful for surmounting difficulties that arise from a two-value schema according to which *theoria* is pursued exclusively as an instrumental or a non-instrumental good. By adopting the tripartite schema, we find ourselves able to accommodate counter-examples, and also, formulate two general hypotheses for testing subsequently. The first hypothesis proposed is that traditional *theoria* is primarily an instrumental good in the sense that its central value depends on obtaining results extrinsic to the theoric activities themselves, and second, to show that while Plato and Aristotle praise philosophical *theoria* primarily on non-instrumental grounds, inspection reveals that they do not entirely reject the idea of *theoria* being useful. Rather, they relegate its utility to a decidedly second place, typically praising *theoria* on non-utilitarian grounds, claiming that it is sought for its own sake, and not for its effects. Part of the task before us, then, concerns the extent to which the positions of Plato and Aristotle about *theoria*'s value constitute a continuation (or a reversal) of the valuation assigned to traditional *theoria*.

---

[3] Two notes: first, while activities are not explicitly mentioned in Aristotle's enumeration of goods in *EN* I 6, they are included in Aristotle's functional description in *EN* I1 (1094a1–5); second, Plato's list of goods in *Rep.* II (357b4–358a2) mentions first intrinsic goods, second, mixed goods, and third, instrumental goods; my inclusion of an intermediate, or mixed, class is due to Plato's lead.

[4] I note that in the tripartite presentation of goods in *Rep.* II, Plato distinguishes what I am calling the instrumental good as a third kind, that which is "onerous but beneficial to us" like medical treatment (cf. *Rep.* 357c5–d1); here the description "what is beneficial but painful" implies that the justification for choosing such a thing is for its effect only: you chose it for its effect despite its being onerous.

6.1.1 The Value of Traditional Theoria

Keeping in mind the tripartite schema of value sketched above, we turn first to the question about why traditional *theoria* was pursued, which, of course, brings up certain divisions within traditional *theoria*, the primary one being that between festival-attendance and sanctuary-visitation. In addition, we note that where traditional *theoria* signifies civic festival-attendance, the practice comprises several different activities: viz., observing festival events, participating in rituals, publicly representing the city, and reporting to the city-council after the event. A similar observation may be offered concerning *theoria* as sanctuary-visitation, in which case, we find individuals seeking cures who are engaged in various subsidiary activities, such as making offerings, undergoing purification, requesting interventions from the deity, and similar actions.[5] Having noted the heterogeneity among the subsidiary activities, it may appear that we are faced with the problem of assessing the value of each constituent activity rather than that of the whole. This problem is more apparent than real, however, for, as Aristotle reminds us, an action or activity that is undertaken for a more proximate end is evaluated relative to that end (cf. *EN* I 1, 1094a14–18; 1.7, 1097a25–32); so, the subsidiary activities of traditional *theoria* are, logically speaking, valuable relative to their overall end, specifically, that of festival-attendance or sanctuary-visitation. So, the value attached to the activities making up civic *theoria*, such as observing festival events or reporting to a city-council, must be considered in relation to the general end of civic *theoria* we noted. In so doing, acknowledging the activities comprising festival-attendance, say, does not threaten to shatter the unity of the general activity. For, as we have noted in Chapter 1, the central meaning underlying traditional *theoria* consists in observing something sacred or something of high significance. To employ the phrasing of a classical scholar, we might consider referring to the common character of festival- and sanctuary-attendance as "watching for a manifestation of a god" (Naiden 2005, 91). It becomes evident that by placing traditional *theoria* under this description, we judge the value of the constituent activities in light of their utility to the overall aim which becomes the

---

[5] The distinction in the two roles is reflected by a lesser-used term *hiketes* ("one who comes/arrives," pl. *hiketai*; on etymology, Beneveniste 1969, 2.254) for one traveling to a healing sanctuary: in general, Naiden (2005) finds the civic *theoros* primarily tied to observation, noting "the *theoros* participates in the spectacle he sees ... [representing] those who cannot attend" (Naiden 2005, 73), whereas the *hiketes* plays a more active part by initiating a request to the god(s) of the shrine, and "when they approve, he and they initiate a relation, such as *xenia*" (Naiden 2005, 74).

primary focus.[6] So, let us investigate the sources of value that appear attached to festival-attendance and sanctuary-visitation.

6.1.2   The Value of Festival-Attendance

The question concerning the value of festival-attendance requires more attention than that of sanctuary-visitation as it has greater complexity. More specifically, we distinguish three levels of value attached to festival-attendance relative to levels of practice, namely, the value to the citizen-delegate, to the city, and to the alliance of city-states. The first aspect, that involving the value to the citizen-delegate, appears to consist primarily in the civic honor conferred on the official *theoros* in virtue of the duties, such as the festival observation, participation, and post-event reporting to the city-council. The second aspect, the value to the city, consists in the public display of the city's status that the delegate's activity produces by displaying the city's status to the general public present at the festival, and indirectly, to other participating Greek cities. If, in addition, the elected delegate is undertaking certain political duties for the city, such as securing interviews with politicians in the host city, these activities, if successful, would provide additional instrumental value to the home city. The diplomatic aspect of civic *theoria* leads us to a third level, the value to the city-states engaged in civic *theoria*. The value of this aspect of civic *theoria* largely depends on the benefit of sharing common religious and cultural beliefs.

At all three levels, civic *theoria* is clearly pursued for its good effects, although each level aims at securing specific benefits. So, for example, the official delegate is seeking the public recognition and honor from the city; the city seeks public confirmation of its status through its display in the festival procession and its rituals, and also seeks to benefit from political alliances with fellow civic leaders.[7] Finally, the city-states involved comprise a network which benefits from the effect of Greek cultural integration and cultural identity that civic *theoria* produces. But at each level, the primary value of festival *theoria* depends on what the activity produces, and so, broadly speaking, is an instrumental good. Yet we need to investigate both civic *theoria* (festival-attendance) and visitation to sanctuaries more

---

[6] To this common feature, we would add the specific end, such that festival-attendance is described as watching for manifestation of the divine in relation to attending festivals, and something similar is added for visitation to sanctuaries.

[7] Rutherford provides analysis of civic *theoria* and inter-state politics with delegates acting as diplomats (Rutherford 2013, 250–63).

closely to determine whether their value is primarily or solely instrumental, and if the former, whether either includes non-instrumental value as well.

We now consider the value attached to the attendance at festivals as it is undertaken, first, by a private individual (citizen, resident alien, or slave), and second, by a city-appointed *theoros*.[8] First, let us suppose an individual is traveling as a private citizen to the festival at Olympia; if the individual is wealthy, he may be sponsoring his own athletes in foot-racing or chariot-racing, as Alcibiades recounts to the Athenian council about his private *theoria* (Thucydides, *Hist*. VI, 16, 2). In such cases, a wealthy, private citizen may have the aim both of observing the events and of attaining the honor or fame attached to sponsoring victorious athletes or teams at the games. In addition, if he is of high social standing, he may be hoping to build or to cement his political standing. Next, consider an individual attending a festival as a city-appointed delegate: his task is more complex in that it combines acting as a civic observer with other duties.[9] For example, an appointed *theoros* is acting as a representative of a home city, first, by observing and taking part in the religious rituals, especially ritual sacrifices, as well as by attending and observing games and second, by playing a political role similar to a foreign ambassador for the duration of the festival. For, the appointed civic *theoros* not only has to show the proper respect and restraint in all his actions during the festival, but must make a personal report to the city-council about his observations and contribution after returning. In this respect, the appointed *theoros* has a crucial task to perform after his responsibilities at the festival are fully carried out: his observations are formally presented before the city assembly of the home city, making the utility of this kind of *theoria* different in kind from that performed by the private citizen.

The complex role of the city-appointed delegates, particularly that of official civic representatives, marks the function as similar to that of a diplomat or an ambassador. Two aspects of civic *theoria* gives rise to the similarity. One arises from the feature internal to the practice of state-appointed *theoria*, namely, that the official *theoros* is acting as the representative of the entire city since the *demos* votes to send out a named individual as the *architheoros* (head delegate) on behalf of the city. So, for

---

[8] We may also distinguish, first, the roles and responsibilities of the *theoroi* as appointed announcers, sometimes also called *presbeutai*, from the festival observers (cf. Dillon 1997, 5–6; Rutherford 2013, 71–76); second, the participant's social, class status makes a difference.

[9] So, we find that certain duties associated with *theoroi*, such as officiating at rituals and acting as envoys, can be seen as reflecting the duties of *theoroi* as magistrates, rather than as sacred observers, as Rutherford claims (2013, 127–41).

example, Demosthenes mentions himself elected as *architheoros* "to lead the common *theoria* on behalf of the city" to the Nemean Festival (ἀγαγεῖν τῷ Διὶ τῷ Νεμείῳ τὴν κοινὴν ὑπὲρ τῆς πόλεως θεωρίαν, Demosthenes 21. 115).[10] The phrase of note in the decree is ". . . on behalf of the city," which reflects the special political status of state-appointed *theoroi*, a status that does not apply to private citizens traveling to festivals. As one scholar notes, "*theoroi* are agents of the political authorities who send them" (Rutherford 2013, 213), and for this reason, they can be charged with carrying out activities that would be considered improper for private citizens.[11] So, for example, an official *theoros* may be directed to meet with or give advice to leading politicians of the festival host city or to visit host cities while he is attending a festival.[12]

A third level of value that arises from civic *theoria* is that, by providing benefits to Greek city-states it comprises a form of political alliance that transcends individual states. The role of civic *theoria* in supporting this kind of association is explained by the fact that the organization of panhellenic festivals (Olympian, Pythian, Isthmian, Nemean) supports a network of shared religious and political values.[13] We may conceive civic *theoria* contributing to a pan-Greek alliance in two ways: in the short term, through the laws extending truces (*spondai*) among the participating cities for the festival period during which attendants could travel freely through the territories of the city-states, including those engaged in war.[14] Over the long term, civic *theoria* provides palpable, beneficial effects in cementing the network of Greek festival cities through shared laws and practices. The supporting argument here is that by providing space in which Greeks met one another within the structure of shared cultural practices such as theatrical performances, athletic events, and religious rituals, civic *theoria*

---

[10] A similarly worded honorary decree mentions electing Kallias of Sphettos as *architheoros* to lead the Athenian *theoria* to Alexandria "on behalf of the city" (*SEG*, 28.60.56–59).

[11] Formally appointed *theoroi* to festivals are typically sent by individual cities, but in some cases were sent by a federation, like the Thessalian League, or an organization, like the Delphic Amphiktiony (the states administering the Delphic sanctuary) or the Dionysiac artists, organizations of professional musical performers for *theoriai* (for discussion, see Rutherford 2013, 214, cf. 29, 66, 210, 245).

[12] E.g., Demosthenes acting as *architheoros* to Olympia (324 BCE) wants to use his position to interview Nikanor to discuss Alexander's exile's decree (Dillon 1997, 22).

[13] Having said this, it should also be pointed out that the interconnected network of festival cities and sanctuaries depended on various specific factors, including proximity and distance of sites; special connections forged among the two; long-held traditions of *theoriai*, like that of Athens to Delos; reciprocity between cities based on festivals; see Rutherford (2013, 297–303).

[14] Dillon (1997, 20) notes that another term for *spondai* is *ekecheira*, used for political truces; for discussion about truces, see Rutherford (2013, 71–92), Dillon (1997, 1–8).

as a practice promotes inter-state alliances as well as shared cultural ideals. Most classical scholars thus allow that civic *theoria* has the effect of spreading Greek religious and cultural values, even if they differ about the degree to which civic *theoria* promotes strong panhellenism.[15] So, for example, a classicist arguing on the side of civic *theoria* effecting panhellenism has observed that "*theoria* brought foreign Greeks together … to witness spectacles and participate in rituals" so that while a *theoros* maintained his own political identity, "he participated in events that celebrated a Greek identity over and above that of any individual city-state" (Nightingale 2004, 35). Another scholar similarly comments that while Greeks traveled to festivals as members of individual city-states, these same festivals provided the means through which a broader Greek identity could be forged.[16] In summary, this overview about *theoria* as festival-attendance shows that the practice produces substantial benefits to the alliance of Greek cities as well as to the individual attending as an official delegate and also to the participating cities.

6.1.3   The Value of Sanctuary-Visitation

The value of visiting healing sanctuaries, in particular, allows a simpler analysis in that, at base, we see individuals traveling to healing sanctuaries, like Delphi, with a single aim, to seek help in curing physical ailments.[17] A case in point is provided by Euripides' story of Creusa's *theoria* to Delphi in the *Ion*, where Creusa is traveling to Delphi to find a remedy for infertility, with the value of her *theoria* depending on her success. Of course, visitation to healing sanctuaries may be undertaken by state groups, as well as by private individuals, but the overall aim remains the same. In general, we find that a *theoria* to a healing sanctuary involves arriving at a shrine and asking the god to help cure some bodily ailment. Specifically, the healing *theoria* typically includes the performance of a special sequence of actions, including making an offering to the god, purifying oneself,

---

[15] For example, Scullion's skeptical view on the issue leads him to find "panhellenic *theoria* a fleeting and elusive thing" (Scullion 2005, 128), a view that contrasts with that of Elsner and Rutherford who find that "the panhellenic *theoria* of the 5th century BCE was an expression of shared religious and cultural traditions of participating states" (Elsner and Rutherford, 2005, 260).

[16] As she notes, given that "the *polis* anchored, legitimated, and mediated all religious activity" (Sourvinou-Inwood 1990, 297), cited by Nightingale (2004, 52).

[17] Travel to oracular sites, such as at Delphi, Thebes, or Dodona, differs in its aim from travel to sanctuaries for medical cures, yet, as one classicist observes, both involve traveling to find "solutions to specific problems" – we might imagine those of personal health or political success, say – and he considers them falling under the same class (Dillon 1997, 60).

asking for and receiving divine help so as to achieve one's desired end, such as curing an illness or a disorder. Some visitors to the sanctuary also pay fees to stay overnight in the sanctuary in anticipation of receiving special dreams that may aid them in their cure.[18] Among these activities, it seems clear that some, such as purification, may have been thought to provide intrinsic value to the individual.[19] But, once again, since such activities are undertaken for the sake of being healed, this value is secondary to the overall end. In general, then, if an activity is undertaken as means to an end, this end provides the standard for the activity. Thus, subsidiary activities undertaken for the sake of bodily curing have instrumental value, namely, a value relative to being healed. It may be noted that in some cases of traditional *theoria*, like travel to healing sanctuaries, individuals may even experience hardship in the constituent activities as well as in the traveling to the sites, and such cases closely resemble Plato's description of "onerous but beneficial" goods (*Rep.* 357c6–d1). But overall, it appears that the primary value of traditional *theoria*, whether we consider travel to healing sanctuaries or attendance at festivals, depends on the benefits obtained, such as being cured, lessening physical pain, or receiving a civic honor. Although we find several distinct ends among these, they are pursued for a utilitarian aim: their good consisting in the final goal of the action.

In addition to having instrumental value, it seems likely that some subsidiary activities in traditional *theoria* are pursued for intrinsic value as well. So, it would not be surprising if individuals attending theoric festivals also enjoyed the experience, quite apart from whatever benefits the activity provided. For example, it seems obvious that being an observer or participant at festival events affords the individual a pleasant, perhaps a thrilling, visual or auditory experience: recall the lovers of spectacles in *Rep.* V rushing around to festivals, seeking more spectacular experience (*Rep.* 475d–e). But this aspect of festival-attendance – the immediate experience sought by thrill-seeking fans of spectacles – does not outweigh the overall valuation of the practice for its results. At most, I think we may concede

---

[18] The process is called "incubating," according to Dillon (1997, 75); he also mentions that major healing sanctuaries, like Epidauros and Kos, tended to be full of sick pilgrims, which implies an extended duration of stay.

[19] Rutherford (2013, 192–95) claims that the standard rituals in *theoria* at sanctuaries (e.g., contact with *proxenos*, sacrifice, procession) involve the element of being in "proximity to or contact with the god" (2013, 193); in addition, Dillon (1997, 204–14) mentions specific prohibitions at healing sanctuaries such as abstinence, cleansing, refraining from misconduct like drunkenness, thieving, and the like.

that festival-attendance may be valued for the experience as well as for the benefits. But in deciding whether to place traditional *theoria* under Plato's class of mixed goods mentioned in *Rep*. II, we note that Plato's analysis tends in a different direction than our analysis of traditional *theoria*. For, Plato's class of intermediate goods, which includes seeing, knowing, and being healthy, are things valued "for their own sake and for the sake of what comes from them as well" (*Rep*. II, 357c1–2).[20] The goods that Plato describes are primarily valued for themselves, and secondarily for their results, as both sentence structure and logic require. First, Plato sets the phrase "what we love for its own sake" in primary place and "what comes from it" in secondary place; hence, it makes no sense to claim that someone loves something both for itself and for its results to the same degree. Second, since Plato's examples of seeing, knowing, and being healthy are understood as being primarily loved for themselves, they cannot be equally valued for their results. However – and here we add emphasis – since according to our analysis of traditional *theoria*, the primary value of the activities depends on what they produce, not in the activities themselves, they would not be placed in the class of mixed goods that Plato names in *Rep*. II. If there were a class of intermediate goods that consisted in things valued primarily for their results and secondarily for their intrinsic value, some activities of traditional *theoria* might belong to this. But the result about intermediate goods leaves open the question concerning whether Plato and Aristotle consider *theoria* to belong to such a class or to one of the others.

6.2 Plato's Valuation of *Theoria*

The topic of assessing the value of *theoria* for Plato requires a bit of clarification as it may be construed as implying either of two kinds of analysis, one concerning the value for Plato that philosophical *theoria* has for those who would become philosophers, and the other, the value that theoric language has in Plato's works. The focus of the present chapter, predictably, concerns the first topic, but we give brief attention to the second as well. We open the investigation by recalling that Plato employs theoric terminology in two distinct ways. More specifically, he puts the

---

[20] Aristotle finds that sight (of all the special senses) belongs to things loved for their own sake (*Meta.* I, 1, 980b22–24); yet it is also valued for its use as being "the most important for the necessities of living" (*DS* I, 437a5–6) and for its utility for stages of cognition, see *An. Po.* II 19, cf. Salmieri (2010), Tuominen (2010).

theor/eo/ia family of terms to use primarily in relation to two contexts of meaning: (i) to traditional *theoria*, and (ii) to philosophical contemplation. Furthermore, while he uses theoric language in both contexts, the technical employment of such terminology appears in the second context where the specific reference is to the intellectual activity of apprehending forms. Since we have identified this activity as identical with Platonic *theoria*, our present inquiry about the value of *theoria* to Plato is devoted largely to assessing what worth Plato attaches to this specific activity. However, since Plato often employs theoric terminology in a double context of meaning, describing philosophical *theoria* against the broader backdrop of traditional *theoria* (i.e., festival-attendance), we need to consider how he employs traditional *theoria* in this context. A key text illuminating both uses occurs in *Rep.* V where Plato describes the followers of traditional *theoria*, "the lovers of sights and sounds," as dreamers who pursue appearances of the beautiful by attending spectacles at festivals (cf. *Rep.* 476b1–5). Since the followers of traditional *theoria* are in epistemic confusion, mistaking beautiful appearances for the beautiful, this group provides Plato with a perfect foil to describe philosophers, the true seekers of beauty (cf. *Rep.* 476c2–7). Plato reflects the difference in terminology, calling the festival-goer "a lover of spectacles" (*philotheamonas*) and terming the philosopher is "a lover of the spectacle of truth" (*philotheamonas tes aletheais* [τοὺς τῆς ἀληθείας ... φιλοθεάμονας], 475e3–4).[21] Plato employs theoric terminology here with pedagogical intent, contrasting the differences between two kinds of followers and two ways of thinking; one easily pronounces the instrumental value of such contrasts. We can discern a similar intent in the way in which Plato uses references to theoric events to construct ring compositions in certain dialogues, which, again, may be assumed as constructed for teaching purposes. In brief, the value of Plato's theoric terminology used as compositional elements in several dialogues concerns the poetic and philosophical effects they have on the reader or listener, whether the terms are deployed in a straightforward, critical, or ironical tone, which indicates their having instrumental worth.

6.2.1   Plato's Valuation of Philosophical Theoria

Let us turn to the philosophical question concerning the value that Platonic, or philosophical, *theoria* possesses for Plato. To do this, let us

---

[21] Plato expresses the epistemic contrast in two apposite phrases, "the lover of the spectacle of truth" and "the lover of spectacles," which reflects the core idea that seeing a Platonic "spectacle" is not akin to watching a theatrical appearance, but is apprehending being, the ground of all appearances.

locate it in relation to one of the three classes of goods Plato describes in *Rep.* II (357b–d) that we sketched above. Our evidence points to it belonging to the second class described as including the things that are both good in themselves and good for their effects. However, Plato presents the intermediate class of goods in a rather ambiguous way, leaving it unclear how the two goods are conjoined. More specifically, we need to decide how something loved "for itself" (αὐτοῦ χάριν) and something loved "for what comes from it" (χάριν ... ἀπ' αὐτοῦ γιγνομένων, *Rep.* 357c1–2) are being weighed against one another. Taking a perfectly natural way of conjoining the two, Grube and Reeve seem to let the thing loved for itself take precedent in reading: "Is there a kind of good we love both for its own sake and also for the sake of what comes from it?" (357c2–3).[22] This reading suggests that the thing loved for itself has primary value and its effect has secondary value. Moreover, Socrates' examples, the verbal nouns "knowing" (*to phronein*), "seeing" (*to horan*), and "being healthy" (*to hygienein*) (*Rep.* 357c2–3), lend themselves to this reading.[23] For, it is natural to conceive the states of seeing, knowing, and being healthy as valued first for themselves, and then also for what comes from them. We will pursue the weighing of the two values further in a moment. At this point, the first question at hand concerns whether Plato would place the activity of philosophical *theoria* among this class of the "finest" goods, namely, those valued for themselves and also for their effect (cf. *Rep.* 358a1–2).

Let us approach the issue by investigating the other alternatives, namely, that *theoria* might belong to one of the other classes described at *Rep.* II, namely, being loved for itself or loved for its effects (cf. *Rep.* 357b3–d3). It is immediately obvious that Plato would not include *theoria* in the third class, the kind valued only for its effects, such as undergoing physical training, taking medicine or undergoing medical treatment (cf. *Rep.*357c5–6). For while these goods are useful, no one would choose them for themselves as they are strenuous or painful; we choose them only for their beneficial results (cf. *Rep.* 357c5–d3). Yet it is obvious that Plato does not believe philosophical *theoria* is good for its effects alone. As we have seen, Plato gives many arguments showing philosophical *theoria* is loved for itself and is an intrinsic good.[24] One might wonder, then, whether this kind of *theoria* is valued only for itself, like "joy and other

---

[22] The Greek line runs thus: ὃ αὐτό τε αὐτοῦ χάριν ἀγαπῶμεν καὶ τῶν ἀπ' αὐτοῦ γιγνομένων (*Rep.* II, 357c1–2).

[23] Plato repeats the list at *Rep.* 367c19–22, adding hearing (*akouein*) as part of the class; Plato earlier specifies justice (*dikaiosune*) in this class, *Rep.* 358a1–2.

[24] E.g., since Platonic *theoria* consists in apprehending forms, it is evident that Plato finds this activity of intrinsic value.

harmless pleasures" (*Rep.* 357b6). In reply, we might foreclose this possibility by recalling Plato's comment about mixed goods as comprising "the finest" kind (*Rep.* 358a1) from which we might infer that *theoria* must possess good effects as well. Yet, surely, a more persuasive argument would show where Plato affirms that *theoria* brings about good results, and what these are.

We can find no better evidence of Plato's position about the mixed, or intermediate, value of philosophical *theoria* than by turning to the passages on *theoria* from *Rep.* VI–VII. Our starting point is the cave analogy in *Rep.* VII where the budding philosopher achieves the ascent from the cave, studies the forms, and returns to the cave (city) to practice politics (cf. *Rep.* 519b–520d). The analogy reflects two aspects of *theoria* and two corresponding sources of value: the philosopher who has ascended engages in philosophical *theoria* for its own sake, and in returning to the city, proves its instrumental value. From the perspective of the complete, fully trained philosopher that Plato presents in *Rep.* VII, these two aspects are not contradictory, but complementary: philosophical *theoria* constitutes an intrinsic good to the philosopher whose political wisdom provides an instrumental good to the city (i.e., this wisdom is the "that by which" civic justice is secured). In this context, Glaucon's familiar objection to Socrates that the city does philosophers a disservice by returning them to the city (*Rep.* VII, 519d9) glosses over two aspects of the philosophers' education that moderates their self-interest. One concerns the process of character education that philosophers undergo, enabling them to consider themselves part of the city the good of which they are actively seeking, i.e., to make civil society "more harmonious with itself" (*Rep.* 519e3–4). A theoretical determinant is also involved, a second element that secures the change from egoistic thinkers wishing to remain unattached to the city to politically engaged philosophers is provided by the performance of philosophical *theoria*. What needs to be made explicit about the activity concerns its efficacy in maintaining moral virtues, like justice, in the souls of the philosophers who will be rulers.[25] Thus, to the standard objection that *kallipolis* is unjust by compelling philosopher-rulers to act against their own self-interest, the reply is found in Cooper's comment that "Plato's just man is no egoist," someone who neither "does everything out of concern for his own good" nor "does anything for this reason" (Cooper 1997, 27).

---

[25] This glosses over one aspect of Plato's virtue that needs emphasis, namely, that one good quality of virtuous actions is that they maintain virtue as a state (cf. *Rep.* IV, 444d–e), just as healthy actions produce health; cf. Aristotle, *EN* II 1 (1103ab31–b2).

The explanation of how the transformation comes about becomes clear in subsequent discussion.[26]

Nonetheless, there is good evidence about the transformative aspect of philosophical *theoria* in the psychological change brought about by the philosopher's education, as described in *Rep.* VII. Socrates states that education (*paideia*) is not concerned with adding knowledge to souls without knowledge but involves a kind of psychological revolution, literally, "a turning around of the whole soul" (ὅλῃ τῇ ψυχῇ ... περιακτέον, *Rep.* 518c7),[27] and, more relevant to the problem at hand, is that the revolution cannot be achieved without studying forms, particularly, the form of the good due to its motive force on the soul.[28] Here Plato's reasoning should be stated in full: "The power to learn is in everyone's soul, and the instrument with which one learns is like an eye that cannot be turned around from darkness to light without turning the whole body. This instrument cannot be turned ... without turning the whole soul until it is able to study (θεωμένη) that which is (τὸ ὄν) and the brightest thing that is, the one we call the good" (τοῦτο δ᾿ εἶναί φαμεν τἀγαθόν, *Rep.* 518c4–518d1). Plato is making two significant claims about *theoria* that have an impact on its value: first, the philosopher's education vitally depends on and culminates in the study (*theoria*) of being, i.e., the forms, and especially, the form of the good; second, the study of the form of the good (and other forms) is that which produces the complete change of vision in the philosopher. So, the study of forms is neither an accidental nor a partial cause to the change in vision; rather, such study is that which allows for and contributes to the "turning of the whole soul" (cf. *Rep.* 518c7). Yet, one might pose the objection that the reversal, or revolution, of the soul, might equally lead to egoism, not eradicate the vice.

In response, an explanation about the means by which the philosopher's psychology is transformed is found in *Rep.* VI. Socrates here explains that the philosopher "who studies (*theomenous*) things that are organized and always the same" will "imitate them and become as like them as he can" (*Rep.* 500c3–5), so becoming "as orderly and divine as a human being can"

---

[26] The problem of unresolved egoism and compulsion of philosophers to return to the city is presented in Annas (1985, 265-71), to which Cooper (1997), Kraut (1997), and Vlastos (1997) offer the correct and persuasive replies, as our discussion shows.

[27] Adam sees Plato here as contrasting the Sophists' idea of education with his own (Adam 1965, vol. 2, 98-99).

[28] I am not sure I concur with Cooper's final assessment of Plato's just person as "a sort of high-minded fanatic," but agree that this person is not even a covert egoist (Cooper 1997, 28).

(*Rep.* 500d1–2).²⁹ In brief, let me suggest that since Platonic *theoria* is the activity of studying forms, and these possess properties of order and eternality, the act of consciously knowing them enables the philosopher to achieve internal psychic harmony, justice in the soul. This line of argument is suggested by recent approaches offered by Kraut, Vlastos, and, to a lesser extent, Burnyeat, according to which studying forms or mathematical objects has a determinative effect on the philosopher's moral character. To begin, Kraut maintains that knowing the forms enables philosophers to become more virtuous by imitating the properties of harmony, balance and proportion that forms possess, and, in so doing, they become harmonious in themselves (Kraut 1997, 213). A similar idea is offered by Vlastos in arguing that for Plato, forms exert a powerful pull on the philosopher's moral character, an attraction that is as effective as their epistemic force, and which is often under-appreciated by Plato scholars.³⁰ Finally, in a related line of argument, Burnyeat (2000) claims that the study of mathematics constitutes a kind of moral education in that the structures and properties that mathematics studies are the same that the philosopher-rulers must implement in the best city.³¹ The general implication drawn in all three accounts is that studying the forms has profound moral, as well as epistemological, implications for the philosopher's soul.

A more naturalistic account concerning the way in which moral and epistemological effects are linked is provided by Menn (1995) who discusses the role of *nous* in relation to a harmonious human soul.³² Based on *Timaeus*, Menn claims that Plato considers *nous* a cause in two senses, first, as a formal cause in our souls in which "souls can participate," and second, as an efficient cause in that *nous* "acts on souls much as it does on bodies" (Menn 1995, 47). Leaving aside the details of the larger process of the

---

²⁹ The passage recalls the description of moderation (*Rep.* 430e, 432a) and justice (*Rep.* 432a–b) in *Rep.* IV, but here moral change is stimulated by theoretical study of forms, not by the habitual training, as in *Rep.* II–III (cf. *Rep.* VII, 522a–b); for similar passages about studying forms in *Rep.* VI–VII, see *Rep.* 496a–c, 515a–516b, 522e–523a, 525a, 525d, 531c–d, 532b–e.

³⁰ Vlastos (1997, 189) mentions the line above-mentioned from *Rep.* VI, "the philosopher, consorting with the divine and harmonious . . . will himself become as harmonious and divine as any human may" (*Rep.* 500c2–4); to him, Plato's notion of the philosophical vision of form almost comprises a kind of religion (cf. Vlastos 1997, 190).

³¹ While Kraut (1997, 197–201) does not refer specifically to the effect of studying mathematics, as Burnyeat does (2000, esp. 42–56), in both fields, the philosopher studies harmony, balance, proportion, and by imitation, such study produces similar changes in moral character; cf. also Reeve (2006, 72, 78).

³² Menn's work on the causal role of *nous* in late dialogues like *Timaeus* adds a distinct level to the previous scholarly explanations.

world-soul, when it comes to ordering the human soul, *nous* restores harmony to the violent motions of our soul caused by our birth. The restoration is achieved, first, by habituation as we begin "the right habituation of the sub-rational motions" so that the circuits of the soul are restored to their order (cf. *Tim.* 44b2–6). And significantly, second, it is by education, specifically, by studying the heavenly bodies with our eyes which enables "seeing the circuits of *nous* in the heavens ... and we stabilize the wandering motions in ourselves" (cf. *Tim.* 47b6–c4).[33] On Menn's reading, then, the human soul becomes more harmonized by regulating its inner irregular motions to become more uniform, more similar to circular motion. The preceding suggestions are illuminating with regard to attaining a balanced *nous* but leave a gap concerning the role philosophical *theoria* plays in the transformation and maintenance of a balanced soul. What we may add to the naturalistic account of regulating the inner motions is that the activity of consciously understanding forms and their properties affects the whole soul, and further, if becoming wise implies Platonic justice, then the soul has become god-like (Sedley 1999, 314). For, as Sedley has pointed out, Platonic justice implies "becoming as like god as possible" (*homoiosis theoi*), an idea that recalls Diotima's closing assertion that anyone "who has nurtured true virtue becomes dear to the gods" (*Symp.* 212a5–6).[34]

The account of the psychological transformation described in *Rep.* VI–VII concerning the value of studying forms is completed by the discussion about the effects of such study, primarily on society but also on philosophers themselves. As we have seen, the activity of studying forms is valuable in itself in that it constitutes the exercise of the highest faculty, an activity that enables thinkers' moral and intellectual virtues to flourish. Yet the same activity gives rise to social benefits as well. For, exercising Platonic *theoria* consists in a philosopher grasping, not only the fact, but the manner in which forms are causes of becoming in the sensible domain: this comprises theoretical knowledge, which, in turn, leads to empirical knowledge. As the discussion of the cave analogy in *Rep.* VII (519d–520c) implies, having advanced theoretical knowledge of forms provides the benefit of carrying over to moral and political knowledge, which justifies the principle concerning the philosophers' return to rule in *kallipolis*. In

---

[33] Tr. Menn (1995); the present *Tim.* passage is discussed in more detail (Menn 1995, 53–54).

[34] Sedley (1999, 314); broadly speaking, he develops the notion of *homoiosis theoi* as a central goal of Platonic virtue, mapping its appearance in *Rep.*, *Phdr.*, *Tim.*, and finding its echo in Aristotle's recommendation to "become immortal as far as possible" (*EN* X 7, 177b33).

brief, Platonic *theoria* is shown to have beneficial results that flow from the philosophers' moral character and epistemic success that ensure the practical applications of their knowledge are just for the city. In summary, the activity of philosophical *theoria* seems properly placed in the intermediate group of goods, which includes knowing (*to phronein*) and seeing (*to horan*).

Having reached this conclusion, let me add a further point about the likely weighing of the intermediate class of goods that we touched on earlier, even though Plato's discussion pertaining to philosophical *theoria* in *Rep*. VI–VII does not include this level of detail. In brief, there are three ways we might be said to value something belonging to the intermediate class of goods. Let us differentiate these as Type I and Type II and allow that Type I has two variants. Thus, let us define: Type I (a) as obtaining when we value an activity primarily for itself and secondarily for its results; Type I (b) as obtaining when we value an activity primarily for its effects and secondarily for itself; Type II as obtaining when we value something for itself and for its results equally. Using these distinctions, the valuation of *theoria* may appear as: (i) Type I (a), valued primarily for the activity itself, and secondarily, for its results, or (ii) Type I (b), valued primarily for the results, and secondarily, for the activity itself, or (iii) Type II, valued equally for the activity itself and for its results. If we proceed on the assumption that Platonic *theoria* belongs to the intermediate category of goods described in *Rep*. II, our problem becomes which of the three value-relations described it best fits.

Let us examine the three possibilities as they apply to Platonic *theoria*. While the texts on *theoria* vary, an initial argument against Type I (b) depends on Plato's insistence that the activity of *theoria* itself has the highest value, and so, *theoria* is not being valued primarily for its results. If this is true, the issue would be to decide whether there is more evidence supporting Type I (a) or Type II. Let us begin by examining the evidence against Type I (b): we derive the negative conclusion from the (implausible) notion that for Plato the primary value of philosophical *theoria* resides in its result. This idea is implausible inasmuch as it would require us to hold that the apprehension of forms is valuable primarily for its results, say, for its application as statecraft. While there may, in fact, be considerable value in statecraft, there is much other evidence to reject the view of Type I (b) arising from, say, Plato's line of argument in *Rep*. VII that culminates with description of *theoria* of forms, especially, the form of the good, as being the highest or Diotima's description of *theoria* as being close to a divine state (cf. *Symp*. 210d–211d). Reaching a negative result thus leaves us with two possibilities: (i) Type I (a) obtains, meaning that Platonic *theoria* is valued primarily for the activity and secondarily for its results, or (ii) Type II obtains, meaning that Platonic *theoria* is valued for the activity and its results equally. We shall see that these options are not equally plausible, the first one having more intuitive and textual support than the second.

Taking a synoptic view of the texts surveyed about Platonic *theoria*, the most plausible and well-supported option is Type I (a), according to which *theoria* is valued primarily for itself and secondarily for its results. The supporting argument for this option runs as follows: (i) Platonic *theoria* is the highest activity (*Rep.* 479e5, 500c3–5); (ii) Platonic *theoria* consists in contemplating forms, the highest objects (*Rep.* 500c3–5, 532c5–6); (iii) the activity of Platonic *theoria* is valuable in itself; (iv) Platonic *theoria* provides practical benefits, such as statecraft (cf. *Rep.*520c–d); (v) the activity of *theoria* is more valuable than statecraft; (vi) so, the activity of *theoria* is primarily valued in itself and secondarily valued for its benefits.[35] If this argument represents something of Plato's view, it follows that Platonic *theoria* and its benefits are not equally valuable for Plato. Therefore, we are justified in excluding Type II valuation according to which *theoria* is valued for the activity itself and for its benefits equally. The pivotal argument against Type II valuation consists in the idea that *theoria*, the intellectual activity with the highest objects has the greatest intrinsic value, and this value outweighs its instrumental value.[36] This result is also consonant with the view taken about the philosopher-rulers in *Rep.* VII: Glaucon finds a difficulty in philosophers being required to return to the city (cf. *Rep.* 519d9), and Socrates replies (using forms of αναγκάζειν) that the measure is necessary and just (cf. *Rep.* 519e4, 520a6–7, 520e2, 521b5). The best reading of the reply is, first, that the philosophers are sufficiently trained and educated so that their return to the city is not onerous, and second, that they consent to follow the law concerning their duty to rule since it is just. From the perspective of philosophers as theoreticians, the activity is good in itself, but since it is just that the philosophers return to the city as rulers, they will do so, not due to harmful coercion.[37] This outcome does not violate the standard of

---

[35] Also noting the objects of metaphysics are higher and more noble than those of politics, cf. sun, line, cave in *Rep.* V–VII.

[36] This result follows even if we add the positive effects on the soul that *theoria* of the forms produces, for while thinking of the forms produces good effects, their value cannot be better than their cause.

[37] As I read Plato, the activity of *theoria* perfects our moral and intellectual virtues, setting up a reciprocal reinforcement with such actions preserving the virtuous states (cf. *Rep.* 444c–e).

Platonic justice, for the city, receiving the benefits of the philosophers' *theoria*, is made just and the philosophers, in active engagement of *theoria*, reinforce justice and other virtues in their souls.[38] Based on the prior considerations about the value of philosophical *theoria* in the *Republic*, it appears most plausible to conclude that its primary value arises from the activity itself and its secondary value from its benefits.[39]

6.2.2   Conclusion: Plato's Valuation of Theoria

In the middle period dialogues, Plato frequently considers the value of traditional *theoria* from the standpoint of philosophical *theoria*, and, predictably, finds it wanting. As we have seen, he typically contrasts philosophical and traditional *theoria*, highlighting the differences in terms of activities, aims, and practitioners. Considering the contrast between philosopher and lover of spectacles at *Rep.* V (475d–480a), we find: (i) first, from an epistemic standpoint, the festival-goer scores far below the philosopher by confusing the many beautiful sights and sounds with the beautiful itself, choosing to pursue the appearances of beauty rather than its form. Second, (ii), from a moral standpoint, the festival-goer cannot lay claim to moral excellence as he is lacking in theoretical knowledge, often displaying his lack of moderation in his desire for more spectacles. Plato's appraisal of the two kinds of *theoria*, philosophical and traditional, does not (and perhaps cannot) reflect a positive valuation for the latter kind whenever it is seen in comparison with the former kind as is found in the extended discussions in *Republic*, *Symposium*, and *Phaedo*. There are, however, a few additional references to theoric practices similar to traditional *theoria* in the *Laws* that do not contain any comparison to Platonic *theoria* and seem to show the practices as valuable for what they produce. For example, we find *theoria* as a developed state practice (and so, similar to traditional *theoria*) appearing in *Laws* Book XII (950d–952d), where discussion includes the notion of citizens traveling abroad.[40] More specifically, it is suggested that the city of Magnesia allows select virtuous citizens to travel to other cities with the purpose of learning about their

---

[38] This claim restates my earlier argument that in *Rep.* V–VII the activity of *theoria* itself transforms the moral character of the philosopher; it does not lead to this transformation as a distinct result of the activity.

[39] Nor does the evidence from other key dialogues where *theoria* figures in a central role, such as *Phaedrus*, *Phaedo*, or *Symposium* lead to a different conclusion.

[40] Plato makes clear reference to traditional *theoria* in virtue of the cultural ambassadors sent out to other cities, and by referring to the delegate as *theoros* (*Laws* 951c6).

regimes and laws in order to educate lawmakers and improve their laws (cf. *Laws* 951a–c). Although here Plato tells us little of what the ambassadors that he refers to as *theoroi* do on their trips apart from learning about the laws of cities they visit, the overall description bears a strong resemblance to the city-appointed *theoros* we have met in discussing traditional *theoria*. So, it appears that when Plato is not focusing on the activity of philosophical *theoria*, especially as it figures in the formation of a *kallipolis*, he is willing to consider the positive pragmatic value of traditional *theoria* and its attendant activities.

Finally, brief mention may be made of Plato's use of the concept of traditional *theoria* to construct ring compositions where, it is clear, the theme of festival-attendance and its feature of circularity have utility value to him. In general, *Republic* and other theoric dialogues reflect two uses of traditional *theoria*: (i) as a way of implementing the form of ring composition; (ii) as a contrastive device differentiating philosophy as truth-seeking from festival-attendance as perceptual entertainment. In casting traditional *theoria* as a foil to philosophy, Plato highlights the epistemic contrast between traditional *theoria*, a dream-like state that distracts its followers from truth-seeking, and philosophical *theoria* that aims at genuine knowledge. As we recall from *Rep.* V, while the former leads its adherents away from truth, the latter involves followers "... who study the things themselves that are always the same in every respect" (τοὺς αὐτὰ ἕκαστα θεωμένους καὶ ἀεὶ κατὰ ταὐτὰ ὡσαύτως ὄντα, *Rep.* 479e5), an activity that is, first, good in itself and also, for what it produces.

6.3   Aristotle's Evaluation of *Theoria*

6.3.1   The Dual Valuation of Theoria

At first glance, it may seem reasonable to assume that philosophical *theoria* has the same "mixed" value for Aristotle as it does for Plato. Under this assumption, we might expect to find their accounts about the value of *theoria* overlapping in that both hold the view of *theoria* as being primarily good in itself, and secondarily, good for its effects. Yet, an initial acquaintance with Aristotle's remarks about *theoria* suggests the opposite position: Aristotle seems everywhere to emphasize *theoria*'s lack of utility as a value-making feature. To cite but one key passage from *EN* X 7, we recall Aristotle stating that political actions are noble, but unleisurely, because they aim at some result – making them in part useful – whereas *theoria* is superior in that "it aims at nothing beyond itself" (*EN* 1177b17–20).

Nor is the lack of utility belonging to *theoria* unique to *EN* X 7, as it is also evident in *EE* and *Protrepticus*. On the whole, Aristotle's praise of *theoria* as being good in itself and not for its effects is so familiar that several scholars consider Aristotle's evaluation of *theoria* to depend entirely on its uselessness.[41] Yet while this interpretation of Aristotle's valuation of *theoria* is understandable, it does not reflect the whole picture, as will become clear given due consideration.

Although Aristotle clearly underscores the non-utilitarian value of philosophical *theoria* in his central discussions, such as at *EN* X 7 (cf. 1177b12–22), *EE* (1215b2–3), and *Protrepticus* 9 (53.15–26), three arguments may be raised in favor of re-evaluating the textual evidence concerning its value. First, where Aristotle makes an emphasis on *theoria*'s lack of utility, it seems likely that he does so (at least partly) for rhetorical reasons: as Walker points out, Aristotle wishes to distinguish his position from that of Isocrates, who argues that the only value of philosophy is utilitarian.[42] Second, claiming that *theoria* has value in itself does not preclude *theoria* having positive benefits, as we found to be the case with Plato. Third, and perhaps most compellingly, the textual evidence canvassed does not lead to the conclusion that *theoria* lacks benefits and is valuable only in itself. In fact, passages in *EN* and *Protrep.* support the view that the activity of *theoria* is valuable for what it produces as well as for the activity itself.

The following discussion about Aristotle's valuation of philosophical *theoria* is presented in two parts: the first section is devoted to showing why *theoria* is valuable in itself, and the second to showing how the activity brings about good results. The analysis will also show that in regard to the weighing of *theoria*'s goods, we conclude that the primary valuation of *theoria* is as an activity good in itself, and the secondary valuation is as an activity that produces good effects. In my overall view, Aristotle is arguing that, being the highest activity, *theoria* is choice-worthy and good in itself, but the activity yields beneficial results as well. Aristotle's mixed valuation (viz., good in itself and for its effects) of philosophical *theoria* is similar to what we found in Plato.[43] In the first part of the discussion, we employ some conclusions reached in Chapter 3 concerning the nature of *theoria* as

---

[41] For example, see Broadie (1991, 392), Nagel (1980, 11–12), Wilkes (1980, 346–47), Nightingale (2004, 187–89).

[42] For discussion about Aristotle's rejection of Isocrates' view, see Walker (2018, 38–40).

[43] A suggestion concerning why both would place *theoria* in the intermediate class relates to a shared, general inference about forms, namely, that since forms are the causes of being, apprehending forms (or, *theoria*) implies having some knowledge about their application to the material realm; Plato draws this connection (cf. Reeve 2006, 77–79), as does Aristotle's theory of scientific knowledge of the natural world.

a complete activity to support the conclusion that Aristotle views *theoria* as most valuable in itself. The key text here consists in the discussion about *theoria*, human and divine, in *EN* X 7–8. Yet, the final section of *EN* X 7 where Aristotle urges us to "try to make ourselves as immortal as possible" (EN 1177b33–34) contains a slight suggestion about another way in which to view *theoria* as well, namely, as an activity that yields practical benefits. Our presentation of this aspect of the question about the valuation of *theoria* consists in two parts, one advancing a negative conclusion, the other, a positive conclusion about the work that *theoria* provides to other faculties. In the latter regard, Walker's views about the practical benefits of contemplative *nous* prove very fruitful for this leg of the investigation (Walker 2018).

6.3.2   Theoria *as Good in Itself*

The primary value that Aristotle finds in philosophical *theoria* arises from its nature as the activity of the highest faculty (*nous*), which, being directed at specific objects, is related to our scientific understanding (*episteme*). According to our analysis of Aristotle's discussion in *EN* X 7, *theoria* consists in an activity of the highest faculty directed at the highest objects of study (*EN* 1177 a12–14, a19–22). Since the aim of the activity is grasping forms or essential properties of composite and incomposite substances, the intrinsic value of *theoria* cannot be overstated, having the highest intrinsic value of any complete activity. Furthermore, as a complete activity, human *theoria* is essentially complete, continuous, leisurely, self-sufficient, chosen for itself, and pleasant (cf. *EN* 1177a21–22, 1177b19–22). As such, it shares certain features with divine *theoria*, to which it may be compared. Recalling *EN* X 8, we know that *theoria* is the unique activity that the gods enjoy since partaking in anything else like moral activity would be inconsistent with their divine nature (*EN* 1078b10–18).[44] So, if we subtract action and production from the gods' activities as living things, the sole activity remaining is contemplative (*theoretike*); hence, he observes, human *theoria* is the activity that is most similar to the gods' activity, and so is "most conducive of happiness" (*EN* 1178b20–22).[45]

---

[44] In *EN* X 8 (1078b10–18), Aristotle argues it is absurd to think of the gods needing to make contracts, return deposits, and the like; supposing them as concerned with practical actions is unworthy, inconsistent with their nature as "most happy and blessed" (*EN* 1178b8–9).

[45] The Greek lines run: τῷ δὴ ζῶντι τοῦ πράττειν ἀφαιρουμένου, ἔτι δὲ μᾶλλον τοῦ ποιεῖν, τί λείπεται πλὴν θεωρία; ὥστε ἡ τοῦ θεοῦ ἐνέργεια, μακαριότητι διαφέρουσα, θεωρητικὴ ἂν εἴη· καὶ τῶν ἀνθρωπίνων δὴ ἡ ταύτῃ συγγενεστάτη εὐδαιμονικωτάτη (*EN* 1178b20–22).

We may conclude that human *theoria* has two central pillars supporting its intrinsic value: first, it is the highest activity, being complete, self-sufficient, most continuous and pleasant; second, it is the activity most similar to gods' activity, even though humans cannot engage in it continuously.[46] For, human beings' composite nature involves other obligations and needs, moral and political ones, that, of course, do not affect divine nature; in any case, the absence of fully continuous *theoria* for humans is deflected by his suggestion about extending the activity over a lifetime. Specifically, he suggests that theoretical activity expanded over a lifetime outweighs other pursuits to make human life "complete in happiness" (*EN* 1177b24–25). Does this suggestion, then, not imply that to be happy, we should only engage in *theoria*, and if so, how does this square with his statement that only the gods can think continually? On the contrary, the most plausible interpretation of his claim is that, while humans cannot exercise *theoria* continually, they may construct a life around theoretical activity which promises the most happiness. Furthermore, it does not imply that the happiest people are those who withdraw from society to engage solely in theoretical contemplation, but that engaging in theoretical activity is accompanied by benefits that naturally spill over from the theoretical faculty to the lower faculties, and in so doing, aid them.

The view that *theoria* has positive benefits as well as being good in itself, of course, requires further support: in what follows, we develop an account setting out the lines of connection between the theoretical intellect and action to account for the influence of the former on the faculties concerned with moral action. On this writer's estimation, it seems reasonable – perhaps even inevitable – to suppose that intellectual faculties, like theoretical *nous*, would have an effect on non-theoretical faculties, such as moral deliberation. But can this claim withstand scrutiny? It may be objected, after all, that nowhere in Aristotle's central discussion of *theoria* in *EN* X 7 and 8 do we encounter a claim about its usefulness or benefits – and this view is not contradicted by *Protrep.* 9, where *theoria* is described as the exercise of a theoretical faculty apparently lacking practical application. In fact, as we noted, the view of *theoria* as essentially useless is widespread in the literature.[47] Two replies may be brought to bear against this line of interpretation. First, as we have already noted, the argument that *theoria*

---

[46] For, as he observes, a purely theoretical life "would be more than human" (*EN* 1177b24–25).

[47] See, for example, Broadie (1991, 392), Nagel (1980, 11–12), Wilkes (1980, 346–47), and Nightingale (2004, 187–89).

cannot have practical benefits since it belongs to a theoretical faculty is weak: nothing prevents the exercise of a theoretical faculty from producing benefits to a non-theoretical faculty, especially when we consider it belongs to a complex network of human capacities. Second, indirectly or directly, Aristotle countenances the possibility of practical benefits arising from theoretical activity in *EN* X 7–8 and *Protrep.* 10. To begin, the closing section of *EN* X 7 (1177b26–1178a8) includes lines that indirectly refer to benefits following from theoretical activity when he praises the theoretical way of life for being closely aligned with human happiness. Here he recommends that we employ our intellectual faculty (*nous*) in such a way as "to live in accordance with what is highest in us" (*EN* 1177b33–34), concluding that the theoretical way of life is the happiest (cf. *EN* 1178a7–8). Now since humans cannot engage in *theoria* continually, the most obvious sense in which his claim about "the life of the intellect" (*ho kata ton noun bios*) leading to the happiest life (*EN* 1178a6–7) is to be understood is that the theoretical way of life produces benefits for living the happy life. So it is that the closing lines about *theoria* in *EN* X 7 point toward a way of balancing two seeming incompatible ends for humans, the one concerning engaging in continual *theoria* (impossible for humans), and the other concerning intermittent, human aims. His solution proposes a way of life guided by the theoretical faculty: this succeeds in being at once the most divine and the most human, not because it encourages withdrawal from social relations and obligations, but because it allows the results from theoretical understanding to pass over to moral deliberation.

However, the way in which the theoretical faculty is connected to the practical faculty is open to different interpretations. In recent scholarly work, Kraut (1989, 87–88) and Lear (2004) argue that moral virtue can be seen as an "approximation" of philosophical *theoria*, a line of argument which, although persuasive, takes us in the direction of linking moral virtue to *theoria* in terms of its intrinsic value, which is not the one we are seeking to develop.[48] What we are seeking is evidence that Aristotle finds *theoria*, an activity prized for its intrinsic worth, also valuable for its benefits. To this second topic, the most recent scholarly work is that of Walker (2018). My view generally concurs with that of Walker but differs slightly: in brief, we share the view that the activity of *theoria* provides benefits to moral virtue but differ about the degree and kind of connection

---

[48] For example, what Lear argues is that since excellent moral activity is an "approximation of *theoria*," we may find the same value linked to moral virtue as *theoria*, namely, that it is intrinsically good (Lear 2004, 85, 91–92), cf. Broadie on the approximation thesis (Broadie and Rowe 2002).

the speculative and practical intellect have. The general view Walker develops is that the speculative *nous* provides rules or directions to the agent's deliberative capacity prior to acting. Aided by his reading of *Protrep.* 10, Walker holds that, for Aristotle, our speculative intellect aids our practical intellect by means of illuminating the "boundary points" (*horoi*) of practical reasoning. Let us develop this position briefly below, while mentioning certain points of difference.

6.3.3   The Benefits of Theoria

On Walker's view, the utility of *theoria* depends on certain connections shared by the activity of *theoria*, the faculty of *nous*, and deliberation; here he provides two main lines of argument to support his thesis, one epistemological, the other psychological. The first line of argument centers on the notion that in *EN*, Aristotle thinks of complete virtue as requiring theoretical knowledge, and more specifically, knowledge of the reason why that relates to human nature (Walker 2018, 132). The deeper, scientific understanding of human nature, he argues, is that which Aristotle finds necessary to distinguish the decent person or the person of natural virtue from the fully virtuous person. According to Walker, the *phronimos* knows the ethical "why" and not merely the ethical "that" – more specifically, the *phronimos* is the one who knows the "boundary points," or *horoi*, of practical reasoning (Walker 2018, 135–36). From passages in *EN, EE*, and *Protrep.*, he develops an account of the way in which the *phronimos* "sees" the necessary boundary points for acting.[49] By providing the boundary points for practical reason to grasp, contemplative *nous* "guides" the human faculties for action.[50] The necessary connection between contemplative *nous* and *phronesis* is explained by the fact that the superior epistemic understanding supplied by *theoria* is what provides the information needed for practical reasoning since "the *phronimos* must understand the human good theoretically" (Walker 2018, 138).[51] Following this sketch, we may appreciate how the activity of *theoria* is considered to be

---

[49]   He uses parts of *EN* I 13, *EN* X 9, *EE* V 13/*EN* VI 13, *EE* VIII 3, and *Protrep.* 10 (55.14–65.2) in showing how the *phronimos* grasps the boundary points needed in practical reason (cf. Walker 2018, 136–39).

[50]   So, the practical ability of grasping boundary points in *phronesis* complements the theoretical understanding resulting from contemplation; "contemplative *nous* thus … authoritatively guide[s] the lower human functions" (Walker 2018, 139).

[51]   So, this leg of the argument relies on an epistemic link between contemplative and practical *nous*: only scientific understanding can provide the boundary points necessary for complete moral comprehension (full *phronesis*).

useful in a robust sense: it works as part of contemplative *nous* which provides theoretical information to *phronesis* and so "completes practical reasoning" (Walker 2018, 139).[52]

It should be noted that Walker does not claim that grasping the boundary points is a sufficient condition for practical reason, only a necessary condition (Walker 2018, 139). This distinction is apt and useful in that it would be incorrect to suppose that complete moral virtue can be won simply by an understanding of boundary points; clearly, their grasp is not sufficient for practical wisdom. But if it is necessary to have such a grasp to possess full practical wisdom, as he proposes, the range of *phronimoi* is limited by the restriction to those who possess *episteme*, and, in my view, the requirement constitutes too high an epistemic bar for those aspiring to attain moral virtue.[53] Aristotle's discussions of the connection between moral virtue and *phronesis* as well as of the moral and intellectual virtues in *EN* VI seem to suggest a looser, less determined role for any theoretical elements in moral reasoning.[54] While I agree that full practical reasoning of the *phronimos* requires contribution by a higher faculty, like *nous*, the references to *nous* coupled with action in *EN* point to the practical intellect as a faculty that "sees" the right situation to perform a certain kind of action (e.g., *EN* II 19, 1109b18–23; IV 5, 1126b2–4; VI 2, 1139a26–33, 1139b4, cf. VI 8, 1142a22–30; VII 6, 1150a5), and in this regard, the contribution from *nous* seems to be highly indexed to contextual situation, rather than arising from theoretical understanding.[55]

[52] As to which objects of speculation are useful for the practical intellect, Walker suggests the theoretical *nous* is developed by the contemplation of friends and God, which contribute to one's self-knowledge and so enable us to grasp the boundary points of practical reasoning (Walker 2018, 158–63).

[53] Walker's condition poses a rather high epistemic bar for the *phronimos* who must grasp, say, the form of human being to be fully morally virtuous, i.e., know the reason why of the moral virtues; for, it is implausible to deny that those who have achieved virtuous character states through repeated right action and who meet the cognitive conditions for deliberate action are practically wise because they lack the boundary points supplied by contemplative *nous*.

[54] Consider, for example, that in *EN* VI, the states of intellectual excellence, such as theoretical wisdom (*sophia*) and scientific understanding (*episteme*), differ in kind and subject matter from that of practical wisdom (*phronesis*), making the proposal that full *phronesis* essentially depends on a theoretical element from *sophia* implausible.

[55] Admittedly, other references to contemplative *nous* or *nous* in its truth-seeking capacity arise in *EN*, e.g., *EN* VI 6, 1141a3–8; VI 8, 1142a27–30; X 7, 1177a13, a20, a21 (cf. *DA* 432b27), but these are clearly not action-guiding cases; cf. in *EE*, references to *nous* characterize it rather as a ruling element in the soul (e.g., *EE* 1246b14; cf. *EN* 1168b5, 1169a17, 18, 1177a13) or as opposed to appetite (e.g., *EE* 1240b34) than as truth-seeking.

The other supporting line of argument Walker advances about the utility of *theoria* and contemplative *nous* arises from Aristotle's theory of the relations among capacities of the human soul. In this second line of defense, Walker presents what he terms a "naturalistic" view of *nous* and its activity *theoria* which is persuasive for two reasons. First, its opposite, the non-naturalistic view of contemplative *nous*, presents it as a power standing over and above the "lower" faculties of the soul (e.g., perception, desire, choice) that sub-serve it, and it has no part in their functioning.[56] Walker rightly rejects this view, that of "the detached *nous*," in favor of one according to which there are reciprocal relations holding between higher and lower faculties: for example, the nutritive capacity sub-serves and supports the perceptive capacity, and yet, while the latter does not sub-serve the former, it guides and benefits the nutritive capacity (Walker 2018, 64). If we extend the analogy to the relation of the contemplative *nous* and the lower faculties, we might suggest that the lower faculties sub-serve *nous* (and not the reverse), and yet, contemplative *nous* may guide and benefit them. In this fashion, contemplative *nous* counts as the highest faculty supported by lower faculties, like nutrition and perception, but the relation allows for a certain reciprocity of utility. The second reason recommending this view of the faculties is related to Aristotle's natural teleology, and specifically, the principle that "nature does nothing in vain" (cf. *DA* III 12, 434a31). On Aristotle's natural teleology, we have the general view that biological kinds, like human beings, possess naturally ordered capacities fitted for their ends. So, to suppose the ordered capacities of some natural kind might prove "useless" for the functioning of its other natural capacities, like desire and perception, is incompatible with this telic naturalism.[57] However, the contradictory of this claim, that the human faculty of contemplative *nous* works not only "upwards" in the apprehension of truth but "downwards" by aiding practical reason, is both consistent and more reasonable.

Having laid out the grounds for which we are justified in calling contemplative *nous* and *theoria* useful to the lower faculties, and specifically, to the production of right action, we are in a better position to re-read the ending of *EN* X 7. In the final section that we examined previously, viz., *EN* 1177b26–1178a8, Aristotle put forward a single,

---

[56] This view coincides with the abovementioned view of *theoria* as "useless," described by Broadie (1991, 392), Nagel (1980, 11–12), and Wilkes (1980, 346–47).

[57] It is of course clear that the lower capacities in mortal, living things, like the nutritive capacity, support and serve the higher capacities, like thinking (cf. *DA* II, 1–2); the issue at hand concerns whether the higher serve any purpose to the lower capacities.

dramatic claim: one should make *theoria* and contemplative *nous* the center of one's life. The suggestion naturally brings up questions such as not only, "Why should one do so?" but also "Can one do so – for isn't this a superhuman life?" These questions are put to rest when armed with the recent knowledge about the feasibility and utility of contemplative *nous*. For, we see at once that the activity of this *nous* is integrated with the reasoning that issues in action. According to Walker, contemplative *nous* supplies the necessary boundary points for practical reason; in my view, the contribution is less determinate, more emergent, with the long-term effect of exercising *nous* bleeding down to the faculties concerned with action. On my view, the suggested relationship between the activity of *theoria* and its effect is one of super-addition, which we may compare to the relation of pleasure to certain complete activities (cf. *EN* X 4, 1174b23–33).[58] On the picture being suggested, the activity of *theoria* has a cumulative effect on the whole soul, including both affective and cognitive aspects of character. So considered, the activity of *theoria* is not a means to something else, but conveys positive results through itself, in the way that Aristotle suggests that pleasure is carried along with specific activities, like seeing or thinking.[59] More specifically, in *EN* X 4, he claims that pleasure arises "as a superadded completion" of the activity (*hos epigignomenon ti telos*), adding a comparison to "the bloom of those in their prime" (*EN* 1174b31–33).[60]

My suggestion is supported by what I take as a two-step argument for adopting the theoretical way of life in the focal section of *EN* X 7 (1177b27–1178a8). In the first step, he states it is possible by pointing out we have a shot at divinity through our intellect: "someone who lives thus does not do so in virtue of something human, but in virtue of

---

[58] First, a useful note by Gauthier and Jolif observes some commentators (Zell, Ramsauer, Susemihl) bracketing *EN* 1174b26–31 as inauthentic for interrupting the flow of argument about pleasure at 1174b23–26 and 1174b31–b33 which makes a continuous whole (Gauthier and Jolif 1970 vol. 2, 842); second, the substantial point is that pleasure is super-added, or perhaps "supervenes," on the complete activity, compared to (standard translation) "the bloom of those in their prime" (*EN* 1174b31–33). Commentators vary as to the weight of the simile, with Hadreas (1997) disputing the metaphorical comparison as rendered, Bostock (1988, esp. 251–53) analyzing the issue of pleasure "completing" activities, on which cf. Aufderheide (2016, esp. 290–93), and Gonzalez (1991, 145–49).

[59] The phrase "carried along" is meant to imply the relation of super-addition but without specific metaphysical commitments, like "metaphysical" or "ontological grounding" considered in McLaughlin and Bennet (2018): https://plato.stanford.edu/entries/supervenience.

[60] In more detail, Aristotle gives us a double analogy in *EN* X 4 (1174b23–26) to contrast the relation of pleasure to an activity: thus, the faculty of perception and the sensible object complete perception in different ways, and similarly, health and the physician fulfill being healthy in different ways; however, pleasure completes the activity in a different sense – by being a "super-added completion" or "perfection" (see Burnet 1900, 453 fn., *EN* 1174b31–33).

something divine in him" (*EN* 1177b27–28).[61] For, he reminds us, "our intelligence (*nous*) is divine in comparison with human [and] the life according to it is divine in comparison with human life" (*EN* 1177b30–31).[62] Here Aristotle is not making the point, as it may first appear, that engaging in *theoria* itself is more than human or that a life lived according to *nous* is more than human, but the contrary. He means that the theoretical life is the truly human life: as he reminds us, we should not try to live safely, as some would advise, saying that humans should have only "human thoughts" or "mortal thoughts" (*EN* 1177b32–33). Rather, he urges us to strain toward the upper limit of our human nature, stating that this comprises the best human life, "trying to make ourselves immortal as far as possible and doing everything to live in accordance with what is best in us" (*EN* 1177b33–34).[63] It is evident that what is "best in us" refers to our intelligence (*nous*) (*EN* 1177b30–31), and that living in accordance with this faculty implies "making ourselves immortal as far as possible." What might this mean? To begin with, we know that as human beings we cannot make ourselves immortal by continual *theoria*-thinking – while possible for the gods, it is impossible for us. However, we may approximate the condition by placing the faculty of intelligence (*nous*) at the center of our lives. In so doing, we engage in the highest activity, *theoria*, and enjoy benefits, the fulfillment of the activity that comes about from the theoretical way of life. Where does the text in *EN* X 7 (1177b27–1178a8) support this idea? To begin, the injunction "to become immortal as far as possible" (ἀλλ᾽ ἐφ᾽ ὅσον ἐνδέχεται ἀθανατίζειν) is given in reply to those who tell us to think only mortal thoughts (*EN* 1177a32–33) but is clarified by the second part of the line: we are "to do everything to live in accordance with what is highest in us" (πάντα ποιεῖν πρὸς τὸ ζῆν κατὰ τὸ κράτιστον τῶν ἐν αὐτῷ, *EN* 1177b33–34). Placing emphasis on the phrase "living in accordance with what is highest is us," i.e., living in accordance with *nous*, the recommendation to become immortal as much as possible implies living a certain way of life by placing *theoria* at its center.

But it also implies something more, as Socrates' closing thought to Glaucon in *Rep.* X recommends: we will "always hold to the upward path,

---

[61] The Greek runs: οὐ γὰρ ᾗ ἄνθρωπός ἐστιν οὕτω βιώσεται, ἀλλ᾽ ᾗ θεῖόν τι ἐν αὐτῷ ὑπάρχει (*EN* 1177b27–28).

[62] The Greek runs: (εἰ δὴ θεῖον ὁ νοῦς πρὸς τὸν ἄνθρωπον, καὶ ὁ κατὰ τοῦτον βίος θεῖος πρὸς τὸν ἀνθρώπινον βίον (*EN* 1177b30–31).

[63] The Greek is: ἀλλ᾽ ἐφ᾽ ὅσον ἐνδέχεται ἀθανατίζειν καὶ πάντα ποιεῖν πρὸς τὸ ζῆν κατὰ τὸ κράτιστον τῶν ἐν αὐτῷ (*EN* 1177b33–34).

practicing justice with reason in every way; that way, we will be friends to ourselves and to the gods" (621c4–7). As Sedley has pointed out, Platonic justice implies "becoming as like god as possible" (*homoiosis theoi*), an idea that recalls Diotima's closing assertion that anyone "who has nurtured true virtue becomes dear to the gods" (*Symp.* 212a5–6).[64] The Platonic recommendation fits well with the closing of Aristotle's discussion on human *theoria*, as Sedley observes (1999, 325). For, Aristotle closes *EN* X 7 with two reasons for making one's intelligence (*nous*) the basis of one's life: first, it comprises the best part of oneself, and so it would be odd "not to choose to live one's own life, but someone else's" (*EN* 1178a2–4), and second, since intelligence is proper to humans, "the life guided by intelligence will be the best and most pleasant" (*EN* 1178a5–7). Two comments are in order: first, these lines reflect a connection between exercising human intellect and human living, and second, this is what makes us god-like, using contemplative *nous* in acting virtuously. The textual evidence is clear in this passage: the closing section of *EN* X 7 (1177b26–1178a8) contains seventeen lines with eight references to "way of life" (βίος) or "live" (ζῆν) that provide support for a non-trivial connection between contemplative *nous* and action. By extension, then, Aristotle cannot be supposing that the activity of our intellectual faculty, *theoria*, is one having no relation to life and action; rather, it is something closely related to our living. It is also closely related to what we are, for our intelligence is "the best and ruling part" of us, and "what each one is" (*EN* 1178a2–3). So, the theoretical way of life for Aristotle is not "disinterested" in the sense of lacking connection to the lived world, as some have argued, even if the activity of *theoria* itself aims at truth, not action. By placing Aristotle's comments about *theoria* being an activity that is the highest (*EN* 1177a19), most self-sufficient (*EN* 1177 a27–28), and loved for its own sake (EN 1177b1–2) in context, we discern the link between contemplative *nous* and action. For, theoretical activity is that which makes a happy life complete. It is therefore necessary to leave behind the view that Aristotle's account of *theoria* entails it is useless as some scholars maintain. While Aristotle often emphasizes that *theoria* is chosen and loved for its own sake, this is quite compatible with benefits arising from the activity, the discussion then leading us to the analogy of the way pleasure completes an activity that is described in *EN* X 4 (*EN* 1174b31–33). According to the parallel, the benefits may be

---

[64] Sedley (1999, 314); broadly speaking, he develops the notion of *homoiosis theoi* as a central goal of Platonic virtue, mapping its appearance in *Rep.*, *Phdr.*, *Tim.*, and finding its echo in Aristotle's recommendation to "become immortal as far as possible" (*EN* X 7, 177b33).

conceived as completing the activity of *theoria* just as pleasure completes certain activities, namely, perceiving (*aesthesis*), thinking, (*dianoia*), or study (*theoria*), according to Aristotle (*EN* 1174b20–21). Taking a longer view about the valuation of *theoria*, we conclude that both Plato and Aristotle assess philosophical *theoria* as having mixed value in that the activity has both intrinsic and instrumental value, with more weight on the former. In comparison, traditional *theoria*, which we judged as having primarily instrumental value, has some intrinsic value as well.

Concluding Remarks

The significance of traditional *theoria* to the philosophical thought of Plato and Aristotle is indisputable, reflecting the central role that the practice plays in the two philosophers' accounts of *theoria*. Plato makes explicit, and sometimes ironic, use of the tradition at several levels in his dialogues. To mention one example, in *Rep.* VI we find Plato mentioning and then re-conceiving *theoria* – first, he takes it as festival-attendance, which he describes as akin to mere dreaming (*Rep.* 476b1–5) – and then he transforms it into genuine philosophical inquiry. Yet, the Platonic ideal of philosophical study preserves various features characteristic of traditional *theoria* including its observational component, its religious objective, and its cosmopolitanism.[1] While Aristotle does not engage with traditional *theoria* in the systematic way that Plato does, he follows Plato's lead in regard to the activity being directed to intelligible objects of a divine nature, refining Plato's insights about philosophical *theoria* as consisting in the apprehension of form. Taking another step back, we might achieve a more comprehensive view of traditional and philosophical *theoria* together. From this perspective, we distinguish four common elements between traditional and philosophical *theoria* in general, namely, (i) the *theor/eo/ia* family of terms signifying the apprehension of the divine or of high significance; (ii) the concept of pilgrimage, or moving from what is familiar and mundane to what is unfamiliar and sacred; (iii) cyclical motion or traversing a circular route, figuratively or literally; (iv) engaging in an activity or activities having great intrinsic and extrinsic worth.

With regard to the fourth element, our investigation reveals that while traditional and philosophical *theoria* are assessed as having both intrinsic

---

[1] The claim to cosmopolitanism is made connecting the relatively inclusive scope of traditional *theoria* similar to the notions of Platonic dialectic and philosophical *theoria* being available to humans simply as thinkers; the first wave proposal in *Rep.* V (451d–457a), Socrates' geometrical demonstration with the slave, *Meno* 82b–86b; cf. Ch. 1, sec. 1.5.

and extrinsic worth, its value depends on the activity involved. For example, in festival-attendance overall, the primary value of the practice resides, in my view, in the benefits and advantages the city receives, such as public recognition of the city's status and wealth, the honor to the city, its increased alliances with other cities, and similar benefits. As well, traditional *theoria* has value to the festival-delegate in the form of public honor, one aspect being an intrinsic good, another being the benefits that result; additionally, a *theoros* likely enjoys the experience of attending traditional *theoriai*. Yet, it seems that in traditional *theoria* the balance tips toward the instrumental side of value rather than toward that of intrinsic value. In philosophical *theoria*, however, the scale reads the other way: the primary value of the activity lies in its intrinsic worth, and its instrumental value is considered secondary. Thus, Plato and Aristotle alike accord more significance to the intrinsic value of philosophical *theoria* as an activity of contemplative *nous* than to its benefits. This difference in relative valuation, in part, springs from the practical orientation of traditional *theoria* in comparison with philosophical *theoria*. In Plato's hands, *theoria* becomes an activity associated with the highest theoretical faculty, one which, while it may produce beneficial results, deserves the highest valuation for its activity alone, a view with which Aristotle concurs.

In addition to the lines of continuity associated with the activity of traditional or philosophical *theoria*, significant similarities associated with the term *theoros* deserve mention as well. From the standpoint of traditional *theoria*, the term *theoros* typically signifies an individual acting as a city-designated attendant – or, to a lesser degree, a private citizen attending festivals or visiting sanctuaries informally. The terminological connection appears to arise in the activity of *theoria* as going to and attending festivals, and is then extended to the practitioner of the activity, the *theoros*. Following the extension seen in traditional *theoria*, philosophers employ the notion of the *theoros* as the one who engages in *theoria*, although since their idea of *theoria* depends on philosophical intellection, the corresponding notion of the *theoros* differs from the traditional one. In Plato's reconceptualization of the *theoros*, the festival-attendant of traditional *theoria* is transformed into the philosophical inquirer, the individual seeking genuine truth about the causes of phenomena, like the beautiful, and not seeking pleasant sights and sounds. Thus, in Plato's reconfiguration in the *Republic*, the *theoros* becomes the escaped cave-dweller, and in the *Symposium*, the aspirant of the beautiful itself described in Diotima's speech. Yet, like the traditional *theoros*, the Platonic *theoros* experiences a "return" that recalls that of the city-appointed *theoros*. For, allowing for certain differences, both figures undertake a pilgrimage whose end concerns the apprehension of something sacred, one that follows a circular path and has high value (intrinsic or extrinsic). Of course, where the traditional *theoros* experiences a literal return to his starting point, namely, the home city, the Platonic *theoros* experiences the "return" to the empirical starting points when he returns to the city which represents the application of scientific knowledge to politics. In addition, one of the most distinctive and original connections that Plato forges with traditional *theoria* consists in his use of the ring structure to emphasize the elliptical path traveled by the traditional *theoros*.

A final word may be offered concerning the conceptual exchange or lines of influence existing between the long-standing practice of *theoria* and the fourth-century philosophical innovators, Plato and Aristotle. Despite their re-envisioning of *theoria* as an intellectual activity aimed at comprehensive knowledge, Plato and Aristotle do not reject the practical dimension of traditional *theoria*, i.e., its role in shaping political and religious ideals for the city, as well as for the individual. In this regard, our philosophers acknowledge and support the Greek understanding of *theoria* as comprising a significant practice for the *polis*. As well, however, both thinkers depart from the way in which traditional *theoria* defined the activity of festival-attendance and its representative, the *theoros*. Plato, in particular, places special significance on the *theoros* and *theoria* in his epistemological theory while remaining highly critical of their roles within the traditional practice. For Plato, the traditional festival-delegate who participates in religious rituals is someone he finds philosophically unsuitable: untutored and inexpert, lacking the theoretical knowledge the Platonic *theoros* possesses. Aristotle's view of the traditional *theoros* is not as critical as Plato's but he shares his revisionary conception of the *theoria* as truth-seeking, oriented toward scientific knowledge. Yet, theoretical wisdom and science name human excellences for both Plato and Aristotle that, despite Aristotle's characterization of the former as self-sufficient (*EN* 1177a27–28), are exercised in a human setting, the city. Hence, a central feature of traditional *theoria* persists in the philosophers' views of *theoria* as theoretical activity, for it is connected to character virtue, and so, to the good of civil society. Similarly, the activities of traditional *theoria* and its practitioner, the *theoros*, are embedded as part of a flourishing city.[2] In addition to looking toward the city to ground the

---

[2] Despite scattered references to the isolationism of Plato's philosophers-rulers in *Rep.* VII, their good is, nonetheless, bound up with the city; in *Laws* XII (950d–952d), we find Plato returning to more

good of the virtues, the two philosophers take it that the activity of *theoria* draws the thinker closer to the gods by visually apprehending what is eternal and divine, and in this respect also philosophical *theoria* continues and refines a central, defining feature of traditional *theoria*.

An awareness of the "rootedness" of traditional *theoria* and its continuity in the accounts of Plato and Aristotle also suggests a few surprising results. First, it becomes understandable why Plato and Aristotle do not characterize the pursuit of *theoria* as isolated from a larger community or describe individuals who engage in *theoria* as seeking to separate themselves from practical concerns. From this standpoint, it would be misguided to assume that Plato or Aristotle consider someone choosing *theoria* as a way of life (*bios*) as electing a life isolated from the political sphere – in so doing, we assume the life of a religious recluse for comparison, which is erroneous. A better comparison for the philosophical *theoros* would be the engaged scientist, someone who, in seeking wisdom about the causes of things, understands and absorbs the world. For, while philosophical *theoria* consists in seeking wisdom of divine causes (viz., forms), this does not prevent experts in *theoria* from extending their knowledge to the sensible world, marking a return to it. We may employ an analogical figure that Aristotle mentions in *EN* I 4, the elliptical racecourse, which he gives in relation to explaining Plato's distinction between the way up to first principles and the path down from them. Specifically, it seems that the racecourse analogy is used to suggest one leg of the course as representing the starting point, what is better known to us, and the other leg as what is better known in itself (cf. *EN* 1094b32–1095b4). In this context, he claims that we begin with "the that," or the moral fact (which is more known to us) when we begin our practical reasoning,[3] and yet, if we are to complete the image, we may consider the moral expert, or *phronimos*, as one who completes the course, moving from what better known to us to what is better known in itself and then returning to its application in practice.

Both thinkers assert that the philosopher active in *theoria* is engaging with the highest objects, things best known in themselves, and in this regard, both regard *theoria* as akin to divine activity. Yet possession of the highest knowledge, even if it approaches the divine, does not rest solely in theoretical expertise but yields positive results. Suggestive accounts of the

---

traditional *theoria* with civic ambassadors; similarly, Aristotle ends his account of *theoria* in *EN* X 7–8 with a return to politics in *EN* X 9, stating ethics is a part of politics, "the aim is not to study and attain knowledge ... but to do [it]" (*EN* 1179b1–2).

[3] For, as in other fields of inquiry, we begin with what is more known to us; accepting something as a fact becomes our starting point (*EN* 1095b3–4, 1095b6–7).

totalizing effect of *theoria* abound in Plato as, for example, in his descriptions of the philosopher's vision of forms in *Symposium* (210a–212b) and *Republic* (Bk. VII, 516a–c), and while Aristotle lacks Plato's dramatic turn of phrase, his descriptions about *theoria* as an activity at *EN* 1177a15–b26, and *theoria* as "a way of life" (*bios*) at *EN* 1177b27–1178a8 reflect a conception similar to Plato's. Furthermore, finding that both forge a link between theoretical and practical aspects is fully reasonable: it would be less plausible to suppose that full theoretical excellence would be separated *de re* from practical, or moral, excellence, especially considering the exhaustive moral training Plato and Aristotle require as preliminary to theoretical study. So, it does not appear far-fetched to see Aristotle's notion of extending *theoria* as a way of life suggested in *EN* X 7 as reflecting a Platonic view about the value of *theoria* both as intrinsically good and practically necessary. Both Plato and Aristotle hold that apprehending the causes of substances, including compound substances like humans, enables philosophers to grasp what follows from them in the sense of knowing how to apply theoretical knowledge to an empirical realm. In this regard, we may appreciate that in their accounts of *theoria*, not only Plato but also Aristotle come full circle concerning the way its practitioners return from theoretical heights to political society. In this respect, we find a similarity to traditional *theoria* – as an embedded political practice – in the practical effect of philosophical *theoria*. But in regard to the activity of *theoria* itself, Plato stands firmly opposed to philosophers following traditional *theoria*: it is epistemically risky, leading them to pursue beautiful appearances instead of beauty itself. On the whole, then, Plato considers traditional *theoria* unscientific, proposing to replace the traditional practice with philosophical *theoria*. Here Aristotle would concur that a philosophical *theoros* is not a festival-goer pursuing spectacles but a philosopher searching for the divine in "a vision of form," striving to become in some sense god-like in knowledge.[4] Yet, for both thinkers, in seeking metaphysical and epistemological truth considered "divine" (*theion*),[5] philosophical *theoria* contributes to our ethical character. Thus, setting aside Plato's criticism of traditional *theoria*, we may comprehend the promulgation of moral ideals as the larger aim that connects philosophical *theoria* with traditional practice.

---

[4] See Vlastos (1997, 190); cf. Kraut (1997, 213); for Aristotle, cf. *EN* 1177b30–1178a2; on *homoiosis theion*, see Sedley (1999, 314).

[5] Thus, Plato refers to forms, see *Phd.* 81a3, 83e1, 84a1; *Rep.* 500e3, 517d5, 611e2 (Des Places 1970, vol. 1, 247), Aristotle similarly qualifies the objects of *theoria* in *EN* X 7–8, e.g., 1177a13–22, 1178b21–23, 1179a23–33.

Bibliography

Achtenberg, Deborah. 1995. "Human Being, Beast and God: The Place of Happiness According to Aristotle." In M. Sim, ed., *The Crossroads of Norm and Nature: Essays on Aristotle's Ethics and Metaphysics*, 25–50. Lanham MD: Rowman & Littlefield.

Ackrill, J. L. 1978. "Aristotle on 'Good' and the *Categories*." In J. Barnes, M. Schofield, and R. Sorabji, eds., *Articles on Aristotle: Ethics and Politics*, vol. 2, 17–24. New York: St. Martin's Press.

——— 1980. "Aristotle on *Eudaimonia*." In A. Rorty, ed., *Essays on Aristotle's Ethics*, 15–34. Berkeley, CA: University of California Press.

Adam, James. 1965. *The Republic of Plato With Critical Notes, Commentary, and Appendices*. 2 vols. Cambridge: Cambridge University Press.

Adkins, A. W. H. 1978. "*Theoria* versus *Praxis* in the *Nichomachean Ethics* and the *Republic*," *Classical Philology* 73: 297–313.

Anastasiades, I. 2004. "Idealized *Schole* and Disdain for Work: Aspects of Philosophy and Politics in Ancient Democracy," *Classical Quarterly* 54, 1: 58–79.

Annas, Julia. 1985. *An Introduction to Plato's Republic*. Oxford: Clarendon Press.

——— 1999. "Becoming Like God: Ethics, Human Nature, and the Divine." In J. Annas, ed., *Platonic Ethics, Old and New*, 52–71. Ithaca, NY: Cornell University Press.

Armstrong, John. 2004. "After the Ascent: Plato on Becoming Like God," *Oxford Studies in Ancient Philosophy* 26: 171–83.

As, Imdat, and Daniel Schodek. 2008. *Dynamic Digital Representations in Architecture*. London and New York: Routledge.

Ast, Friedrich. 1956. *Lexicon Platonicum, sive, Platonicarum Index*. 3 vols. Bonn: R. Habelt.

Aufderheide, Joachim. 2016. "Aristotle against Delos: Pleasure in *Nicomachean Ethics*," *Phronesis* 61: 284–306.

Baker, Samuel. 2016. "The Metaphysics of Goodness in the Ethics of Aristotle," *Philosophical Studies* 174, 7: 839–56.

Barnes, Jonathan. 1993. *Aristotle Posterior Analytics. Translated with Commentary*. Second Edition. Oxford: Clarendon Press.

——— 2002. *Aristotle Posterior Analytics. Translated with Commentary*. Oxford: Clarendon Press.

2004. *The Complete Works of Aristotle. The Revised Oxford Translation.* 2 vols. Princeton: Princeton University Press.

Barnes, J., M. Schofield, and R. Sorabji, eds. 1978–1979. *Articles on Aristotle.* 4 vols. New York: St. Martin's Press.

Barney, Rachel. 2010. "Platonic Ring-Composition and *Republic* 10." In M. McPherran, ed., *Plato's Republic: A Critical Guide,* 32–51. Cambridge: Cambridge University Press.

Bedu-Addo, J. T. 1991. "Sense-Expereince and Argument for Reollection in Plato's *Phaedo,*" *Phronesis* 36, 1: 27–60.

Beneveniste, E. 1969. *Les Vocabulaires de Institutions Indo-Européenes.* Paris: Minuit.

Berryman, Sylvia. 2002. "Continuity and Coherence in Early Peripatetic Texts." In I. Bodnár and W. W. Fortenbaugh, eds., Eudemus of Rhodes. *Rutgers University Studies in Classical Humanities,* 157–69. New Brunswick: Transaction Publishers.

Bill, C. P. 1901. "Notes on Greek θεωρός and θεωρία," *Transactions of the American Philological Association* 32: 196–204.

Bluck, R. S. 1955. *Plato Phaedo. Edited with Introduction and Notes.* Indianapolis: Bobbs-Merrill.

Boardman, John. 1999. "The Parthenon Frieze: A Closer Look," *Revue Archéologique* 2, 99: 305–30.

Bolton, Robert. 1991. "Aristotle's Method in Natural Science: *Physics* I. 1." In L. Judson, ed., *Aristotle's Physics: A Collection of Essays,* 1–30. Oxford: Clarendon Press.

2005. "Perception Naturalized in Aristotle's *De anima.*" In R. Salles, ed., *Metaphysics, Soul, and Ethics in Ancient Thought: Themes from the Work of Richard Sorabji,* 209–44. Oxford: Clarendon Press.

Bonitz, Hermann, Bernhard Langkavel, and Jürgen Bona Meyer. 1870. *Index Aristotelicus,* 2nd ed. Graz: Akademische Druck- u. Verlagsanstalt.

Bostock, David. 1986. *Plato's Phaedo.* Oxford: Oxford University Press.

1988. "Pleasure and Activity in Aristotle's *Ethics,*" *Phronesis* 33, 3: 251–72.

Brennan, Teresa, and Martin Jay, eds. 1996. *Vision in Context: Historical and Contemporary Perspectives on Sight.* New York: Routledge.

Broadie, Sarah. 1991. *Ethics with Aristotle.* Oxford: Oxford University Press.

Broadie, S., and C. Rowe, 2002. *Aristotle: Nicomachean Ethics. Translation, Introduction and Commentary.* Oxford: Oxford University Press.

Brown, Eric. 2000. "Justice and Compulsion for Plato's Philosopher-Rulers," *Ancient Philosophy* 20: 1–17.

Buck, Carl D. 1953. "ΘΕΩΡΟΣ." In G. E. Mylonas and D. Raymond, eds., *Studies Presented to David Moore Robinson on His Seventieth Birthday,* vol. 2, 443–44. Saint Louis, MO: Washington University.

Buddensiek, Friedemann. 2009. "Contemplation and Service of the God: The Standard for External Goods in *Eudemian Ethics* VIII 3," *Bochumer Philosophisches Jahrbuch für Antike und Mittelalter* 14: 103–24.

Burger, Rona. 1995. "Aristotle's Exclusive Account of Happiness: Contemplative Wisdom as the Guise of the Political Philosopher." In M. Sim, ed., *The Crossroads of Norm and Nature: Essays in Aristotle's Ethics and Metaphysics*, 79–98. Lanham, MD: Rowman & Littlefield.

Burnet, John. 1900. *The Ethics of Aristotle*. London: Methuen.

ed. 1900–1907. *Platonis: Opera*. Oxford: Clarendon Press.

1989. *Plato Phaedo. Edited with Introduction and Notes*. Reprint of 1911 edition. Oxford: Clarendon Press.

Burnyeat, Myles. 1976. "Plato on the Grammar of Perceiving," *Classical Quarterly* 26, 1: 29–51.

1981. "Aristotle on Understanding Knowledge." In E. Berti, ed., *Aristotle on Science: Proceedings of the Eighth Symposium Aristotelicum*, 97–139. Padua: Editrice Antenore.

1999. "Culture and Society in Plato's *Republic*," *Tanner Lectures on Human Values* 20: 215–324.

2000. "Plato on Why Mathematics Is Good for the Soul." In T. Smiley, ed., *Mathematics and Necessity: Essays in the History of Philosophy*, 1–81. New York: Oxford University Press.

2008. *Aristotle's Divine Intellect*. The Aquinas Lecture 28. Milwaukee, WI: Marquette University Press.

Bush, Stephen. 2008. "Divine and Human Happiness in *Nichomachean Ethics*," *Philosophical Review* 117: 49–75.

Bywater, I., ed. 1894. *Aristotelis: Ethica Nicomachea*. Oxford: Clarendon Press.

Cairns, Francis, and Malcolm Heath, eds. 1998. *Papers of the Leeds International Latin Seminar, Tenth Volume, 1998: Greek Poetry, Drama, Prose, Roman Poetry*. Leeds: F. Cairns Publications.

Chantraine, Pierre. 1968. *Dictionnaire étymologique de la langue grecque: histoire des mots*, vol. 2. Paris: Klincksieck.

Charles, D. 2014. "*Eudaimonia, Theôria*, and the Choice-worthiness of Practical Wisdom." In P. Destrée and M. Zingano, eds., *Theoria: Studies on the Status and Meaning of Contemplation in Aristotle's Ethics*, 89–109. Leuven: Peeters.

Charles, D., and D. Scott. 1999. "Aristotle on Well-Being and Intellectual Contemplation," *Proceedings of the Aristotelian Society, Supplementary Volume* 73: 205–42.

Chroust, Anton-Hermann, trans. and comm. 1964. *Aristotle: Protrepticus – A Reconstruction*. Notre Dame, IN: University of Notre Dame Press.

Chroust, Anton-Hermann, 1965. "A Brief Account of the Reconstruction of Aristotle's *Protrepticus*," *Classical Philology* 60, 4: 229–39.

Colaner, Nathan. 2012. "Aristotle on Human Lives and Human Natures," *History of Philosophy Quarterly* 29, 3: 211–26.

Cooper, John. 1986. *Reason and the Human Good in Aristotle*. Indianapolis: Hackett.

Cooper, John. 1997. "The Psychology of Justice in Plato." In R. Kraut, ed., *Plato's Republic: Critical Essays*, 17–30. Lanham, MD: Rowman & Littlefield.

Cooper, John, and D. S. Hutchinson. 1997. *Plato: Complete Works, Edited with Introduction and Notes*. Indianapolis and Cambridge: Hackett.

Curzer, Howard J. 1991. "The Supremely Happy Life in Aristotle's Nicomachean Ethics," *Apeiron: A Journal for Ancient Philosophy and Science* 24, 1: 47–69.

Dahl, Norman O. 2011. "Contemplation and *Eudaimonia* in the *Nichomachean Ethics*." In J. Miller, ed., *Aristotle's Nichomachean Ethics: A Critical Guide*, 66–91. Cambridge: Cambridge University Press.

Dehart, Scott M. 1995. "The Convergence of *praxis* and *theoria* in Aristotle," *Journal of the History of Philosophy* 33: 7–27.

Des Places, Edouard. 1970. *Platon Œuvres Complètes. Tome XIV: Lexique de la langue philosophique et religieuse de Platon*. Paris: Les Belles Lettres.

Destrée, Pierre, and Marco Zingano, eds. 2014. *Theoria: Studies on the Status and Meaning of Contemplation in Aristotle's Ethics*. Leuven: Peeters.

Diels, H., and W. Kranz, eds. 1951. *Die Fragmente der Vorsokratiker*. Berlin: Weidmann.

Dillon, Matthew. 1997. *Pilgrims and Pilgrimage in Ancient Greece*. London: Routledge.

Donini, Pierluigi. 2014. "Happiness and Theôria in Books I and X of the *Nicomachean Ethics*." In Pierre Destrée and Marco Zingano, eds., *Theoria: Studies on the Status and Meaning of Contemplation in Aristotle's Ethics*, 7–20. Leuven: Peeters.

Dorter, Kenneth. 2006. *The Transformation of Plato's Republic*. Lanham, MD: Lexington Books.

Dougherty, Carol, and Leslie Kurke, eds. 1993. *Cultural Poetics in Archaic Greece: Cult, Performance, Politics*, Cambridge, MA: Cambridge University Press.

Douglas, Mary. 2007. *Thinking in Circles: Essays in Ring Composition*. New Haven: Yale University Press.

During, I. 1961. *Aristotle's Protrepticus: An Attempt at Reconstruction*. Stockholm: Almqvist & Wiksell.

Elsner, J., and I. Rutherford, eds. 2005. *Pilgrimage in Graeco-Roman & Early Christian Antiquity: Seeing the Gods*. Oxford: Oxford University Press.

Engelmann, Edward M. 2007. "Scientific Demonstration in Aristotle, *Theoria*, and Reductionism," *Review of Metaphysics* 60, 3: 479–506.

Evans, M. G. 1955. "Aristotle, Newton, and the Theory of Continuous Magnitude," *Journal of the History of Ideas* 16: 548–57.

Farwell, Paul. 1995. "Aristotle and the Complete Life," *History of Philosophy Quarterly* 12, 3: 247–63.

Ferejohn, Michael. 2006. "Knowledge, Recollection, and the Forms in *Republic* VII." In G. Santas, ed., *The Blackwell Guide to Plato's Republic*, 214–33. Oxford: Blackwell Publishing.

Festugière, A. J. 1936. *Contemplation et Vie Contemplative Selon Platon*. Paris: J. Vrin.

Franklin, Lee. 2005. "Recollection and Philosophical Reflection in Plato's *Phaedo*," *Phronesis* 50, 4: 289–314.

Galli, Marco. 2005. "Pilgrimage as Elite *Habitus*: Educated Pilgrims in Sacred Landscape During the Second Sophistic." In J. Elsner and I. Rutherford, eds., Pilgrimage in Graeco-Roman & Early Christian Antiquity: Seeing the Gods, *253–90*. Oxford: Oxford University Press.

Gauthier, René. 1958. *La Moral d'Aristote*. Paris: Presses Universitaires de France.

Gauthier, René, and Jean Jolif. 1970. *L'Ethique a Nicomaque. Introduction, Traduction, et Commentaire*. 2 vols. Louvain: Publications Universitaires.

Gibson, Twyla. 2011. "The Philosopher's Art: Ring Composition and Classification in Plato's *Sophist* and *Hipparchus*." In K. Carlson, K. Fagan, and N. Klanenko-Friesen, eds., *Orality and Literacy: Reflections Across Disciplines*, 73–109. Toronto: University of Toronto Press.

Gill, Mary Louise. 1971. "Matter and Flux in Plato's *Timaeus*," *Phronesis* 32: 34–53.

Goldhill, Simon. 1996. "Refracting Classical Vision: Changing Cultures of Viewing." In T. Brennan and M. Jay, eds., *Vision in Context: Historical and Contemporary Perspectives on Sight*, 15–28. New York: Routledge.

———. 2000. "Placing Theater in the History of Vision." In N. K. Rutter and B. Sparkes, eds., *Word and Image in Ancient Greece*, 161–79. Edinburgh: Edinburgh University Press.

———. 2007. "What Is *Ekphrasis* For?" *Classical Philology* 102, 1: 1–19.

Goldhill, S., and R. Osbourne, eds. 1992. *Art and Text in Ancient Greek Culture*. Cambridge and New York: Cambridge University Press.

Goldin, Owen. 1996. *Explaining an Eclipse: Posterior Analytics 2.1–10*. Ann Arbor: University of Michigan Press.

Gonzalez, Francisco. 1991. "Aristotle on Pleasure and Perfection," *Phronesis* 36, 2: 141–59.

Gotthelf, Allan. 1988. "The Place of the Good in Aristotle's Natural Teleology," *Proceedings of the Boston Area Colloquium of Ancient Philosophy* 4, 1: 113–39.

Graham, Daniel. 2013. *Science Before Socrates: Parmenides, Anaxagoras, and the New Astronomy*. Oxford: Oxford University Press.

Grand-Clément, Adeline. 2015. "*Poikilia*." In P. Destrée and P. Murray, eds., *A Companion to Ancient Aesthetics*, 406–21. Chichester: Wiley-Blackwell.

Grube, G. M. A., and C. D. C. Reeve, trans. 1992. *Plato: Republic*. Indianapolis: Hackett.

Hadreas, Peter. 1997. "Aristotle's Simile of Pleasure at *Nicomachean Ethics* 1174b33," *Ancient Philosophy* 17, 2: 371–74.

Heinaman, Robert. 1994. "Kosman on Activity and Change," *Oxford Studies in Ancient Philosophy* 12: 209–18.

Hett, W. S., ed. and trans. 1936. *Aristotle: On the Soul, Parva Naturalia, On Breath*. Cambridge, MA: Harvard University Press.

Hicks, R. D. 1907, reprint 1976. *Aristotle: De Anima*. Cambridge: Cambridge University Press.

Hill, Susanne. 1995. "Two Perspectives on the Ultimate End." In M. Sim, ed., *The Crossroads of Norm and Nature: Essays on Aristotle's Ethics and Metaphysics*, 99–114. Lanham, MD: Rowman & Littlefield.

Holm, Adolf. 1894–1902. *The History of Greece from its Commencement to the Close of the Independence of the Greek Nation.* 4 vols. London and New York: Macmillan.

Hudry, Jean-Louis. 2009. "Aristotle on Time, Plurality, and Continuity," *Logical Analysis and History of Philosophy (Philosophiegeschichte und Logische Analyse)* 12: 190–205.

Hulme, C. 1962. *The Religion of the Greeks and Romans.* London [Translation of Kerenyi 1942].

Hutchinson, D. S., and M. R. Johnson. 2005. "Authenticating Aristotle's *Protrepticus,*" *Oxford Studies in Ancient Philosophy* 29: 193–294.

2017. *Aristotle Protrepticus, or Exhortation to Philosophy.* www.protrepticus.info/protr2017x20.pdf.

Irwin, Terence. 1981. "Homonymy in Aristotle," *Review of Metaphysics* 34: 523–44.

1990. *Aristotle's First Principles.* Oxford: Oxford University Press.

Jaeger, W., ed. 1957. *Aristotelis: Metaphysica.* Oxford: Clarendon Press.

Jay, Martin. 1996. "Vision in Context: Reflections and Refractions." In Teresa Brennan and Martin Jay, eds., *Vision in Context: Historical and Contemporary Perspectives on Sight,* 1–11. New York: Routledge.

Jost, Lawrence. 2014. "*Theos, Theôria,* and *Therapeia* in Aristotle's Ethical Endings." In Pierre Destrée and Marco Zingano, eds., *Theoria: Studies on the Status and Meaning of Contemplation in Aristotle's Ethics,* 287–312. Leuven: Peeters.

Keaney, John. 1992. *The Composition of Aristotle's Athenian Politeia.* Oxford: Oxford University Press.

Ker, James. 2000. "Solon's *Theôria* and the End of the City," *Classical Antiquity* 19, 2: 304–29.

Kerenyi, Karl. 1942. *Die Antike Religion: Eine Gundlegung.* Amsterdam. Translated in C. Hulme, 1962. *The Religion of the Greeks and Romans.* London.

Keyt, David. 2014. "The Meaning of *Bios* in Aristotle's *Ethics* and *Politics.*" In P. Destrée and M. Zingano, eds., *Theoria: Studies on the Status and Meaning of Contemplation in Aristotle's Ethics,* 52–59. Leuven: Peeters.

Koller, Hermann. 1958. "*Theoros* und *Theoria,*" *Glotta* 36, 3/4: 273–86.

Korsgaard, Christine M. 1983. "Two Distinctions in Goodness," *Philosophical Review* 92, 2: 169–95.

Kosman, L. A. 1973. "Understanding, Explanation, and Insight in Aristotle's *Posterior Analytics.*" In E. N. Lee, A. P. D. Mourelatos, and R. M. Rorty, eds., *Exegesis and Argument,* 374–92. Assen: Van Gorcum.

1984. "Substance, Being, and *Energeia,*" *Oxford Studies in Ancient Philosophy* 2: 121–49.

Koutras, D. N. 2004. "Man's Place in the World According to Aristotle," *Diotima: Review of Philosophical Research* 32: 93–98.

Kowalzig, Barbara. 2005. "Mapping Out *Communitas*: Performances of *Theoria* in their Sacred and Political Context." In J. Elsner and I. Rutherford, eds.,

Pilgrimage in Graeco-Roman & Early Christian Antiquity: Seeing the Gods, 41–72. Oxford: Oxford University Press.

Kraut, Richard. 1989. *Aristotle on the Human Good*. Princeton: Princeton University Press.

1995. "Reply to Professor Roche." In M. Sim, ed., *The Crossroads of Norm and Nature: Essays on Aristotle's Ethics and Metaphysics*, 139–48. Lanham, MD: Rowman & Littlefield.

1997. "The Defense of Justice in Plato's Republic." In R. Kraut, ed., *Plato's Republic: Critical Essays*, 197–221. Lanham, MD: Rowman & Littlefield.

Lannstrom, Anna. 2011. "A Religious Revolution? How Socrates' Theology Undermined the Practice of Sacrifice," *Ancient Philosophy* 31: 261–74.

Lear, Gabriel Richardson. 2004. *Happy Lives and the Highest Good: An Essay on Aristotle's Nicomachean Ethics*. Princeton: Princeton University Press.

2014. "Approximation and Acting for an Ultimate End." In P. Destrée and M. Zingano, eds., *Theoria: Studies on the Status and Meaning of Contemplation in Aristotle's Ethics*, 61–88. Leuven: Peeters.

Lee, Edward. 1966. "On the Metaphysics of the Image in Plato's *Timaeus*," *Monist* 50: 341–68.

1976. "Reason and Rotation: Circular Motion as the Model of the Mind (*Nous*) in Later Plato," in W. H. Werkmeister, ed., *Facets of Plato's Philosophy*, 71–102. Assen: Van Gorcum.

Lesher, James. 1973. "The Meaning of '*Nous*' in the *Posterior Analytics*," *Phronesis* 18: 44–68.

ed. 2010. *From Inquiry to Demonstrative Knowledge: New Essays on Aristotle's Posterior Analytics*. Kelowna, Canada: Academic Printing & Publishing.

Levin, Susan. 1996. "Women's Nature and Role in the Ideal *Polis*: Republic V Revisited." In J. Ward, ed., *Feminism and Ancient Philosophy*, 13–30. New York and London: Routledge.

Liddell, H. G., and R. Scott, eds. 1968. *A Greek-English Lexicon*. Oxford: Oxford University Press.

Lindsay, Judson, ed. 1991. *Aristotle's Physics: A Collection of Essays*. Oxford: Oxford University Press.

Liu, Wei. 2011. "An All-Inclusive Interpretation of Aristotle's Contemplative Life," *Sophia: International Journal for Philosophy of Religion, Metaphysical Theology and Ethics* 50, 1: 57–71.

Long, A. A. 2011. "Aristotle on *Eudaimonia*, *Nous*, and Divinity." In J. Miller, ed., *Aristotle's Nichomachean Ethics: A Critical Guide*, 92–113. Cambridge: Cambridge University Press.

Loraux, Nicole. 1993. *The Children of Athena*. Trans. Caroline Levine. Princeton: Princeton University Press.

Maher, Daniel P. 2012. "Contemplative Friendship in *Nicomachean Ethics*," *Review of Metaphysics* 65, 4: 765–94.

Majithia, Roopen N. 2006. "Function, Intuition and Ends in Aristotle's *Ethics*," *Ethical Theory and Moral Practice* 9, 2: 187–200.

Mansion, S. 1960. "Contemplation and Action in Aristotle's *Protrepticus.*" In I. Düring and G. E. L. Owen, eds., *Aristotle and Plato in the Mid-Fourth Century, Papers of the Symposium Aristotelicum held at Oxford in August 1957*, 56–75. Göteborg: Almqvist & Wiksell.

Marconi, Clemente. 2009. "The Parthenon Frieze: Degrees of Visibility," *Anthropology and Aesthetics* 55–56: 156–73.

McLaughlin, Brian, and Karen Bennet. 2018. "Supervenience." *Stanford Encyclopedia of Philosophy.* https://plato.stanford.edu/entries/supervenience.

McPherran, Mark. 1996. *The Religion of Socrates.* University Park, PA: Pennsylvania State University Press.

2013. *Socratic Theology and Piety.* London: Bloombury Academic.

Menn, Stephen. 1994. "The Origins of Aristotle's Concept of *Energeia*: *Energeia* and *Dunamis*," *Ancient Philosophy* 14: 73–114.

1995. *Plato on God as Nous.* Carbondale, IL: Southern Illinois University Press.

Mirus, Christopher V. 2004. "*To Hou Heneka* and Continuous Change," *Newsletters for the Society for Ancient Greek Philosophy* 5, 1: 1–19.

Morgan, Michael L. 1983. "The Continuity Theory of Reality in Plato's *Hippias Major*," *Journal of the History of Philosophy* 21: 133–58.

Morris, Ian. 1998. "Poetics of Power: The Interpretation of Ritual Action in Archaic Greece." In Carol Dougherty and Leslie Kurke, eds., *Cultural Poetics in Archaic Greece: Cult, Performance, Politics*, 15–45. Oxford: Oxford University Press.

Morrow, Glenn. 1963. *Plato's Cretan City: A Historical Interpretation of the Laws.* Princeton: Princeton University Press.

Mylonas, George E., and Doris Raymond, eds. 1953. Studies Presented to David Moore Robinson on His Seventieth Birthday, *vol. 2.* Saint Louis, MO: Washington University Press.

Nabielek, Marcus. 2010. "Aristotle's Double Solution to Zeno's 'Dichotomy': Sign of a Radical Revision?" *Análisis Filosófico* 30, 2: 245–59.

Nagel, Thomas. 1980. "Aristotle on *Eudaimonia.*" In A. Rorty, ed., *Articles on Aristotle's Ethics*, 7–14. Berkeley: University of California Press.

Naiden, Fred. 2005. "*Hiketai* and *Theoroi* at Epidauros." In J. Elsner and I. Rutherford, eds., Pilgrimage in Graeco-Roman & Early Christian Antiquity: Seeing the Gods, 72–95. Oxford: Oxford University Press.

Nehamas, Alexander, and Paul Woodruff. 1989. *Plato Symposium Translated with Introduction & Notes.* Indianapolis: Hackett.

Neils, Jenifer. 2001. *The Parthenon Frieze.* Cambridge: Cambridge University Press.

Nightingale, Andrea. 2001. "On Wondering and Wandering: *Theoria* in Greek Philosophy and Culture," *Arion* 9: 111–46.

2004. *Spectacles of Truth in Classical Greek Philosophy: Theoria in its Cultural Context.* Cambridge: Cambridge University Press.

2005. "The Philosopher at the Festival: Plato's Transformation of Traditional *Theoria.*" In J. Elsner and I. Rutherford, eds., *Pilgrimage in Graeco-Roman &*

Early Christian Antiquity: Seeing the Gods, 151–80. Oxford: Oxford University Press

Norman, R. 1969. "Aristotle's Philosopher God," *Phronesis* 14: 63–74.

Nussbaum, Martha. 1986. *The Fragility of Goodness: Luck and Ethics in Greek Tragedy and Philosophy*. Cambridge: Cambridge University Press.

1990. "Transcending Humanity." In *Love's Knowledge: Essays on Life and Literature*," 365–91. Oxford: Oxford University Press.

1995. "Aristotle on Human Nature and the Foundations of Ethics." In J. Altham and R. Harrison, eds., *World, Mind and Ethics: Essays on the Ethical Philosophy of Bernard Williams*, 86–131. Cambridge: Cambridge University Press.

Olfert, C. M. M. 2014. "Incomplete Activities," *Apeiron* 42, 2: 230–44.

Ostwald, Martin. 2000. *Aristotle Nicomachean Ethics Translated with Introduction and Notes*. Upper Saddle River, NJ: Prentice Hall.

Owen, G. E. L. 1978. "Aristotelian Pleasures." In J. Barnes, M. Schofield, and R. Sorabji, eds., *Articles on Aristotle: Ethics and Politics*, vol. 2, 92–103. New York: St. Martin's Press.

Panayides, Christos Y. 2007. "Aristotle on First Principles and Divine Contemplation," *Skepsis: A Journal for Philosophy and Interdisciplinary Research* 18, 1–2: 114–23.

Patzig, Gunther. 1979. "Theology and Ontology in Aristotle's Metaphysics." In J. Barnes, M. Schofield, and R. Sorabji, eds., *Articles on Aristotle: Ethics and Politics*, vol. 3, 33–49. New York: St. Martin's Press.

Peck, A. L., and E. S. Forster, eds. and trans. 1937. *Aristotle: Parts of Animals, Movement of Animals, Progression of Animals*. Cambridge, MA: Harvard University Press.

Pistelli, H. G. 1888. *Iamblichi Protrepticus*. Teubner: Bibliotheca Scriptorum Graecorum et Romanorum Teubneriana.

Polansky, Ronald. 2007. *Aristotle's De Anima*. Cambridge and New York: Cambridge University Press.

Poulakos, John, and Nathan Crick. 2012. "There is Beauty Here, Too: Aristotle's Rhetoric for Science," *Philosophy and Rhetoric* 45, 3: 295–311.

Rackham, H., ed. and trans. 1926. *Aristotle: Nicomachean Ethics*. Cambridge, MA: Harvard University Press.

ed. and trans. 1935. *Aristotle: Athenian Constitution, Eudemian Ethics, Virtues and Vices*. Cambridge, MA: Harvard University Press.

Rausch, Hannelore. 1982. *Theoria: von ihrer sakralen zur philosophischen Bedeutung*. München: Fink.

Redfield, James. 1985. "Herodotus the Tourist," *Classical Philology* 80: 97–118.

Reeve, C. D. C. 2006. *Philosopher-Kings: The Argument of Plato's Republic*. Indianapolis: Hackett.

2012. *Action, Contemplation, and Happiness: An Essay on Aristotle*. Cambridge, MA: Harvard University Press.

2014a. *Aristotle Nicomachean Ethics. Translation with Introduction and Notes*. Indianapolis: Hackett.

2014b. "Aristotelian Immortality." In P. Destrée and M. Zingano, eds., *Theoria: Studies on the Status and Meaning of Contemplation in Aristotle's Ethics*, 335–43. Leuven: Peeters.

Roche, Timothy. 1988. "*Ergon* and *Eudaimonia* in *Nicomachean Ethics* I: Reconsidering the Intellectualist Interpretation," *Journal of the History of Philosophy* 26: 175–94.

1995. "The Ultimate End of Action: A Critique of Richard Kraut's Aristotle on the Human Good. In M. Sim, ed., *The Crossroads of Norm and Nature: Essays on Aristotle's Ethics and Metaphysics*, 115–38. Lanham, MD: Rowman & Littlefield.

Rønnow-Rasmussen, T. 2002. "Instrumental Values: Strong and Weak," *Ethical Theory and Moral Practice* 5, 1: 23–43.

Roochnik, David. 2009. "What Is *Theoria*? *Nicomachean Ethics* Book 10.7–8," *Classical Philology* 104, 1: 69–82.

Rorty, A. O. 1980. "The Place of Contemplation in Aristotle's *Nichomachean Ethics.*" In A. Rorty, ed., *Essays on Aristotle's Ethics*, 377–94. Berkeley: University of California Press.

Roselli, David. 2009. "*Theorika* in Fifth-Century Athens," *Greek, Roman, and Byzantine Studies* 49: 5–30.

Ross, W. D., ed. and comm. 1924. *Aristotle's Metaphysics*. 2 vols. Oxford: Clarendon Press.

ed. 1950. *Aristotelis: Physica*. Oxford: Clarendon Press.

1955/2001. *Aristotle: Parva Naturalia. Revised Text with Introduction and Commentary*. Oxford: Clarendon Press.

ed. 1956. *Aristotelis: De Anima*. Oxford: Clarendon Press.

ed. 1958. *Aristotelis: Topica et Sophistici Elenchi*. Oxford: Clarendon Press.

ed. 1964. *Aristotelis: Analytica Priora et Posteriora*. Oxford: Clarendon Press.

Rowe, Christopher J. 1993. *Plato, Phaedo* (Cambridge Greek and Latin Classics). Cambridge: Cambridge University Press.

2014. "The Best Life According to Aristotle and Plato: A Reconsideration." In P. Destrée and M. Zingano, eds., *Theoria: Studies on the Status and Meaning of Contemplation in Aristotle's Ethics*, 273–86. Leuven: Peeters.

Rutherford, Ian. 1995. "Theoric Crisis: The Dangers of Pilgrimage in Greek Religion and Society," *Studi e materiali di storia delle religione* 61: 276–92.

1998. "*Theoria* as Theatre: Pilgrimage in Greek Drama." In F. Cairns and M. Heath, eds., *Papers of the Leeds International Latin Seminar, Tenth Volume, 1998: Greek Poetry, Drama, Prose, Roman Poetry*, 131–56. Leeds: F. Cairns Publications.

2000. "*Theoria* and *Darśan*: Pilgrimage and Vision in Greece and India," *Classical Quarterly* 50, 1: 133–46.

2013. *State Pilgrims and Sacred Observers in Ancient Greece: A Study of Theoria and Theoroi*. Cambridge: Cambridge University Press.

Salmieri, Gregory. 2010. "*Aisthesis, Empeiria*, and the Advent of Universals in *Posterior Analytics* II 19." In J. H. Lesher, ed., *From Inquiry to Demonstrative*

Knowledge: New Essays on Aristotle's Posterior Analytics, 155–85. Kelowna, Canada: Academic Printing & Publishing.

Sattler, Barbara. 2012. "A Likely Account of Necessity: Plato's Receptacle as a Physical and Metaphysical Foundation for Space," *Journal of the History of Philosophy* 50, 2: 159–95.

Scarry, Elaine. 1999. *On Beauty and Being Just*. Princeton: Princeton University Press.

Schomakers, Ben. 1994. "The Blindness of Contemplation on Thinking According to Aristotle," *Revista Filosófica de Coimbra* 5: 121–60.

Scullion, Scott. 2005. "'Pilgrimage' and Greek Religion: Sacred and Secular in the Pagan Polis." In R. Elsner and I. Rutherford, eds., *Pilgrimage in Graeco-Roman & Early Christian Antiquity: Seeing the Gods*, 111–30. Oxford: Oxford University Press.

Sedley, David. 1999. "The Ideal of Godlikeness." In G. Fine, ed., *Plato 2: Ethics, Politics, Religion, and the Soul*, 309–28. Oxford: Oxford University Press.

2006. "Form-Particular Resemblance in Plato's *Phaedo*," *Proceedings of the Aristotelian Society* 106: 311–27.

2017. "Becoming Godlike." In C. Bobonich, ed., *The Cambridge Companion to Ancient Ethics*, 319–37. Cambridge: Cambridge University Press.

Shields, Chris. 1999. *Order in Multiplicity: Homonymy in the Philosophy of Aristotle*. Oxford: Clarendon Press.

2007. "Forcing Goodness in Plato's *Republic*," *Social Philosophy and Policy* 24, 2: 21–39.

2015. "Fractured Goodness: The *Summum Bonum* in Aristotle." In J. Aufderheide and R. M. Bader, eds., *The Highest Good in Aristotle and Kant*, 83–111. Oxford: Oxford University Press.

Shorey, Paul. 1895. "The Idea of the Good in Plato's *Republic*: A Study in the Logic of Speculative Ethics," *Studies in Classical Philology* 1: 188–239.

Sihvola, Juha. 1993. "Why Does Contemplation Not Fit Well into Aristotle's *Eudaimonia?*" *Arctos* 27: 103–21.

Silverman, Alan. 1992. "Timaean Particulars," *Classical Quarterly* 42, 1: 87–113.

Slings, S. R. 2004. *Plato Clitophon. Edited with Introduction, Translation and Commentary*. Cambridge: Cambridge University Press.

Sourvinou-Inwood, C. 1990. "What is *Polis* Religion"? In O. Murray and S. Price, eds., *The Greek City from Homer to Alexander*, 295–322. Oxford: Clarendon Press.

Sparshott, Frances. 1982. "Aristotle's *Ethics* and Plato's *Republic*," *Dialogue* 21: 483–99.

Steiner, Deborah. 2015. "Figures of the Poet in Greek Epic and Lyric." In P. Destrée and P. Murray, eds., *A Companion to Ancient Aesthetics*, 31–46. Chichester: Wiley-Blackwell.

Stigen, A. 1961. "On the Alleged Primacy of Sight, with Some Remarks on *Theoria* and *Praxis*, in Aristotle," *Symbola Osloenses: Norwegian Journal of Greek and Latin Studies* 37: 15–44.

Stillwell, Richard. 1969. "The Panathenaic Frieze: Optical Relations," *Hesperia: Journal of American School of Classical Studies at Athens* 38, 2: 231–41.

Stocks, J. L. 1936. *"Schole,"* *Classical Quarterly* 30, 3–4: 177–87.

Thesleff, Helgar. 1993. "Looking for Clues: An Interpretation of Some Literary Aspects of Plato's Two-Level Model." In G. Press, ed., *Plato's Dialogues: New Studies and Interpretations*, 17–45. Lanham, MD: Rowman & Littlefield.

Tréheux, Jacques. 1953. "La Réalité Historique des Offrandes Hyperboréennes." In G. E. Mylonas and D. Raymond, eds., *Studies Presented to David Moore Robinson on His Seventieth Birthday*, vol. 2, 758–74. St. Louis, MO: Washington University.

Tuominen, Miira. 2010. "Back to *Posterior Analytics* II 19: Aristotle on the Knowledge of Principles." In J. H. Lesher, ed., *From Inquiry to Demonstrative Knowledge: New Essays on Aristotle's Posterior Analytics*, 115–43. Kelowna, Canada: Academic Printing & Publishing.

Tuozzo, Thomas M. 1992. "Contemplation, the Noble, and the Mean: The Standard of Moral Virtue in Aristotle's Ethics," *Apeiron* 25: 129–54.

   1995. "Aristotle's Theory of the Good and its Causal Basis," *Phronesis* 60, 3: 293–314.

Turner, Edith, and Victor Turner. 1978. *Image and Pilgrimage in Christian Culture: Anthropological Perspectives*. New York: Columbia University Press.

Upton, Thomas. 1981. "A Note on Aristotelian *Epagoge*," *Phronesis* 26, 2: 172–76.

   1987. "Infinity and Perfect Induction in Aristotle," *Proceedings of the American Catholic Philosophical Association* 55: 149–58.

   2004. "Truth vs. Necessary Truth in Aristotle's Sciences," *Review of Metaphysics* 57, 4: 741–53.

Van Otterlo, W. A. 1948. *De Ringcompositie als opbouwprincipe in de Epische Gedichten von Homerus*. Amsterdam: Nederlansche Academie van Wettenschappen.

Vellacott, Philip. 1972. *Euripides Bacchae and Other Plays*. Harmondsworth: Penguin.

Vlastos, Gregory. 1989. "Was Plato a Feminist?" In Daniel Graham, ed., *Studies in Greek Philosophy*, vol. 2, 133–43. Princeton: Princeton University Press.

   1997. "A Metaphysical Paradox." In R. Kraut, ed., *Plato's Republic: Critical Essays*, 181–95. Lanham, MD: Rowman & Littlefield.

Von Fritz, Kurt. 1945. *Nous, Noein* and Their Derivatives in Pre-Socratic Philosophy Part I," *Classical Philology* 40, 4: 223–42.

Walker, Matthew. 2010. "The Utility of Contemplation in Aristotle's *Protrepticus*," *Ancient Philosophy* 30: 135–53.

   2018. *Aristotle on the Uses of Contemplation*. Cambridge: Cambridge University Press.

Walzer, R. R. and J. M. Mingay, eds. 1991. *Aristotelis: Ethica Eudemia*. Oxford: Clarendon Press.

Ward, Julie K. 2008. *Aristotle on Homonymy: Dialectic and Science*. Cambridge: Cambridge University Press.

2018. "*Theoria* as Practice and as Activity." In R. Radice and M. Zanatta, eds., *Aristotele e le Sfide del Suo Tempo*, 235–50. Milan: Editioni Unicopli.

Warden, J. R. 1971. "The Mind of Zeus," *Journal of the History of Ideas* 32, 1: 3–14.

Webb, David. 2010. "The Structure of *Praxis* and the Time of *Eudaimonia*," *Epoche: A Journal for the History of Philosophy* 14, 2: 265–87.

White, Michael. 1980. "Aristotle's Concept of *Theoria* and the *Energeia-Kinesis* Distinction," *Journal of the History of Philosophy* 18: 253–65.

Wiitala, Michael. 2009. "Contemplation and Action within the Context of the *Kalon*: A Reading of the *Nicomachean Ethics*," *Proceedings of the American Catholic Philosophical Association* 83: 173–82.

Wilkes, Kathleen. 1980. "The Good Man and the Good for Man." In A. Rorty, ed., *Essays on Aristotle's Ethics*, 341–58. Berkeley: University of California Press.

Woods, Michael, trans. 1992. *Aristotle Eudemian Ethics, Bks. I, II, and VIII*. Oxford: Clarendon Press.

Worman, Nancy. 2015. "Stylistic Landscapes." In P. Destrée and P. Murray, eds., *A Companion to Ancient Aesthetics*, 291–306. Chichester: Wiley-Blackwell.

Zeitlin, Froma. 1992. "The Artful Eye: Vision, *Ecphrasis*, and Spectacle in Euripidean Theater." In S. Goldhill and R. Osbourne, eds., *Art and Text in Ancient Greek Culture*, 138–96. Cambridge: Cambridge University Press.

Zeyl, D. 1975. "Plato and Talk of a World of Flux," *Classical Philology* 79: 125–48.

Index of Passages

General Index

Acropolis, 32, 118
activity (*energeia*). *See* Aristotle
agalmata, 118–20, 122, 125–26, 128, 135–36, 152–53
analogy
cave analogy. *See* Plato
racecourse. *See* Aristotle
theoria and pilgrimage, 7–8, 27, 35–36, 99–101
anamnesis. *See* Plato, recollection, *See* recollection
Aristophanes, 6, 23, 29, 31
Aristotle
activity (*energeia*), 87, 104, 114, 140–41, 147, 154
eudaimonia, 45, 88–89, 103, 105, 110
knowledge of god, 145, 147–48, 150–51
motion (*kinesis*), 104–5
pleasure, 90–92, 102–3, 105–7, 144
political life, 101, 103, 113
potentiality, 104
racecourse analogy, 62–63, 187
scientific knowledge, 45, 47, 115, 145, 147–48, 151–53
sense-perception, 106, 109, 115
and memory (*mneme*), 115, 131, 153
substantial forms, 141, 145
theoretical wisdom (*sophia*), 88, 91–92, 107, 186
theoria
as activity of *episteme*, 147, 150
as complete activity, 10, 91, 103–4, 108, 112–14, 151, 174
as leisurely, 89, 93–94, 96–97, 108, 112, 174
definition of, *EN* X 7, 114, 147
linked to highest happiness, 110
objects of *theoria*, 139, 141–45, 147, 150–53
value of *theoria*, intrinsic and instrumental, 174–76, 183
virtue (*arete*), 87, 89, 92, 97, 107, 111, 146, 176–79

Barney, R., 4, 57–59, 66
Beauty itself. *See* Plato
bookending. *See* ring composition
Burnet, J., 88, 147–48
Burnyeat, M., 4, 57–59, 66, 167

circular motion
and ascent. *See* Plato, *Republic*.
and pilgrimage, 6–8, 25, 35, 120, 124, 168
and Platonic *theoria*, 8, 53, 61–63, 66
and ring composition, 53
contemplation (*theoria*), 1–3, 10, 40–41, 43, 46–48, 103, 133, 163, 175
Cooper, J., 165

Delphi, 13, 15, 29, 31–32, 118–22, 160
dianoia (reasoning), 91, 106, 137, 182
Dillon, M., 3, 18, 20
divine (*theion*)
divine *theoria*, 109, 116, 139–40, 174
human *theoria*, 87, 107–9, 115–16, 139–40, 147, 174–75, 182
Dorter, K., 57
Douglas, M., 55–56

education
and *theoria*, 28–29, 34, 37–40, 64–65, 135, 165–68
in Plato. *See* Plato
elliptical motion. *See* circular motion
eudaimonia (happiness). *See* Aristotle, *eudaimonia*
Euripides, 6, 23, 29, 31–32, 95–96, 118, 120, 126–28, 136, 160

festival attendance, 13–14, 23, 77
Form of the Good. *See* Plato
forms. *See* Plato, *See* Aristotle, substantial forms
frieze. *See* Parthenon

206